Tahu - Potiki

GENEALOGY

A genealogy given by Eruera Stirling showing the links
that led to his taumau marriage with Amiria O'Hara, and
relationships between the main characters in her life story.

Te Haemata = Te Pakira

Te Aotiraroa = Te Ao Whanui

Ngarehutai

Te Ara Taua

Te Wahi-Tapu

Matahira

Kahutawhiti

Amiria = Wiremu Parata Moihi Ka   Mereana = Henare
                                         Mokikiwa   Kaiwai

Hera   Heni   = Petuere   Ani   1.   2.   3.   4.
Kaiwahie   Hautao   Awatere   Kahutawhiti = Kawhi = Harry = Watene = Wirihana   Tamati
                                                   Kena   O'Hara   Campbell   Tatai   Kaiwai

        Arapeta   Maraea   Ani   Amiria   Te Kuatau   Watara
        Maru-Ki-Tipua   or Te O   Herbert = Kahu   Manutahi   Wi
        Awatere   = Manukau Wright   Tawhiti   O'Hara

Tamahae   Marama   Te Kepa Takataka   Kingi Hori Te Ariki-Tapu-Ki-Waho
Bernard   Pankhurst   -o-Rangi   (adopted)

Webster
295 Richbank

AMIRIA

The Life Story of a Maori Woman

Amiria is Amiria Manutahi Stirling, and this is her life story, the remarkable account of a woman born on the East Coast eighty years ago.

The story begins with Amiria's birth at Tuparoa, a childhood spent in both her grandmother's raupo hut and the magnificent Williams homestead Kaharau; it takes the reader through Amiria's schooldays, her *taumau* (arranged) marriage to Eruera Stirling, farming on "The Coast" and latter days in Auckland, where the Stirlings still live as prominent elders.

The autobiography is based on a collection of taped interviews by Anne Salmond, senior lecturer in Anthropology at the University of Auckland, whose book *Hui: A Study of Maori Ceremonial Gatherings* was one of this country's publishing landmarks in 1975. Amiria and Eruera Stirling were the source of much of *Hui*, and it wasn't a complete surprise then that Amiria herself should become the subject of another, more personal story.

Her remembrances, told in a charming narrative style, form a significant, often moving, advance in ethnographic texts of this kind. It is authentic and cuts to the very heart of Maori experience, conveying to the reader a deep understanding of what it is to be Maori.

Amiria is available in both cased and limpbound editions.

By the same author:
Hui (1975)

AMIRIA

The Life Story of a Maori Woman

AMIRIA MANUTAHI STIRLING

as told to
ANNE SALMOND

A. H. & A. W. REED
Wellington - Sydney - London

First published 1976

A.H. & A.W. Reed Ltd
182 Wakefield Street, Wellington
53 Myoora Road, Terrey Hills, Sydney 2084
11 Southampton Row, London WC1B 5HA
also
16-18 Beresford Street, Auckland
165 Cashel Street, Christchurch

ISBN 0 589 00978 8

Typography and layout by Kevin Woolcott

Jacket design by Trevor Plaisted

Typeset and Printed by NZ Consolidated Press Ltd,
Wellington

Contents

List Of Photographs

List Of Maps

Acknowledgments

A number of individuals and institutions gave generous help in the work of compiling this text, and I want to thank them one by one.

Firstly, my thanks to the University Grants Committee, who allocated money to pay Mrs Rangi Motu for her expertise in transcribing the tapes; to Peggy and Peter Kaua and Barbara Allum in Gisborne, and Cheryl Sutheron in Auckland for reading the script and offering helpful comments; and to my mother Joyce Thorpe, who both read the script and collected some background material.

The Gisborne Art Gallery and Museum staff gave free access to their photographic and clipping files; Mr Dumbleton, the Editor of the *Gisborne Herald* loaned a number of old photos from the newspaper's collection; Dr Peter and Elizabeth Hinds in Gisborne helped with enquiries about the 1914–15 epidemic on the Coast; and the Land Inquiry Officer for the Tai Rawhiti District of the Maori Land Court searched out material on the "Kaharau" block. Sir Robert Hall gave freely of his time to collect invaluable background material in Gisborne, enlisting the help of Mr and Mrs C. K. Williams, Mr and Mrs H. E. Williams and Mrs S. H. Burdett as he went — my thanks to all of these people for their generous co-operation.

Miss Alice Berridge of Queen Victoria School discovered the date that Kuatau Campbell was a pupil there, Michael King and Graeme Butterworth helped to date some of the events in Ngata's career, and the Alexander Turnbull Library and the Department of Education in Wellington both helped with enquiries about "Wellington Ladies' College". The staff of the H. B. Williams Memorial Library in Gisborne located material on the Williams family, and the staff in the photographic sections of the Auckland War Memorial Museum, the Auckland City Library, the Alexander Turnbull Library in Wellington and the Hocken Library in Dunedin all helped with photographic material for the book. Mrs Phyllis Walker of Waihau Bay, Eva Eruera and Te Iritana Stirling at Raukokore, Dave White of the Whakatane and District Historical Society, Wiremu Maxwell at Opotiki, Sir Robert Hall, and the archivist at the Whakatane Museum also helped generously in the search for old photos.

For contemporary photographs of the Stirlings and the places with which they were most closely associated on the Coast, I'd like to thank my husband Jeremy, Marti Friedlander, and Robin Morrison. Mitch Henry and Stephen Barnett copied some of the Stirling family portraits, and Mitch Henry put them back together again. Sue Stenner typed the manuscript and most of the original transcripts.

Finally, my aroha to Eruera and Amiria and their family, who have made this book a work of love.

Anne Salmond

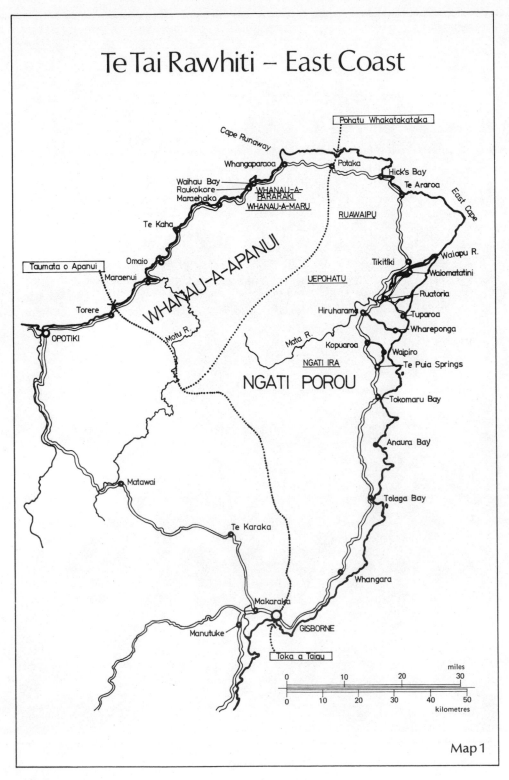

Te Tai Rawhiti – East Coast

Pohatu Whakatakataka

Cape Runaway

Whangaparaoa   Potaka

Waihau Bay   Hick's Bay
Raukokore   Te Araroa
Maraehako   WHANAU-A-
PARARAKI
WHANAU-A-MARU   East Cape

Te Kaha   RUAWAIPU

Taumata o Apanui   Omaio   Tikitiki   Waiapu R.

Maraenui   UEPOHATU   Waiomatatini

WHANAU-A-APANUI   Ruatoria

Torere   Hiruharama   Tuparoa

OPOTIKI   Motu R.   Whareponga

Mata R.   Kopuaroa   Waipiro

NGATI IRA   Te Puia Springs

NGATI POROU   Tokomaru Bay

Anaura Bay

Matawai   Tolaga Bay

Te Karaka

Whangara

Makaraka

Manutuke   GISBORNE

Toka a Taiau

	miles
0 10 20 30	
0 10 20 30 40 50	kilometres

Map 1

xi

Amiria Stirling.

CHAPTER ONE

My Young Life As A Child

I can't tell you much about how I was born. I just know it was about eighty years ago, on the sixteenth of August at Tuparoa. My mother was Ani Kahutawhiti and my father was Harry O'Hara, a tailor at Tuparoa making riding breeches and divided skirts. He wasn't her first husband though. She was married before to Kawhi Kena from North, and she lived with him at Poutou until he died. After that she came back home to Tuparoa.

In those days, Tuparoa was the township, Ruatoria wasn't even started. It was a *beautiful* town too. There was a big hotel and the Farmers', and the big Williams' shop which was run by the Ludbrooks, and the blacksmith's. Then of course, there was my father's business — he was the only tailor there, and when he died there was no more. He did these divided skirts and riding breeches, and my mother used to go there house-keeping and that's how he fancied her. Harry thought, well, he'll come to Auckland and ask his parents about his marriage to this Maori girl. He came to Auckland and told his mother that he was going to get married, and his mother said,

"Oh yes Harry, what is it? The pakeha girl?"

"No, it's a Maori."

When he said it was a Maori, oh . . . she shot up, she didn't like it.

"No," she said, "No!"

They wouldn't have a Maori, not a Maori.

"You'll have to marry to your own people."

And Harry said,

"Well, I can't help it. I *am* going to marry this woman! You don't know the Maori people; you've got to live with the Maori people, Mum, to understand them. They're lovely people if you know them, and I know them because I live there amongst them, and they're the people that got me on my feet. I'm the only tailor in the district and most of my customers are Maoris, so I'm all right. But I just want you to say 'yes' about this."

"No!"

"All right, well you go your way, I'll go my way. I can't help it, I am going to marry that woman."

"If you do, we won't have you, we're finished with you. We don't want to have any more to do with you!"

He walked out, then he thought, so he went back again.

"Mum, what about my family? If I have children would you accept them? I have made the mistake, but what about my family?"

"No." She would not have anything to do with a Maori family. Then Harry thought — this is the end, so he left and came back to Tuparoa.

He took sick a few years afterwards, not long after I was born. He asked my

Tuparoa 1905.

mother to get a doctor, and she went and got a tohunga. The tohunga came and started to do water and all this sort,[1] and Dad got wild, because he said he wanted a doctor. But you couldn't get a doctor in the country in those days and that's how he lost his life.

Before he died, he asked Mum to come over to the bedside. He wanted a quiet talk with her, because he didn't want the tohunga and all the other Maoris sitting around to hear what he was saying. He was talking to her quietly about me, about the baby, to make sure I marry back, marry a pakeha.

"When she's old enough to get married, Ani, promise me that you will see that she marries a pakeha — I was the one that made the breakage with my family, but perhaps my daughter will mend that break. If she marries back, then maybe my family will accept my daughter."

My mother said,

"I will Harry. I'll do that for you. I'll see that your daughter will marry back. I was the cause of the trouble, so you leave that to me."

They hugged one another, and shook hands on it. He was happy before he died. And he left all the money from his business to see that I get the best of education at a good school, not just the Maori school.

After he died Mum couldn't keep up the business, she didn't know how to do tailor's work. She cleared up the shop and sold everything, then she travelled

---

[1] "Doing water" refers to a tohunga's use of sacred water to lift a tapu.

around and stayed with relations for a while. Her elder sister Hera Kaiwahie came and took me to Waipiro Bay.

Several years afterwards my mother got married to Watene Campbell and they had a daughter, Kuatau. My aunt Mereana Mokikiwa thought seeing that Ani has married, she may as well get me and bring me to Taumata-o-mihi. Ani's all right, she's having another family, but my aunt was feeling lonely. Her own son Tamati Kaiwai had gone away and she lived by herself in her little thatched hut. So Mereana came to Tuparoa and asked my mother to give her the pakeha.

"I've come to fetch the mokopuna pakeha, Ani. I want you to let me look after her. You've already got children and you're pregnant again, so it's better if you give her to me."

"Is that what you want?" my mother said.

"Yes. I'm lonely."

So then my mother said,

"All right."

She packed my things and the old lady Mereana brought me on horseback to Taumata-o-mihi. When I settled there, all the old people round the marae thought I was their mokopuna, they owned me. They'd say to the old lady,

"If you go somewhere, give us the mokopuna pakeha to look after."

Hakopa Haerewa and his wife Te Awhimate.

In those days my hair was red; I had fair, fair hair, so they called me turehu after the fairy people, all those sort of names.[2]

When Mereana went out to work at the Williams, sometimes Tapita, Hunia Te Iri's wife, would look after me until the old lady came back from Kaharau. Another time it would be Hakopa Haerewa and his wife Te Awhimate. Their two daughters Areta and Kareti were my friends, although Areta was older than me, but Kareti and I were about the same age. They were the ones that took me to school. The old lady said,

"I think Areta, you better take this Amiria to school now, because she needs to go to school."

So we went to school at Hiruharama. The funny thing was, Areta didn't put down my pakeha name O'Hara, she put me down as Haerewa. I suppose it was because they felt I was their sister. I could have claimed Hakopa Haerewa's money, I teased Titihuia about that. Matter of fact, I didn't even know about it until I asked for my pension.

I had another trouble with my pension too — I couldn't prove my age, no certificates in those days, so I couldn't get my pension for two whole years. In the end it was Eva Williams that wrote to them and fixed that up.

My grandmother Mereana started with the Williams family when T. S. Williams came to Ruatoria. He came to Ngati Porou looking for a property, and when he saw Kaharau he asked the people who owned that land. They sent him to Mereana Mokikiwa, because her husband Henare Kaiwai was dead at that time; just she and I were living in the little raupo hut. He bought the land and built his house there, and when he got word that his family was coming from England, he asked Mereana if she would come to clean the house and put it in order. The old lady said,

"Ae, Te Wiremu . . . yes, I would come. But what about my mokopuna?"

"Bring your mokopuna with you, Mereana."

So that's how I went there and lived with the Williams, right from a child. I can remember the day when they got there, they gave me the biggest fright of my life. I saw these women get off the buggy, and they were coming with their long dresses. I'd never seen anyone like that before, and I had to run away and hide under the table in the kitchen. I was looking under the table, watching their legs as they went past in the house and oh! the dainty little feet, high heels and all that. I wondered how they could walk in those heels. Grandma was looking for me,

"Where's my mokopuna?"

Then Mrs Williams spotted me under the table.

"Come on dear, come on out here. What's wrong with you?"

I was shaking.

"It's all right, come on. . . ."

Mrs Williams was very good to me and now I appreciate all that, but at the time. . . . These manners, they take a while for any child to learn. She would come and show me my manners — don't do this, don't hold the plate towards you, you hold the plate *away* from you, *don't* make a noise while you're eating! We had to walk to school in the mornings, and as soon as I heard the children laughing and

---

[2] At Amiria's request, double vowels are not marked in this text. They are however, marked in the transcripts available in the University of Auckland and Alexander Turnbull Libraries.

4

playing on the way from Kariaka I had to hurry, because it was miles to walk to Hiruharama. So I'd just run and get my plate, and get the porridge out of the pot and eat it while I was there. I suppose I was making a noise while I'm eating, because Mrs Williams was going past and she said,

"Oh! Amy! What's that I heard just now? Was it one of the pigs?"

They had some little suckling pigs in a pen outside. She was looking around.

"Did one of those get under the table somehow?"

I knew she meant it for me. I said,

"No, Mrs Williams. That was me!"

"You, Amy?"

"Yes."

"Why?" she asked.

"Well I'm in a hurry, all the children are going to school, so I just drank my porridge up like that."

"Ah, that was very naughty. Now, you'd better come here and learn your manners."

She made me sit down, and showed me how to hold my plate.

"Did you say grace?"

"No, I didn't Mrs Williams, because I'm in a hurry."

"Even if you're in a hurry, you must say your grace. Now say it with me. Dear Lord, Bless this food, thank you for this gracious food, Amen."

I started to eat again.

"No! No! That's wrong. You turn the plate *away* from you, *no*, don't make that sound. . . ."

Well, by the time she was finished, the kids had gone way over the hill. When I got out to the road, there was nobody around. I started running barefooted to school, and by the time I got up on the top of the mountain I knew I was too late. It was a cold morning, so I thought *blow* this, I'm going to Te Ahi-a-te-Atua to get myself warm. Te Ahi-a-te-Atua was a big mountain, and there was a bubbling stream that came out from there, you could see it bubbling all the time. In those mornings there was snow on Hikurangi, and the snow was thick on the ground. Most of the children had no shoes at all, you were very lucky to have a pair of shoes in those days, so we all went to school barefooted. If it was very cold, we'd take a few matches and go to Te Ahi-a-te-Atua, and when we got there we'd light a match and throw it into this bubbling stream.[3] It would blow up, light up, and we'd all stand round warming our feet and singing, then we'd run to school. That fire would keep on burning until it rained. I went up there, and I slept for a while. When the children came home from school I waited until they had gone past Kaharau, then I went home to Taumata-o-mihi.

We had a lot of Maori kai in those days. My grandmother used to make kumara kao, and I'd take it to school for my lunch. You had to take the kumara and scrape it, but leave the reddish part of the skin, and put the kumara in the hangi. When it was cooked it was still firm. Then you'd take a lot of ponga leaves to the roof

[3] Probably one of the East Coast oil springs. There have been 30 wells sunk in the area since 1874, all without commercial success.

A raupo hut settlement, East Coast 1907 — Taumata-o-mihi must have looked much like this.

of the old thatched hut, and leave the kumara up there to dry. When it dried it was beautiful. It was so thin you could chew it like chewing gum, and it was soft and sweet.

If there was no bread ready to take to school, I'd just wrap up some kao and put it in my kit. The trouble was, by the time I got to school, the kao would be just about finished. I'd be eating it along the way and my mates would say,

"Huh! Are you eating your school lunch, Amy?"

"I slept in this morning, so I'm a bit hungry."

"What have you got? Kumara kao! Oo, I'll have some, you can have my lunch."

And another one would say,

"Give me some too, Amy."

Pretty soon my lunch would be all gone.

Another thing we took to school was dried shark. When the fish is brought ashore, you cut it into thin slices and hang it it in the sun to dry, then you take it inside and smoke it. It will keep for months and months, you just bundle it up in the storehouse and it'll never go bad. You can eat it raw; it's so thin that you just break it up and chew it. It smells strong but it's got a nice taste.

Then there was a lot of corn-cropping in those days, and some of our kai was made from corn. For kanga waru you'd get a fruit tin and punch nails through it, then put a cloth underneath and start to scrape the corn. Once you've got a big heap, you take the leaves that cover the corn, mix the corn with sugar and a little water and put it on the leaves. Tie this end and that end, then you cook it in the

hangi. It's beautiful!

But my favourite kai was kanga pirau. You put the corn in a clean bag and leave that in running water. When it gets soft it's ready to cook, but it's got a terrible smell. If you like it you don't mind the smell, though — I don't think anything of it. By gee, I can eat a lot of that stuff.

Puha toroi we ate at home or on the marae. There was always puha for the tangi. One old man, Ahipene Mika, whenever he saw puha on the table, you'd hear him calling,

"Wai kohua e, wai kohua e!" — he wanted the water. He reckoned that was the best. I think he was right, because when you look back, the old people of those days lived to a good old age. My grandmother Mereana was 108 years old before she died. They never complained of arthritis, or being blind; they just died of old age. I think it's the fancy foods of today that bring all these diseases.

My grandmother Mereana was a lovely woman, and a nice-looking woman too. There used to be a picture of her in the hotel at Ruatoria. I've been wanting to go there and get that picture, but I don't know if it's still there. Anyway, she was very good to me. I remember the first time she ever gave me a present for my birthday. I was born on the sixteenth of August, and someone was talking to my grandmother about it, and she said,

"That's right, e wareware ana," she'd forgotten about it. She'd never given me a birthday, not even a present. The other women round the pa said,

Mereana Mokikiwa, Amiria's "grandmother."

"You should give your grand-daughter something."

So Mereana asked one woman if she could make a dress for me. Mereana got the measurements, and the woman made this beautiful frock.

Anyhow, this morning my grandmother called me,

"Amiria! Kei whea koe? Come here. . . ."

I went over and she said,

"This is your birthday, sixteenth of August. Did you know that?"

No, I didn't know. In those days kids didn't worry about all those things. This was the first time I realised I had a birthday. She took out this frock and said,

"Now, put it on. Purua ki runga i a koe."

I looked — oh, what a beautiful frock, and I put it on. I looked at it, and it just fitted me so nice.

My grandmother said,

"That woman made a good job of it all right!"

I started showing off, dancing around.

"Now, you look after that frock, eh."

"Can I go and tell Kareti about it, grandma?"

"All right, but you look after that frock."

"Yeah, yeah," I said.

So I ran out of the house to show my friend Kareti Haerewa. Of course, when she saw the frock she said,

"Oer . . . fancy! You got that for your birthday? So this is your birthday?"

"Yes."

"Oh, I've never had a present like that for my birthday . . . that cost a lot of money, that dress."

Then she thought up something, I suppose.

"Let's go and play with the other children."

These kids were playing on the hill, sliding down. They'd get the kouka or cabbage tree, and cut a big branch and then slide on it. You'd hold the stick and sit on the leaves and then slide down the hill. We used to play on manuka horses too, made out of kahikatoa. Somebody might crash down, then *bang!* all down on the ground, and all the others were screaming and laughing. That's the way we enjoyed ourselves, we made all our own toys.

Well, Kareti got a kouka for herself and I got one, and away we went to Tauwharenikau hill, not far from Taumata-o-mihi. All the kids from Kariaka marae and Taumata-o-mihi marae, and even the other marae at Te Raupo that belonged to Warihi Tako, all those kids were playing on the hill.

The next thing, I got this dress dirty. I stood up, and the other kids told me about it.

"Look at your nice frock!"

I started to wonder how I was going to get home without my grandmother seeing this frock. Then she called me, so I had to go. When I went inside grandma said,

"You'd better get some firewood to heat the tea-kettle."

When I went to take the wood in, I wouldn't turn my back. I was facing her all the time, and that's the way I was walking around. I filled up the kettle and backed out. She looked at me,

"Huh! What's the matter with this girl? She doesn't seem to walk straight."
She grabbed hold of me.

"He aha to mate? What's wrong with you? . . ." She turned me around, oh! there you are, this beautiful frock was all dirty. The old lady was so shocked to see that beautiful frock spoiled, that was the first biggest hiding I ever had. She turned me around and gave me the devil of a hiding, and even sacked me.

"You'd better go back to your mother. You can go back to Tuparoa, right now! I don't want you, *bad* girl. . . . Go on, off you go!"

I was howling.

"Go on, go back to Tuparoa. Take your cat Takekore with you!"

I had a cat there that was given to me and they called it Takekore, "good-for-nothing", meaning I'm good for nothing, because grandmother did everything for me. That's what used to make my uncle so mad —

"You get that girl to work!"

Oh it's all right, grandmother would take something that I was doing and put me to something very light. My uncle would say,

"She'll be useless, that girl, because she doesn't know how to work!"

Anyhow, I grabbed the bag of sugar and put all my clothes in it. I didn't forget the cat, I put the cat on top and away I went. Grandma didn't take any notice, she didn't think I would go because Tuparoa was a long way off — over two hundred miles, I'm sure. Well, I went. I went over the hills, past Ruatoria. I went up the gully and down another gully, and up again. By Jove, then I got tired . . . I thought I'd sit down and have a rest. There was a creek there, so I sat underneath the fern-trees and I dropped off to sleep.

It was the dogs that found me. I heard the dogs barking, and that woke me up. I woke up and saw this dog, he was coming closer to me. The cat had his head out of the bag and was trying to jump out, so I squeezed the cat's neck like this; I thought, if the dog bites this cat, the cat is bound to jump up and run away and get lost. So I was holding on to the cat and the bag, and a man came down on his horse.

"Huh, what's that! Somebody must be down there. . . ."

He jumped off his horse and ran; he called out to the dogs to stop barking, then he saw me.

"Oh! What are you doing here, little girl?"

"I've been asleep!" I said.

"What do you want to come here and sleep for?"

"My grandmother sacked me out of the house."

"Who's your grandmother, then?"

"Mereana Kaiwai."

"O yes, I know the old lady. You must be the little girl she brings to Kaharau — I've seen you around."

"Yeah," I said.

"And where are you going to now?"

"I'm going to Tuparoa, to my mother's place."

"Oh no, I'll take you back to Taumata-o-mihi, I'll take you back to your grandmother! I'm the head shepherd of Williams' station, so I know the old lady. I'll take you home."

"No, I don't want to go there, she kicked me out."

"Don't be silly," he said.

"No, no," and I started to cry. "No, I don't want to . . . I'm not going back!"

"Oh all right, you'd better get on my horse. I'll take you to Tuparoa."

So I got up on the bank, and hopped on behind him.

"Would you like to come on the saddle?" he asked.

"No, I'll be all right. I'll hold onto you."

"Well, give me the bag."

"No! My cat might jump out!"

Well, we got to Tuparoa. We came to my mother's house, and she was surprised to see me with my bag and all my clothes.

"Amiria, what's wrong with you? What are you doing with all your . . ."

"Grandma kicked me out."

"Now, what did you do?"

I showed her the frock.

"Ah, pai noa — you deserved it all right. Fancy! Oh, fancy you doing that to your grandma's present for you. . . . You deserved all that hiding. But still, I'll have to let grandma know. I bet she's running all over the place looking for you."

She went down to the town to ring up, because we didn't have a phone in the house. She had to go down to Tuparoa to ring up[4] and tell Mereana that I'm all right, I'm at home. When she rang they couldn't find the old lady. She had got on her horse and was riding round the place looking for me. In the end they found her and told her that I was all right. The next day she came to get me, and took me back to Taumata-o-mihi. And last year when I went to the "C" Company reunion at Ruatoria, I was sitting on the grandstand and looking at this mountain; it brought memories of the dog and the cat and everything to me. I said to some of my friends from here,

"See that hill over there? That's where they found me with my cat in the bag." And they laughed.

Another time, the baby next door nearly got burnt up in their whata. Our house was next door to another family and they had a little whata, a storehouse, where they kept all their kai — kumaras, dried fish and all that. Their daughter had a boyfriend, a shepherd from the Williams' place, and sometimes we'd hear him come whistling through the wiwi and toetoe at the back of Taumata-o-mihi. Those shepherds had their Maori girlfriends to take out, and Keriana was courting with one of these fellas.

She wanted to be away from the old people, so she asked her parents if she could live in this whata. She said there was too much Maori talk and chanting at home, it might be quieter in the whata for the baby. They thought about it — oh, maybe she's right. Her father said,

"All right, Keriana, but you'll have to clean the whata up. We can shift the food to a pit."

---

[4] There were telephones on the East Coast in the period. The Williams' had a private line from shore to inland (Sir Robert Hall, private communication); by 1907 a Native Telephone System was in operation in the Bay of Plenty (see photo p. 65).

Ruatoria and District

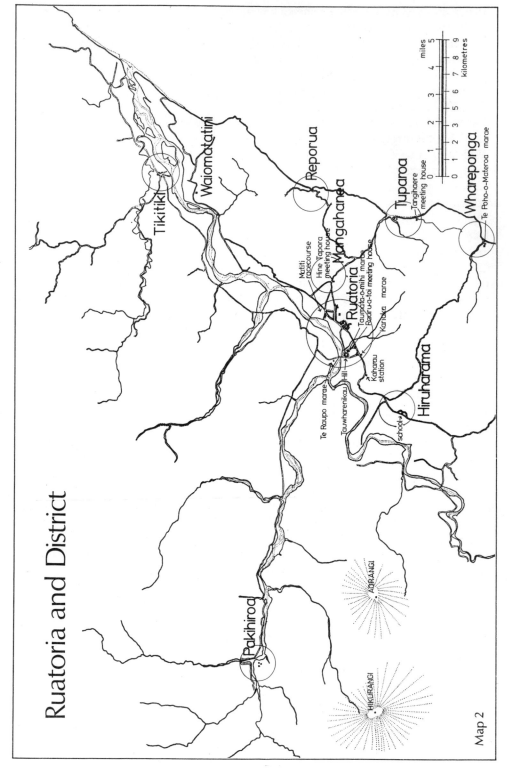

Tikitiki

Waiomatatini

Reporua

Mangahanea

Matiti racecourse
Hine Tapora meeting house
Taupata-o-mihi marae
Ruatoria
Paeirua-toi meeting house
Kariaka marae
Te Raupo marae
Tauwharenikau Hill
Kaharau station
school→

Tuparoa
Tangihaere meeting house

Wharepanga
Te Poho-o-Materoa marae

Hiruharama

Pakihiroa

AORANGI

HIKURANGI

miles
kilometres

Map 2

She tidied the place up and put her bed there, all the baby's clothes and every-thing — it was really neat the way she did it. When you went up the steps there was a little verandah in front; on a nice sunny day she'd just sit out on her whata, and we could see her from the window of my grandmother's bedroom.

"How's the baby?" my grandmother would ask.

"Oh, it's better here, it's quiet for the baby."

But this particular night, I was fast asleep. Suddenly my grandmother yelled out, "Amiria! *Amiria!* Quick, get out of bed. The whata's on fire!"

I got up, half asleep. She grabbed me and opened the window and threw me out of the window.

"Run! Run! Get the baby!"

The baby was howling. As I came out of my sleep, I saw the flames in the whata, and I heard the baby's voice. I crawled through the fence and ran up the steps onto the verandah then opened the door. When I opened the door, all the flames flew out and I stopped. Grandma was running behind me, so she gave me a push. I went in and grabbed the baby, blanket and all, and I got all my hair burnt up.

But the old lady knew what to do, she brought a bucket of water and a wet blanket, and threw this water on me, and covered us both in the blanket. Then she took me out of the blanket and told me to run and get some more water. By the time we turned round to the whata, it was too far gone, we couldn't do anything. Grandma said not to worry, as long as we've saved the baby. Then she asked me to get some potatoes. She took the baby inside, and wrapped it in one of our own sheets. The poor baby was *howling* at the top of her voice. I brought a kit of potatoes, and grandma grabbed some and washed them, then scraped them with a knife.

"Quick, scrape some too, Amiria."

She didn't even bother about peeling them. She got the sheet and tore up the sheet, and wrapped the baby in the potato scrapings. Somehow or other, the baby cooled down. Every now and again she'd howl, but you could see she was easing down a bit. That's when I learned that a potato is the best thing for burns or scalds, because you want something cool. Butter is warm, it's no good, and there's some-thing in the potato that helps the child quicker than anything. When we looked at that baby in the morning — no blisters.

I remember when I grabbed the baby I saw a candle there, and that was how the whata got burned. The baby must have been crying and put her arms out and knocked it over, and started the fire. Keriana had gone off courting. When she came home she had a shock to see the whata burned. She didn't go inside, she hid under the house and was crying under there. When her father found her, poor old Keriana got a thrashing for it. She thought the baby was burnt. After a while her mother and father told her to come and see the baby at our place; when she walked into our house she was crying, and the old lady blasted her off about this,

"Imagine going courting instead of looking after the baby! And lucky Amiria was home with me, because I couldn't have got there quick enough. But she had quick legs to jump and run, and she got in there. Now look at her, she's got no hair!"

There I was, all bald. When Keriana saw me she came and put her arms around me.

13

"Now Keriana, you stop your silly rubbish! One baby is enough for the old people to look after."

She got a hiding from her brother too, and everything.

That was the life in Taumata-o-mihi. It was just a little place in my young days. There was the meeting house, Rauru-a-Toi, not a very big house like the ones they built later at Tikitiki and Waiomatatini; but it was big enough for the people then. And all the people lived in toetoe huts — only Hakopa Haerewa had a nice house. Later on when Hariata married Moko they got a house; and after that, T. S. Williams built a house and gifted it to my grandmother. When the old lady got to a pension age, Thomas Sidney Williams said to her,

"Well Mereana, you're an old-age pensioner now, and there's a pension for you when you retire. But our gift for you will be a house, we'll build a house for you and your mokopuna at Taumata-o-mihi."

The old lady said,

"Ae, Te Wiremu . . . if it's from you, yes."

We couldn't believe it. When they started building, there were one, two, three, four rooms, kitchen and a bathroom — everything. Well! Hakopa Haerewa had a bigger house, but ours was a dainty little house, with everything complete. It had a stove and everything. No lighting the fire out in the cold fireplace and hanging up the billy and the kettle, none of that. The old lady said,

"Ka pai te whare a te pakeha — I do like the pakeha house."

But Tuparoa was the township in my young days. It was only recently in Ngata's time that Mangahanea and Waiomatatini and Waiapu and all those other maraes were built. All the main families, the Milners, and the Haigs and the Koheres,

Amiria outside Rauru-a-Toi meeting house, Taumata-o-mihi, with Mt. Hikurangi in the background.

Hakopa Haerewa's house today.

The house that T. S. Williams built for Mereana.

they all started from Tuparoa. When the roads came through Waiapu and round to Waiomatatini, that's when Ruatoria started. They could get everything brought by boat to Tokomaru Bay and transport it to Ruatoria, there was no need to go to Tuparoa. So Tuparoa was stopped. They bought the hotel and all the shops and shifted them to Ruatoria.

Ruatoria was a real country town in those days. There were horses tied up on the posts, you could see them tearing up the street on horseback, women and all, double-bank. . . . They'd just bring their horses, get off the horse and tie the horse on the verandah post and go in the hotel, have a few drinks I suppose. There were a lot of manukas around by the shop; if there was no room on the verandah for your horse, you could just tie it to a manuka bush.

That's why they called it the cowboy town. You'd see them running up the street on their bare feet, and then they'd hop on their horses and away they'd go, tearing up to Waiomatatini, *singing* away. It was a very happy town. I liked the way they were, the people were nice and good to everybody. Nobody got hit or knocked over, the way they do today. They might look rough, in rough clothes, but they were not rough in their ways. Even the young men, they respected the girls. There might be a coat hanging there and a shirt hanging out of the pants, but they were tidy in their manners. Because as the saying is, the Maoris do train their families kia aroha — to be good to other people.

Top left: Tuparoa in its heyday.

Centre left: When the East Coast road went through.

Bottom left: Tuparoa today — Tangihaere meeting-house.

CHAPTER TWO

Girlhood Days

These are some stories about my days as a girl, full of daring ways and that.

In those times, Ka Waiti and I used to go at the weekends and play football with the other kids. But the trouble was they'd tear our frocks, so we had to borrow a coat. You looked around for a friendly-looking fellow who is good to you, and this fellow Joe Hunia he was good to me. So I'd say,

"Eh Joe, what about giving me your coat?"

"What do you want my coat for?"

"We've got to play football."

"Well, what about if my coat gets torn?" he asked.

"No, it won't get torn, Joe."

"It better not. If it gets torn, you're going to get a hiding from me!"

So the football team of girls would play against the boys, and of course they had had the boys' coats on. This time, poor old Joe got his coat torn all right. By gosh, he kicked my behind! I wrapped up the coat and gave it to him, but he shook it out and had a look — there was a tear. He threw it back at me.

"You've got to damn well sew that up!"

"All right Joe, I'll have to take it home — I haven't got a needle."

"Go on then, take it home!"

So I sewed it up, and brought it back the next day.

When we had dances too, Joe would always come and ask me to dance. He didn't care about dressing up though, he just came any old how.

"Come on Amy, we go and have a dance."

I looked at him, gee whizz!

"Go and put something better on than that rag you got there Joe, you look terrible!"

Then he'd tease me,

"That's not what the old people say. They'll tell you, don't look for the man with the nice collar and tie; find a man with cracked dirty hands, a hard-working man to carry your bucket of water. How about it, Amy?"

He was a hard case alright . . .

The funny thing was, I saw Joe just a few years ago. He'd come back from the war, and we were at a tangi at Ruatoria. He was up on the stage talking away and telling the people what happened when the soldiers were overseas. He'd say something in Italian, and all the people were laughing. I thought gee, that looks like Joe Hunia — but he's dead, it might be his brother. I thought he'd been killed overseas.

After a while he looked down at me, and he asked somebody,

"Who's that woman sitting down there?"

"That's Amiria."

"Hey, that's not Amiria O'Hara is it?"

"Yes, that's her, but she's Amiria Stirling now."

He jumped off the stage and ran to me, and he said,

"Amiria, Amiria, Amiria . . . by Joves, you're a beggar! Remember how you tore my coat?"

"Is that you Joe?" I said.

"Yes, of course it is! You always used to come to me when you wanted a coat to play football."

"But I heard you were dead!"

"Oh they can't kill me, those Germans can't kill me!"

He's dead now, though, poor old Joe. Just recently I heard he'd died.

When I think about dances, it reminds me of one time when Titihuia Haerewa and I wanted to go to a dance at Mangahanea.

Titihuia was Kareti's older sister, and really she wanted to go, but she picked me to help her because I was full of devilment I suppose. She said,

"Amiria, how about you go and steal my uncle's saddle? He's asleep and he's in his little bach."

She asked me to go and steal the saddle because I was only a tiny little brat in those days, so I could sneak into the room and drag the saddle out. Her uncle Reupena Turehu was an old man, and he always slept in his little hut by himself. He kept the saddle beside his bed so nobody could take it. She said,

"You can come to the dance with me if you get that saddle. We can double-bank on my horse."

I thought that was great; usually I couldn't go to dances because I didn't have a horse. We went down to this little bach and we could hear the old man snoring, so we sat and listened. Sometimes he would cough and wake up a bit. After a while he was snoring hard, and Titihuia nodded her head and said to me,

"You go in now, he's fast asleep."

I started crawling in; the door had been left half open to let in the air. She was right behind me and pinched my behind to make me go quicker. I was frightened I might make a noise, and the old man would wake up and catch me. Titihuia pinched me,

"Go on, hurry up! Quick!"

I grabbed the saddle but the stirrups made a ringing noise, and the old man started to cough,

"Uh! Uh!"

I clapped myself down on the floor and wondered if he was going to sit up. He didn't though, so I gradually pulled the saddle away and out of the bach, then ran off with it. We didn't realise that the girth had been left behind until we got the horse in the paddock and caught it. When we put the saddle on — no girth. Titihuia started to growl.

"By Jove! Why didn't you grab everything when you took the saddle? What's the use of this saddle without the girth? Agh!" and she punched me. "You should go back and look for it."

Well, by that time I didn't want to go back.

"No, he might wake up and catch me."

Ruatoria in later years — 1930s.

We started to think perhaps if we just sat on this saddle, if we were careful not to move too much this way or that way, it might be all right. When we got on it was all right and the horse started to canter. We began to sing as we cantered along. But somehow or other, we were going through a track in the bush right below the Ruatoria Hotel, and I saw a manuka bush fallen down and realised it might hit my head. I grabbed it to pull it away, and that's how we fell off. Titihuia called out to me not to hang on to her, to let her go.

"Amiria! Let me go, let go!"

But I thought if I'm going to fall, you're going to fall too; and we both fell onto the ground, the saddle and all. Titihuia got up, she cursed me and hit me. Luckily the horse didn't run away, it just stood there and looked at us.

"Now what are we going to do?" she said.

We decided to hide the saddle in the bush and go bareback to Mangahanea. We got to Mangahanea and we were dancing away; when it was nearly daylight we started to think about coming home.

Titihuia said,

"We'd better go home before daylight, because we have to take the saddle back to the old man's bach and leave it outside. He won't know who took it."

We went back and picked up the saddle, but by the time we got back to Taumata-o-mihi, we noticed the kids playing around, it was daylight.

She said to me,

"By Joves, it's too dangerous! The old man must be awake by now. We'd better leave the saddle just here, he can look for it. We can't take it over there."

We dropped the saddle and ran to the Haerewa home and went to bed. When we were fast asleep we heard Reupena shouting for us, calling out for Titihuia.

"Titihuia! Kei whea koe? Where are you, Titihuia?"

We just lay there, pretending not to hear him. He came into the room —

"Oh, here you are! Where have you put my saddle?"

We were pretending to be all sleepy, as if we couldn't hear him very well, when all of a sudden someone spotted the saddle on the bank. But they had a suspicion. We didn't give in, but someone at Mangahanea told on us.

"Titihuia and Amiria must have stolen the saddle, because they were here last night."

So they caught on to us, and we got another hiding for that. Titihuia got the worst though because she was the eldest. That's why, I suppose, whenever I talked to her about it, she used to get annoyed with me.

In those times too, the Ngati Porou people started dairy-farming. Apirana Ngata called the people to a big hui at Porourangi to talk about it. He told them that the Taranaki people had already started dairying, and they were doing very well.

Sir Apirana Turupa Ngata.

21

Sir Maui Pomare had helped to set his people up in dairying and now Api wanted to do the same for Ngati Porou. It would help to clean all the rubbish off the land and grass it, and if all went well a factory could be set up at Ruatoria.

"There will be a factory at Ruatoria, and every month . . . there's your cheque! Once you're set up dairying, we'll have something to show to the Government — then we can ask for housing. So this is my request to you, Ngati Porou; that you start milking cows."

Then the Ngati Porou orators spoke.

"Ah, all right Api, you ask the Government for the money to start this, and when we get our money — all right."

"The Government will help you," Apirana replied, "but it won't be a gift. You'll have to pay it back. When you get your cream cheque, you can pay it back little by little until you've paid your mortgage, then you're right. And the same for your housing. You'll get your house, then the same money will gradually pay off your house. In the finish your family will have a house and a farm and everything."

When the people saw that Apirana could get the money to do this through the Government, they OK'd it.

Then one smart one stood up,

"Ae, Api! But if this is to be the case, we don't want these drovers' cows they bring around here. We want the *best* breed, and that's Sir Maui Pomare's cows from Taranaki. Then we'll start milking."

The money came from Wellington and the cows from Taranaki, and pretty soon Ngati Porou were doing very well. They composed a song about it, "The Cream Song"; it had beautiful actions too:

VERSE ONE

Tera te mahi pai rawa	*This is the best work,*
E kia ana mai	*So they say,*
Te mahi ra e puta ai	*This work brings*
Nga moni nuinui noa	*Big money.*
E whanga ra, e tama ma	*You wait for*
Ki nga pei marama,	*The monthly cheque*
Kua riro ke, i nga nama	*But it's already gone to pay the debts —*
Aue nga wawata!	*Too bad.*

CHORUS

Aue! E rere ra te kirimi e	*Aue! The cream runs*
Ki roto ki nga kena nei, aue,	*Into the cans.*
Kia tika hawerewere,	*Make sure to aim straight*
Kei rere parorirori	*Don't let it go crooked —*
Kia rite ai nga nama	*We need to settle our debts.*

VERSE TWO

Tera nga tino momo kau	*Those are the best cows*
E kia ana mai	*So they say*
No Taranaki ra ano	*The ones from Taranaki*
Na Maui Pomare	*That belong to Maui Pomare.*
Nga kau ra i rere ai	*Those were the cows*

Te Nati ki te hao,	*The Natis ran to grab —*
He rau mahau, he rau maku,	*100 for you, 100 for me,*
Ka ea nga wawata	*All our hopes are fulfilled.*

CHORUS

VERSE THREE

Tera te pata rongonui	*This is the famous butter*
He Nati te ingoa	*Called "Nati"*
Te wahi ra i mahia ai	*And it's made*
Ko Ruatoria	*In Ruatoria.*
Haramai ra Te Pirimia	*Come, Prime Minister*
Mahau te kawanga	*We want you to perform the grand opening*
Kia pono ai te mahi nei	*So we can believe*
He mahi kai ano!	*This work will make food for us.*

CHORUS

The cream factory was set up, and they made their own butter with its own stamp and everything. It was called "Nati" after the Ngati Porou people, that was their nickname. But years afterwards, things were slackening a bit. The people had to pay off their cows, and Api knew the time was getting a bit close for the Ngati Porou to get all their money in, to show the Government that they were genuine with their mortgages. I think that's why he brought in the Prohibition.

All of a sudden he introduced this law, that the Maoris of Ngati Porou were not allowed to go in any hotel and drink. And when the people found out about this, they just about *killed* Ngata. I heard my own uncle Tamati Kaiwai cursing Apirana on the marae, and telling him off, who the devil does he think he is. That was the first man I ever heard insulting Apirana — I know I felt my blood boiling when I heard him say,

"You're only a mokopuna of Wi Tito[5]!"

Well, tito to us is telling lies. And he said,

"Blow your carved meeting-houses! It's just when somebody dies or there's a meeting or something. What about us? We're still living in raupo huts, we've been living in them all these years. . . . We want a house, Api, a house! You're a *slave,* doing this to us — what about the other Maoris? They can still go in the hotel and have their drink; it's only the Ngati Porou people. You've done this to your *own* people, Api — e hoa!"

I thought, by gosh, you're the first man I've ever heard talking like that to Api. I expected Api to get up and tell him off. Api stood up.

"Have you finished, Tamati?"

"E hoa! *Blow* you."

Api just walked up to the meeting-house, to Porourangi, and he started talking to that house.

---

[5] According to Reweti Kohere, Ngata's true grandfather was a man named Wi Tito. (Kohere 1951, p. 25).

"My ancestors. You hear what this man said, these houses are useless — these houses that I have built, my memorials to you and to Maori tradition. Why did I do it? Because before long the Maori will be lost from the face of the earth, the young people don't appreciate the old treasures any more. Now, you have heard what this man thinks about it. All right, he can scold me — I'm no one, just a mokopuna of Wi Tito. Tamati, I say this to you — you chiefs, you're just like a flower! The pakeha goes and picks the best, the nice-looking bloom, and they put it in a vase on a mantlepiece. What are they for? For the people to admire. That's you! You chiefs are there for the people to look at. But the workers, they are the low-born, the grandchildren of Wi Tito. The old people knew how to choose the hands to work for them, they'd look to the lowly people. They wouldn't choose you, the chiefs! And this is not tito — it's the truth."

I was listening to him talking like that, belittling himself, but I knew he wasn't a low man. He was a great man, and yet he didn't put himself up. That's something I admired in my heart about Apirana. Then he explained to the people.

"Your houses are coming. Once you've paid off the cows, we can raise another mortgage for the houses. But not until you've cleared off the first debt."

It was no use talking to the men about the Prohibition, they only wanted to fight the same as Tamati Kaiwai, so Ngata decided that it would be better for him to get the women interested in it. He talked to some women about getting signatures and they told him that Ani Kahutawhiti would be the right one; she'd be brave enough to go to different homes and get the women to sign and to pass over this white ribbon — she wouldn't be afraid.

Ngata went to Ruatoria and he talked to Ani about it. He said to her,

"It has to be done soon, Ani, so the Ngati Porou can square their debt on the cows, then they can get a mortgage for their houses. *You* are the one to take the papers so the women can sign. But don't let the men know about it, go quickly when the men are out working. As long as you get enough signatures, we'll be right."

My mother said,

"Ae, all right Api, I'll do it!"

That was her. She'd go to one place, and have a look to see if the men were out working. If she saw the children running around she'd ask,

"Where's your father?"

"He's not home, he's gone fencing."

All right, she'd hop there and get the women's signatures. She told them about it.

"Oh, that's a good idea, Ani."

As soon as they signed she'd pass over the white ribbon,

"Put that away, don't let your husband see it."

Once or twice she got caught. One man had gone fencing, but he forgot something so he came back home and caught Mum there. As soon as he saw her, he said,

"What are you doing here?"

"Oh, I've just come to see the family."

"You get the bloody . . . ", he cursed her and pushed her out of the house.

"I know what you're up to. You're nothing but a thief!"

He kicked her out and told his womenfolk never to have anything to do with her. She went away, but she came back when he wasn't around. She wouldn't give in. In

24

Ani Kahutawhiti, Amiria's mother, wearing the white Prohibition ribbon.

the end the women won it, and the Prohibition came to Ngati Porou. Tamati Kaiwai and all his friends thought that this was the big curse on them, so they composed this haka:

Ee . . . i ko Apirana Ngata	*Ee, Apirana Ngata*
Ra ia te tangata	*Is the man*
E takarure mai Poneke e,	*Who keeps coming from Wellington*
Ahaha!	*Ahaha!*
Horahia mai o ture ki ahau,	*Show me your laws!*
Horahia mai o ture ki ahau!	*Show me your laws!*
Ahaha!	*Ahaha!*
Ture reiti koiaraka!	*Rating laws!*
Ture kaunihera koiaraka!	*Council laws!*
Poropeihana koiaraka!	*The Prohibition!*
Ka minamina au ki te wai piro	*I want whiskey*
Kaho kona ki te po	*But it's been sold to the dead!*
Purari paka!	*Bloody bugger!*
Kaura mokai e!	*Slave!*

"Api" leading a haka, 1940.

That was for Api. When this haka started in Ngati Porou everywhere you heard this "Purari paka, kaura mokai e!" Poor old Api.[6] There he was, listening to it, with Tamati Kaiwai jumping around in front of him. But after the years they found out, well, look: they paid off their mortgages, and those people who wanted houses got them. That was Ngata. He was the genuine man. He was good. He wasn't looking for himself, to make himself a big man, a rich man. But today the dairying is finished and the factory closed. I'm sure if Ngata came to life and saw that, he'd run back quickly.

I was about 18 when I went away to school. In those days there was no force for kids to go to school at an early age, and I think I was about six or seven before I started at Hiruharama. I was lucky, though. There was a teacher that came to Kaharau for the Williams children, and Mrs Williams allowed me to go there and listen. I was the baby in the class, sitting at the back and listening to the lessons, but after that I had to go to the Native School. When I got to about 18, my mother

6 Graeme Butterworth has given me another account of the origins of this haka, passed on to him by the late Arnold Reedy. Apparently in 1911 Ngata persuaded the Horouta Maori Council to hold a poll on Prohibition, and by a narrow margin an experimental three-year "dry" period began in the area. When the period lapsed in 1914 the Government refused to finance another poll. The East Coast remained "dry" until 1922 when special enabling legislation finally made a second poll possible. The haka was composed in 1920 by local men, who blamed Ngata for their ten-year drought. Peggy Kaua tells me that Ngata used to take all personal sting out of the haka by leading it himself.

wanted to send me to school with the money my father had put away. She asked Mereana to go and see Mrs Williams about it, because the Maoris in those days were not clever to do those things. Mrs Williams worked everything for them, and the next thing I had to pack up and go to the Ladies' College in Wellington. I felt I couldn't believe it.

My brother-in-law and my sister Ani were living in Lower Hutt at the time, so I stayed with them and started school at the Ladies' College. But I was a funny girl somehow. I got very chummy with a German girl — she seemed to be so lost. Those were the war years, and the other girls didn't look right to her because she was German. She asked me,

"How do you feel here, Amy — are you all right?"

"I don't know," I said. "I suppose I'm a bit lost too, because I'm a Maori. I'm not a pakeha, I'm a Maori. There's a way about some of them that reminds me, 'don't forget you're a Maori'."

"It's the same with me — 'don't forget you're a German'. All because of the war. I'm going to get out of this school, I'm not going to stay here."

"Don't do that, Hilda," I said. "If you're going to go I'll be lonely."

"But I'm not happy at all!"

"Oh," I said, "who cares?", and we carried on for a while. One day Hilda said to me,

"Let's get out of here. I can get us a job in Lower Hutt."

"Can you?"

"Yes."

"Well, not yet. We'll wait until you've got everything all fixed up."

I think someone must have told on us, because the next thing I got a letter to say I have to come home, my grandmother is very sick, she's dying. After that there was a telegram. I wanted to see my grandmother, I didn't want her to pass away without me seeing her, so I went straight home. When I arrived, there was grandma playing patience at home in our house. There was nothing wrong with her. I walked in and she was sitting on the floor playing patience. I said,

"You're all right, you're not sick! I thought you were very sick!"

"Oh, I'm all right now."

I kissed her and rubbed noses to her, and she said,

"I'm very glad to see you. You've been fooling around enough and it's time you came home to make a woman of yourself. You're porangi, a mokopuna porangi!"

"No I'm not, grandma. I'm not crazy. I always remember what you told me."

"Aua, I don't know."

While I was at home Kareti told me that the old people have been planning an arranged marriage for me, a taumau marriage. They wanted me to come home to see if I would agree with it. I think they knew I had a pakeha boyfriend in Wellington too. Well, I wouldn't listen. When I knew my grandmother was all right, I came back to Wellington.

I did have a pakeha boyfriend there too, a boy called George Nelson, and he was a fine-looking fellow. He was at school there with us and that's how I met him. He was very good to me, he would always take me to the pictures and that, he didn't handle me the wrong way. If he went a bit far, I could tell him and he would listen.

"You know, you don't do these things until you're really married, George. So don't think I'm one of those you can please yourself with, I'm *not*. If you treat me that way, I'll never go out with you again. I mean it."

Then he'd start to sing or something, and after a while, we were all right again. One day he took me to his mother's place and she was nice; but in the end he went away to war. Before he went away he said to me,

"Amy, what about going for a trip on the boat?"

"Where to?"

"Oh, anywhere. . . . Wouldn't you like a trip on the boat?"

"Just way out on the harbour?" I asked.

"Yes. There's a lot of people go out."

"Oh, I'd like that, George."

"Well, you meet me down at the wharf. What about Saturday, that's your free day, isn't it?"

"Yes."

"Around about 2 o'clock, I'll be waiting down at the wharf."

When I got to the wharf that day, I saw all these flowers — beautiful! So I thought I'd buy a bunch of red roses. Some were open and some were just budding. I bought this bunch of roses and I took them in my arms, and some biscuits and an ice-cream each. George was waiting there, and when he saw me he said,

"Oh Amy! You look as if you're going to the church. What — are we going to get married?"

"Oh no," I said, "I think I love these roses . . . I'm going to take them home, and put them in my room."

"Yes, they are lovely." He started smelling them.

I gave him an ice-cream and I had an ice-cream, and we went on the boat. We didn't go inside, we sat outside looking at the beautiful day. And we were talking, and he was singing all these songs, and I was singing with him. He sang,

> "Sincerely, oh, oh, oh, sincerely,
> I love you sincerely,
> Please be mine . . . !"

and while he was singing he was picking at my roses and dropping them on to the sea. I didn't know till I saw all the petals on the water, and I turned round and said to him,

"What are you doing, George?"

"Look at the confettis," he said. "That's just like our wedding day, Amy. That's how the confettis . . . "

"Oh," I said. "My roses! You've pulled all the . . . ", and I just about cried. I looked at one — it was almost bare. He said,

"But I like to see them floating away like that — it makes me think of our wedding day, Amy. You wait till I come back. We'll get roses too, on our wedding day, we won't have confettis. I'll buy a bunch of roses and pull all the petals . . . "

Well, that was the last. I never saw George again. He always wrote to me but you see, he was killed over there. His mother was so good to me, she always wrote to me and sent his presents on to me. When my taumau marriage was settled I thought I'd better let her know, so I wrote her a letter. I said, "I'm sorry to have to tell you this Mrs Nelson, but I'm getting married. It's not my wish, it's my people's wish and I

28

have to do what they want — that's the Maori custom. Although I really thought the world of your son, because George was very good to me."

I told her the date we were going to be married, and she sent me a beautiful set of silver teaspoons. I couldn't help it, I cried when I saw them. I thought they were "tear spoons", not tea spoons. She wrote on the card: "Accept these silver tea-spoons, Amy, from the family of George Nelson. Hope you have a happy life, from us all." But I'm glad George didn't know anything about it, I don't think his mother told him.

When I came back to the Ladies' College from Taumata-o-mihi, with all the talk about a taumau marriage and my friend trying to get a job in Lower Hutt, I got all worked up. We ended up by clearing out from school, and I went to Hilda's place in Lower Hutt. We were working at the Woollen Mills and it was a good job, but it didn't last long. The police had an announcement out and everything, and finally they tracked us down at the Mills. My mother came down to Wellington and took me back to Ruatoria.

CHAPTER THREE

The Typhoid Epidemic

When I got home, my mother asked me to go nursing, because a typhoid epidemic had broken out on the Coast. I think she really wanted to get me away from Taumata-o-mihi and the taumau marriage that the old people were planning. All the hospitals were full right from Gisborne down the Bay of Plenty, and there were people lying dead in their houses because there was no one to nurse them — it was terrible.

The best they could in Ruatoria was to put two marquees on the Matiti Race-course, by the Waiapu River. They were calling out for girls to help; there were some Maori nurses there but they had contracted the fever and passed on. So I thought I'd go and be a nurse. When Areta heard about it she said,

"Oh Amy, are you going nursing?"

"Yes, that's it."

"We'll go there, eh?"

"Are you coming too, Adie?"

"Yes. You tell your mother I'm going with you."

Areta was older than me, and she was supposed to be doing mission work at Tokomaru, but she thought she'd like to come with me. When we got to the Racecourse hospital they did give us some training. There were about twenty of us when we started off.

On certain days we had lectures, and a doctor would come in and teach us what to do, how to sponge your patient and take the temperature and all this. The main thing was to wash your hands. The doctors told us that some people are carriers — they can carry typhoid on them, and pass it on. If you are weak in your system, you just grab it like that and you're gone. So you must remember to wash your hands. If you touch your patient, if you lift your patient or wash your patient; when you've finished, wash your hands. If you meet someone on the bus or shake hands at a hui, wash your hands. And disinfection, too — we had a lot of Jeyes' Fluid in those years.

It ended up there were only four nurses left, two day and two night nurses, because we had contracted it too. There would be somebody falling off the bed, and somebody else was delirious and had gone mad, somebody else had passed on. You'd run and catch this one, put her down, and forget about yourself. You only had to put something to your nose and you'd got it. That's how it was in those days.

Every night when we went to bed, Areta would come and say,

"Well Amy, hope to see you in the morning."

"Have a prayer for me," I said.

I'd hold her hand and she held my hand, and we'd say a little prayer in our hearts that we'll come out again the next morning.

We did this every night, even the other nurses.

"Well nurse, are you off now?" I'd say.

"Yes."

"Oh well," and I'd put my arms around her, "see you in the morning, dear."

The next day one of the nurses would be gone, taken away to another hospital. One night, someone asked me,

"Where's Adie?"

"I don't know, she might be in the other marquee down there."

"You'd better go and look for her, she should be here by now."

So I went down there and looked around — no Adie. I saw people all delirious, they were talking away, pulling the blankets off and falling down on the floor. There were not enough nurses to look after them. I couldn't find Adie so I came back and told Mrs Wicksteed, our matron,[7]

"I don't know where Adie is."

"You'd better go and see if she's out of her bed."

When I went in, there she was lying there, she didn't even know me.

"Oh — oh, oh."

I put my hand on her forehead, she was running a temperature. I ran to our matron and told her,

"Adie's sick, she's got a very high temperature."

"Oh, good gracious!"

Mrs Wicksteed came and took her temperature.

"Come on, hurry up, sponge. . . ."

We grabbed the basin and put a towel down, and started spongeing, spongeing, spongeing. You had to sponge the whole body and then afterwards, you just left them there. You couldn't do much. Leave the window open so they get the fresh air, that's all. For months, some of them had nothing but a drink of water, you had to wait until the temperature came down.

Well, Adie was sick for a long time and there were only three nurses left. We were going day and night, day and night. You'd just lie down for a little bit and get up again. I don't know why I didn't go the madhouse, all my relations were dying around me. But I felt that I was fighting somebody, and when I saw one of my relations die I'd get so wild inside, I'd think, why did they die, why? I kept myself going that way, fighting all the time.

Those were the epidemic years — terrible. Sometimes you'd go to a home, because you hadn't seen that family for a while. When you went in they were all dead in the house, all dead. I don't know how I managed, but I got through it. I saw the eldest of all the families of Ruatoria pass on in that epidemic. Lots of families lost the whole family. Well, my thanks to Almighty God that saved me through that, with all my silly ideas. When the epidemic was cleaned up, all over, I decided I'd had enough of nursing so I looked for something else.

---

[7] This particular epidemic has proved difficult to date. Typhoid was endemic in the area from at least 1891 to 1919, and there were a number of major outbreaks during this time. Eruera Stirling tells me he caught typhoid in 1914 during a severe epidemic; according to Mrs B. Burdett of Ruatoria there was a major typhoid epidemic in the area in the years before 1914 (Sir Robert Hall, private communication). Her mother (then unmarried), a Miss McElligot, was the district nurse in charge of a camp hospital on the Matiti Racecourse — Mrs Wicksteed wasn't connected with this hospital.

My grandmother said,

"They want a girl at Kaharau, to work there. They want one cook and one housemaid."

I thought, that'll just do me; I'll go there now because that was my home when I was a little girl. I said to my grandmother,

"You tell Mrs Williams if she still wants a housemaid, well, the housemaid is here — Amiria Manutahi."

"Ae, I'll tell her."

My grandmother was still working there, so she told Mrs Williams about it.

"Oh, is Amy here?"

"Yes, she's been nursing in the epidemic."

"Oh, she was one of the nurses! Of course, tell her to come ."

That's how I went to my old home, Kaharau. The housework suited me, I liked it because it was a big change from all the nursing. Still, the nursing was a help to me when I got settled down.

When I went back to Kaharau I was older of course, and now I understood all their grown-up ideas. I took every interest in the work, and I must thank Mrs Williams for teaching me to do housework. I'm still the housewoman now, and it's been a big help to me.

Kaharau homestead.

Kaharau was a grand house in those days. There was a stable and a man to do the stablework — he'd get the buggy ready and polish up the harness and everything; a fowl-run with a boy to look after it, and the milk-boy to milk the cows — they had a lot of men to do all that work. The family had gone to college, so there wasn't much work on that side, but there was plenty of work in the house. My Aunty Waihuka was the washerwoman, Riria Harrison did the cooking and I helped with the cleaning. There was so much polishing — brasses and silverware, those people ate all out of silver; and beautiful crockery. You got frightened to touch the crockery, it might drop and break.

One time Mrs Williams asked me to iron the family christening robe. It had been sent out from England, and it only went to the first-born of each side of the Williams family. Mrs Williams had been telling us about this robe that was coming from England, and this day she came over to me and said,

"Oh Amy, I want you to clean this frock and iron it for me. I'll show you how to do it."

When she asked me to iron the frock I started to shiver. I thought, oh no, I don't want to touch it, I might spoil it. If something goes wrong it'll be my fault. So I tried to get Riria to do it. She said,

"No. You've got to do it."

Then I went to Aunty Waihuka.

"No . . . no! She picked you to do it, well, *you* do it! Don't try and pass it on to me."

I tried to pretend I had a big job somewhere, I started to clean the silver. I heard Mrs Williams calling,

"Amy, Amy! Where are you?"

"I'm cleaning the silver, Mrs Williams."

"Oh no . . . I didn't tell you to clean the silver. I want you to come here and iron this frock for me."

"I thought you meant. . . ."

"No!"

"Waihuka might do it, you know."

"No, no no, *you* come and do it."

I went to her, and she unwrapped the frock. Oh, I've never seen anything so gracious! I haven't seen that kind of silk since. I don't know what you call it, it looked like muslin but it was all shiny, and it had beautiful threads in it.

"Oh, I don't want to touch it, Mrs Williams."

"Amy, I'll tell you what to do. You just come here and I'll show you."

I cleaned the old stone iron and put it on the stove, then I damped the cloth. There were frills all over this robe, and when Mrs Williams left, I got frightened of it. You had to press inside the frock to bring all the fancy work out. I forgot one part of it and I pressed it the other way. Mrs Williams came back.

"Oh dear me! What have you done, Amy?"

"I haven't done anything, I've only pressed it."

"But you've done it the wrong way!"

Eva came in.

"Tut tut tut! Now look what this girl has done, Eva. I *told* her to press it from the inside. See these French knots, Amy? You have to bring them *out*, not press them down." I don't know how long it took me to press this frock, but I managed in the end. When I finished, Mrs Williams held it up.

"You see how beautiful it is, Amy."

She told me how many years this robe had been travelling amongst the family. When it was finished here, it was going back to England. Her great-great-grand-mother had made it.

33

"Oh! It's all done by hand? I'm going to try and learn these stitches, Mrs Williams."

So Mrs Williams taught me all the fancy stitches, French knots, and how to make those beautiful frills. I did make a christening robe for my family; it was beautiful. It had all the fancy stitches on it, the flowers and petals and the frills, but of course the material was not like the Williams, it was just white muslin. When the minister held up the baby, the frock reached right down to the ground and it matched his robe.

But somehow or other, mine got ruined. I lent it to Arihia, one of the Stirling relations, and I forgot about it. One day I was over at her place and I saw this beautiful underskirt hanging on the line. I went over to look at it; it was my christening robe, cut to make a petticoat. I felt I could do *this* to her. But it was no use fighting over it, it was finished. I'm sure the William's christening robe is still here though, the way they looked after it. Later on I made another robe, but it wasn't as good as that first one.

Another thing I really liked about the Williams was their manners. Riria and I had to take turns to set the table and serve them, and every evening the family would dress up for supper. You'd see them wearing long skirts with big bows, all the jewellery on them and their hair done up — they looked beautiful. The men wore those bob-tailed coats, and in those days it was nothing to have 50 at a weekend for supper, because that's when all the Williamses met — H. B. Williams from Hawke's Bay and all the rest. Riria and I liked to try and forget something just to have a quick look at them, and once Mrs Williams caught me at it.

"What are you doing, Amy?"

"Oh, I forgot Miss Eva's serviette, Mrs Williams, I've got it here in my hand."

"Well, you shouldn't forget — when you've finished setting the table, have a good look to make sure everything is there! You don't keep coming in and out while we are at the table; that's bad manners. In a proper hotel in England, you'd be put off for doing that."

"I'm sorry, Mrs Williams."

"All right, we'll excuse you this time but don't do it again."

And yet I really meant to do that because I wanted to see their manners.

In the morning at breakfast-time, Mr Williams always sat at the head of the table and Mrs Williams sat at the other end, and when the children came in they'd go and kiss their parents on the forehead.

"Good morning, Dad" — Kiss.

"Good morning, Mum" — Kiss.

"Oh good morning, Eva, do sit down."

I thought well, that's it. You don't just sit down and have your meal, you've got to kiss your parents first. When I went back out Riria said to me,

"How is it, Amy?"

"Look here, it's gracious! You really want to see them. You know what it is? They have to kiss the forehead first before they sit down."

"Ne?"

"That's right."

Then we had a laugh about it, because to the Maori way of having a meal you just sit down and in you go. And yet I really appreciated all those beautiful manners.

Mr Williams, of course, he could speak Maori. When there was a tangi the people always came to him to ask for some meat. I remember that; I'd hear him talking Maori to them on the phone, and he'd come out as if annoyed, and he'd see me working in the passage and polishing.

"Good morning, Amy."

"Good morning, Mr Williams."

"That uncle of yours, Tamati Kaiwai! He's your uncle, isn't he?"

"Yes, that's my uncle."

"Oh, he's a horrible man; tangata kino, ne," talking half Maori and half pakeha.

"What's the matter?"

"He wants some meat for the tangi at Taumata-o-mihi. And I told him the shepherds are away, and he started to curse about it, because he wanted some meat."

I thought, oh, I wonder who's dead? Mr Williams said to me,

"Well if he comes here, you tell him I'm not here. He said he's going to get his horse and come here — if he comes here, you tell him I've gone down to Kuhirerere station."

"Oh yes, all right Mr Williams."

Instead of that he didn't go out at all, he went back to the smokeroom, where he smoked.

I thought well, I thought you people are all very perfect, but now I've got to tell a lie, and I'm *not* going to tell a lie to my uncle. If they want meat for the tangi, why not give them meat? You've got plenty of sheep here on the farm. . . . I just kept polishing right along this long corridor. When I got to the end, there was a little porch there where you could look out to Kariaka, and I saw old Tamati coming. He had Hakopa Haerewa with him and another old man from Kariaka, so I went to the smoke-room and said,

"Mr Williams, there's three old Maoris coming up the drive."

"Oh well, tell them . . ."

"I've already told them you're here!"

"You did, did you?"

"Yes."

I didn't, I didn't at all; I thought, I'm not going to tell a lie. So he had to go out and meet them.

"Oh! Tena koutou!"

"Tena koe, Mr Williams."

"All right, come in."

I kept on polishing, I could hear them all talking in the smoke-room.

"We want some meat for the tangi. There's a tangi at the marae. This is our request to you — some meat."

"How much?"

"Oh, three or four sheep perhaps. But two right now."

He had to say yes.

"Well, go to Kuhirerere, the manager will look after you."

But I say this, he was always a big help to my people, although he used to get annoyed with them.

There were several of us working full-time at Kaharau station. Riria Harrison was the other girl in the house, she did the cooking. And the boys around the place were beggars, they thought that because we were Maori girls, they could get what they wanted. One night when I was in bed and Riria was sleeping on the other side of the room, I heard a noise at the window. The next thing I saw someone open the window; it was one of the boys. I said,

"Who do you think you are, just coming in like that? What do you want?"

"I'm looking for you, Amy."

"Well, what is it? What have I done to you?"

"Surely I can just come here and . . ."

"Oh yes, that's what you think! No, not likely . . . and I'm sure if Mrs Williams knew about it, you'd be in big trouble."

"You don't have to tell her."

"I will if you insist to come here. You know it's not right! You don't come and sleep with someone that's not your wife."

Then his mate put his head through the window.

"I want to see Riria. . . . You don't have to go on like that, Riria asked me to come here."

Riria was awake by now and I said to her,

"There's a chap here who wants to see you. He said you asked him to come here."

"No, I didn't! And you boys don't need to think we are Maoris and you can play these games with us. You try it on the pakeha girls and see how they . . ."

This fella said,

"Well, they're all right."

"They might be," Riria said, "but not us! I know what you want, and you're not going to come here and get that."

We shut the window on them and wouldn't let them in. You have to be firm with those beggars, otherwise once you let go, that's it. A little inch, and then further, and then a yard, and that's all. It's best to close down. I always remembered what the old people taught me:

"Amy, be careful, you look after yourself. You can give everything, but one thing must remain tapu to you and you mustn't give that away. Only when you have the ring on your finger, you can give that to your husband. If you fall down on this, you'll have a baby, and that's not fair to the child. So be careful when you go with a man . . . if you give away that treasure, you'll be a slave and a dog! People will laugh at you and say,

"Oh, I've had that one, so now I'll go on to somebody else." In the end you'll be no better than a slave."

The funny thing was, I had that feeling in me too. I didn't mind kissing and all that, but if they went further down, look out!

"You keep your hands to yourself!"

In the end they knew what I was like, and they used to give me cheek. If we were at a dance and they saw me dancing with someone, they'd say,

"You be careful with that girl — *bad* girl, that!"

"Why?"

"E hoa, I tell you, no good. She's a bad girl."

And they'd say to me,

"Are you going to take me back with you tonight, Amy? You and I can be. . . ."

"Be quiet!"

They were hard case all right.

About two years after the epidemic, I caught typhoid. One day my Aunty Waihuka, Tamati Kaiwai's wife, didn't come to Kaharau to do the washing. Mrs Williams came over and said,

"Amy, your aunty didn't come this morning. Now how are we going to manage the washing?"

"She might come later on."

"Oh no, it's a bit late. I think you'd better go and see her — make sure that she'll come tomorrow."

"All right, I'll see her," I said.

"But wait until after three o'clock, Amy. You've got all the brass to polish and the silverware, and Miss Rachel's room to do."

At three o'clock I went down to Taumata-o-mihi. When I got there, Aunty Waihuka was in bed, so I went over and shook hands with her.

"Are you still in bed, Aunty?"

"I feel sick."

"Oh . . . you just want us to do your washing, eh! Mrs Williams wants you to be sure and come tomorrow."

"But I do feel funny, you know," she said.

"Try and come tomorrow, Aunty."

"All right, Amy."

The next day she didn't turn up, so Mrs Williams sent me back again.

There she was in bed. She called out to me,

"I'm sick."

She had a very high temperature. I tried to make her comfortable than I went back and told Mrs Williams that Waihuka was very sick.

"You girls had better get on with the washing, then."

My trouble was, I'd forgotten all about washing my hands and there you are, it was typhoid. The next day, I got it. I woke up with a terrible headache, and when I started to do my work I couldn't carry on with it. I felt dizzy and I had to lie down, then I couldn't get up again. Mrs Williams was looking for me and she asked Riria where I had gone.

"I don't know, she might be outside somewhere."

They had a look round but they couldn't find me, so Mrs Williams came into my room.

"Oh, there you are, Amy! Have you gone back to bed?"

"I'm sick, Mrs Williams."

"Now, what's the matter."

She felt my forehead.

"Oh dear! Tsk."

She rang up the nurse, and got the nurse from Waipiro Bay to come and see me. The nurse examined me and took my temperature, then she said to Mrs Williams,

"She's got typhoid fever."

Look here, Mrs Williams nearly threw me out of the house! She got the stable-boy and everybody else to shift the things out of my room; they put up a tent outside and put me in the tent.

"Get her out of the house quick, hurry up!"

They shut up the room and fumigated it. Everything from that part of the house was taken to the tent; clothes, beds, blankets and linen, chests of drawers and everything, they didn't want them inside. I was rich in my tent with all the things from the Williams's house.

In the end they took me to Taumata-o-mihi marae, but in a tent, not inside the house. Mrs Williams got a special nurse to look after me. I think that's why I pulled through, otherwise I'd have been gone like the rest. And she was always sending somebody to see how I'm getting on — if she didn't come herself, it would be one of her daughters, Rachel or Eva.

One day when I'd got over the worst, my nurse went to Ruatoria. She said,

"Amy, I'm just going to town. What do you want before I leave? Would you like a drink?"

"Oh, can't I have something else, nurse? I've been having this drink of milk, drink of milk . . . I'm tired of that."

"No, you can't."

So I took a drink of milk.

"I won't be long. Before your next drink, I'll be back."

When she went away, I saw some of the children running around outside my tent, eating a watermelon, and I wanted a taste of that melon. I called out,

"Hey, hey! Hey!"

Those kids wouldn't come, they'd been told to keep well away from my tent. I thought, I've got to have some of that melon, so I started to crawl out of bed, and I could see the steps up to the house. I managed to crawl to the house and up the steps.

When I got to the kitchen there was a big watermelon on the table. I found a knife, and had one piece, then another, and another. I had three pieces altogether, then I felt I'd had enough. I got down on the floor again and crawled out into the passage, down the steps and back to my tent. In my tent I was very sick, I was sick all over the bed. When the nurse came back, she screamed,

"Oh! What has this woman been up to? Amy, you've been eating watermelon!"

I started to run another temperature and she had to sponge me and sponge me, and sit me up. When I came back to myself, I was very weak. She said,

"You've been a very naughty girl! Did Waihuka give you that melon?"

"No", I said, "I saw these children eating watermelon and I wanted it so much, but they wouldn't come near me. So I got out of my bed and crawled to the house."

"Oh dear! You crawled over there?"

"Yes."

"You're lucky you survived that, Amy! You're a naughty girl. You know you're not supposed to eat anything; it's a good job watermelon is mainly water."

When I got over that trouble, my hair started to fall out. I was left bald. My grandfather Wiremu Parata had been bald-headed, so they teased me,

"You're Bill Baldie's grandchild all right!"

My mates called me Miss Baldie, but I got a lot of hair after that. I lost all my fair hair, and I got beautiful black hair instead. You know, my grandmother and all the other tipunas on the marae treasured my hair. They used to come and brush it and plait it, they loved playing with it to feel its softness. To the Ngati Porou, a girl's long hair is the "uru mahora", it's a thing of beauty. It was never cut, but when somebody died they would call these girls.

"If any girl wants to give tears to the dead, let her come and have her hair cut."

So they would stand around the coffin with their beautiful long hair, and a woman would cut some hair from each and place it in the coffin. It was one of the most gracious things of the Maori, the time when the young girls gave their "tears" to the dead.

CHAPTER FOUR

My Taumau Marriage

Even while I had typhoid, the old people didn't give in; they were still working on my taumau marriage. Kareti was the one who told me about it. One time we went to a dance at Hiruharama and she said,

"Amy, remember that taumau marriage I told you about? They're still planning it, you know."

"Kareti, I'm sick of that! What are you trying to do?"

"It's not *me*, Amy, it's the old people."

"Oh, what do they want now?"

"They've got a man for you; Eruera Kawhia."

"Don't be silly, that fulla is an old man!"

Eruera Kawhia was an old man in Ruatoria, and I thought Kareti was joking me for all my floating around. I didn't realise that the chap they wanted me to marry was named after that old man.

Years before there had been a death at Whakatane, and Eruera Kawhia and a lot of other people from Ruatoria had gone to the tangi. On the way home, they stopped for a night in the Bay of Plenty and when they called in at Raukokore, someone told them that Mihi Kotukutuku the local chieftainess, wasn't well — she had just had a baby. Old Eruera heard it and he asked what the child was.

"It's a boy."

When he heard that, he wanted the baby to be called after him, Eruera Kawhia. But the other chiefs that were with him said,

"That's only your name on that baby . . . what about us?"

So he suggested that they add Whakatane for the people who had gone to the tangi, then they were satisfied.

Before he left, the old man said to Mihi's people,

"When it comes time for this child to marry, you must return him to Ruatoria."

I didn't know there was all this behind it. Kareti began to explain it to me.

"It's not this old man in Ruatoria, Amy — it's Eruera Kawhia Whakatane *Stirling*. Remember . . . he came here one time, and called in to Taumata-o-mihi."

I did remember that one time when I was at the Williams, I went back home and there was a young boy running around on the marae. Areta told me then that he was their cousin, he was going to Te Aute and his name was Dick.

"That can't be the same fulla. That's Dick . . . "

"It is the same man. Eruera Kawhia — Dick Stirling!"

"Oh well, forget about it!" I said. "I don't want you to talk to me about it . . . he's still at school!"

They kept on planning this though, and all the time my mother was fighting with them. She told Hakopa Haerewa and them to stop it and they told her off. They said it was none of her business.

"You didn't look after this child — we did!"

Then another would say,

"Ae. When her grandmother went to work, Tapita and I kept her. She's *our* mokopuna — you left her behind. So don't talk to us, we have the right!"

There she was, with everyone hoeing into her. She started to think up something to get me right away from this; she thought to herself, the best thing would be to get me to come to Auckland and stay in Auckland — maybe then I'll meet a pakeha, or I might meet some of my father's relations, and they would keep me away from this Maori stuff. Anyway, she planned to take me to the Exhibition in Auckland. She knew that I generally had Wednesday afternoons off from the Williams, and one Wednesday she came up from Tuparoa on horseback. She rang Mrs Williams to ask what time I'd be leaving.

"She generally goes off at three o'clock," Mrs Williams said. "She'll be leaving here soon."

So Mum came up to the Williams place. We didn't go to the pa, we sat out on a bank near Taumata-o-mihi because she wanted to have a quiet talk with me, she didn't want anyone to know. When we sat down on the bank she said,

"Taku korero ki a koe, Amiria . . . do you know your elders want you to have a taumau marriage?"

"What's that, Mum?"

"Well you see, it's not for you to pick the man, it's for them, they pick the man for you. All you have to say is 'Yes', and they'll do everything. It's not your marriage, it's the people's."

"But this Dick Stirling they want, he's only a boy, he's still at Te Aute!"

"That's it. They don't care about anything."

"Oh no, I don't want it, no!" I said, "I don't want it, I want to get away."

"Are you sure?"

"Oh Mum, I don't like that. I want to find my own man, I can find a man myself. I got a lot of boyfriends, pakeha friends and all that. If I want to get married, well, I can choose which one . . ." I was getting all upset.

"Well, this is what I've done for you — I've got your ticket, and we're going on the boat. I'll pay the taxi here from Ruatoria, and we'll go to Tokomaru and get on the *Arahura* [8] and go to Auckland. You pack all your things and everything, and we'll go. I'll stay with you in Auckland until you're really settled down, and then I'll come back."

Poor Mum. She said to me,

"You've got to get away from here. *Never* let those people have what they want!"

Then she told me about her promise to my father on his deathbed, how they shook hands on it, and she promised him that I will marry a pakeha not a Maori.

"So, Amiria, you have to help me keep my promise to your father. If you agree, I want you to shake hands with me too. Will you promise me to marry a pakeha?"

"Yes," and we took hold of each other's hands, and she put her nose to my hand, like that.

"Well, kia kaha! You be strong. Your elder sisters have all married Maoris, but

---

[8] The *Arahura* was a large steamer running along the eastern coast from Auckland to Dunedin.

The *Arahura*.

you must return to your pakeha side, your father's people."

Then she asked me to meet her in Ruatoria the day after next.

"Get all your things, but don't tell your grandma where you're going . . . If you do, they might know that you're leaving. Might be better if you tell her that you're coming to Tuparoa."

"All right, Mum."

She went back to Tuparoa. I went home and started sewing, I wanted to make a nice dress for myself and that, so I started sewing, ironing, and packing up my suitcase.

Old Hakopa had seen her though, and he thought, I'll bet Ani has been here to talk to Amiria about our plans.

He talked to my uncle Tamati, and Tamati said,

"If I see her doing that . . . nati au te kaki, I'll squeeze her neck!"

The next day old Hakopa marched into the house, and there I was, sewing and ironing.

"Oh. Hello mokopuna," he said. "How are you?"

"I'm all right."

"It looks as if you're packing — where are you going?"

"I'm going to Tuparoa," I said.

42

"What's the use of *that?* What do you want to go to Tuparoa for? There's nothing to do there except to look after all your mother's kids! You needn't slave for her. . . . She got married, and brought all that family to the world, let her look after it! Stay here with your tipunas — you belong to us, not her."

I didn't say anything.

He asked me when I was going and I told him tomorrow, I was going tomorrow. He went away, but that night the old people had a meeting, and afterwards Hakopa came back to our house.

"Well, are all your bags packed?"

"Nearly."

He grabbed hold of some of my clothes, and he was packing, helping to pack the suitcase.

"Is there any more?"

"No, that's all."

He put the strap on, got me to write out the tag, then he tied the tag on and took the suitcase and walked out.

I ran after him, I said,

"E koro Hakopa — where are you taking my suitcase?"

"I'm just going to take it to look after it."

"No, no . . . please leave it here!"

"Well when you're ready, come and get it. It's safer in my room than in this house. You don't know who might come and take it away."

So I let him take it. I thought, perhaps he's trying to help. Then after tea that night, he came back again.

"Amiria . . . we want you to come over, we've got something to say to you."

I thought, oh *there* they go again. I wonder if I should go and listen to this. So I just said,

"Yes, all right."

After he'd gone back to his house, I went to the back of our place and whistled to Kareti — "whew! whew!" She came out, looked around and came over.

"Kareti, did you know there's going to be a meeting?"

"Yes. It's that taumau I told you about."

"Well, the old man has been here, he's taken my bag. He said he'll look after it for me."

"Ah . . . I hope so!" Then she looked at me. "What do you think about it, Amy?"

"I don't want it!"

"What are you going to do, then? Are you going to come to the meeting?"

"Well . . . do you think it's safer for me not to go there?"

"I don't know. Perhaps you'd better come. He mightn't give you your bag."

And I thought — Oh! That's why he took the bag.

"I see. In that case I'd better go to the meeting . . . "

When the meeting started, Kareti called out to me and I walked over. But my grandmother felt sorry for me; when I went in she was sitting there, and she looked at me, and I could see tears in her eyes. When I saw that, I knew straight away there was something funny. I sat down, and old man Hakopa stood up and started to preach to me about my childhood days.

"Listen, Amiria Manutahi . . . it wasn't your mother who brought you up, it was us, your tipunas. We were the ones who loved and cared for you. As for your mother, what's the use of that woman! She married another man, had another family — and then she has the cheek to come and lecture us about you. Today, we love you as we always have. We don't want you to be like your mother, one husband dies so she marries another, then he dies and she marries someone else . . . "

Which was right. Wirihana Tatai was her fourth husband, and they didn't like that. They only wanted me, and that was all — she could go her own way. Then they told me why they were so keen on this match, and they explained all about Eruera Kawhia and how his namesake must marry a Ruatoria woman.

"We want you to marry Eruera Kawhia Whakatane, your cousin. He's from here, just like you. On one side he's Te Whanau-a-Apanui, and on his mother's side he's from here. So that is our wish. We only want you to say 'Yes'."

Hika ma! I didn't know what to say.

"Well — what do you say, Amiria?"

"I don't know this man! It might be all right if I did — if a woman sees her man, that's better. You're the ones that know him, not me."

"Never mind that! All we want is for you to agree. . . . As long as you say 'Yes', that's it. We'll be happy then."

"But if I say yes now, I don't want to get married straight away . . . let us be engaged for two years, so we can get to know one another and that."

"Is that what you want?"

"Yes."

"Well, all right."

I thought, that fixes that. As soon as I get my bag, I'm off, I'll never come back.

"All right," I said to them. "Now I'm going to the Exhibition in Auckland with my mother. I will remember about this two years — that's quite a time from now."

"No," said Hakopa. "We don't want you to go. We want you to meet this man now — he's in the Bay of Plenty."

"Why? We've got all this time — two years — to meet him. When I come back from Auckland!"

I knew they'd keeping nagging at me, so I came away and went to bed. Next morning I got ready, and I called out to Kareti to tell the old man that I wanted my bag. He came walking over to our place.

"Now, I want to talk to you, Amiria. . . . You say you're going to the Exhibition in Auckland? Well, Kareti, Areta and I are going there too. We're not going on the launch though, we're going on horseback. Why don't you come with us? I know you haven't got a horse, so I've bought one for you."

I looked at him. "You've bought me a horse?"

"Yes — new saddle, bridle and everything. You're a rangatira woman now, Amiria Manutahi."

"Ohh!" said Kareti. "Fancy that. She's got a horse and I haven't even got one . . . You blooming lucky beggar! He's never bought me a horse."

Then I got excited. In those days I suppose, getting a horse was like getting a motor car. I thought gee, I never owned a horse, and now I will have a horse, and a saddle and everything.

"You don't have to pay any money out either," Hakopa said. "No fares — and when you come back you've still got your horse. You're a lucky girl."

Amiria with the Haerewa Family: (back) Hakopa Haerewa, Bill Butler; (front) Areta Haerewa, Amiria O'Hara, Kareti Haerewa.

Then Kareti went and brought the horse. And when I saw this horse . . . gee whizz! Ka rawe — beautiful! It was a racehorse, too. He told me he bought it from K. S. Williams; but I think Mr Williams only lent it. Kareti saddled it up.

"Come on then! Get on the horse. We're going to Ruatoria." Both of us got on the horse, she came on the back and we went cantering down to Ruatoria — whee! We forgot everything . . . we went right to Mangahanea, came back on the horse whistling and singing all the way home. When we got home and let the horse go out in the paddock, she said

"Gee you're lucky. You're coming with us?"

And I said "Yeah!"

That was it. That afternoon Hakopa asked me if I was coming with them on horseback. I said I was, and he packed everything for me. That was how we came to Raukokore.

It took us about three days to get to the Bay. In those days there was no road like there is now. Heck! It was only pig tracks up the hill and down again. But old man Hakopa always knew someone to stay with; one night in one place then the next day we'd go on to Cape Runaway and stay the night there and so on. And the funny thing was it looked so beautiful, coming from the country. It was all bush in those days, then all of a sudden you'd come out to the beach and see the sea. It was like something wonderful that came to me when I saw the sea. I just stood there and I looked. Then I noticed the sun and I thought — that's funny! It's sunset, but the

Coming to the Sea — Whanarua Bay.

sun is setting into the sea. Yet at home it was always the other way around, the sun rises from the sea. That's why the people call the Coast "Tai Rawhiti", [9] because they see the sun before the rest of the world. I know in my days as a child we would all run in front of the house when we saw a red glow on the sea in the morning and you'd hear the children calling

"Oh — Tama nui te ra! . . . Tama nui te ra!" — meaning the sun is about to come to life, it's been sleeping down there but it's coming up.

"Tama nui te ra!"

You'd see the rays of the sun just creeping up out of the water. And all of a sudden, this red, round, big ball of light — that's Tama nui te ra! It was daylight, sunshine and everything . . . and it sets behind Hikurangi mountain.

But now I saw the sun going down to the sea.

"Kareti," I said. "Is that . . . that sun is not rising. It's going down, isn't it? It looks as if it's just come up and gone down again."

"No," Kareti told me, "that's sunset to them. Not like us in Ruatoria — the sunrise. . . . It's sunset here."

What a queer place this is, I thought. We're sunrise, they're sunset.

[9] "The Coast of the Rising Sun".

Mihi Kotukutuku Stirling.

"We're in the Whanau-a-Apanui area now," she said. "This is the Bay of Plenty. Won't be long, we'll be at Waihau Bay."

"Waihau Bay — where's that?"

And she started to giggle. From that time they started to hide everything from me.

"What did you say, Kareti?"

"Nothing . . . "

The next thing we passed a woman walking. She'd just been to the post office at Raukokore, by the church there. That was Mihi. She called out to the others and I thought, huh, they know that woman. She told them not to wait for her, but to go on home.

47

"Who's that woman?" I asked Kareti. She just giggled, so I took no notice.

When we got to Mihi's place — well, that house in those days! They called it Stirling Castle. Duncan Stirling was a builder and he kept it all painted up; but now its just a wreck of a place. Anyhow we landed there, and we stayed the night. I could see that the old people were having a sort of meeting, but they would always get me to go out somewhere — Kareti would take me for a ride or something.

The next morning, Hakopa told me we were going on to Tauranga. A woman from Tauranga had died at Omaio, and a lot of the local people were going to take death back home. Hakopa thought, because I'm related to the Tauranga people on my mother's side, it would be a good thing for me to go, so we left the horses at Raukokore and went on the launch with all the people from Omaio.

I can remember that marae today, there was a star in front of the front door as you went into the house, but I've never seen it since. Anyway, when we got there, there were a lot of people there, it was a big tangi and the old people were crying. Kareti and Areta told me to listen to them,

"Those old people are talking to you, Amiria, and you're not taking any notice. You listen to them talking!"

"But they're not talking, they're crying."

"To *you*, Amiria — they're having a tangi to you! You listen to them talking, you're not listening."

And then I listened, and it was right, they were talking to me. Another woman had died, a woman from North married to a man from Tauranga, and that day seven cars had come and taken her back to Poutou. The local people wanted her buried in Tauranga, but the father said no, she had to go back home, and they had a big fight at the marae about it. And that's why they were talking to me. Perhaps if we had arrived there a bit earlier, I might have been the one to ask for this woman to be buried here, because the father was a cousin to my mother. But we'd come a bit late.

You see, my mother's mother Amiria, she married Wiremu Parata Moihi Ka, and he was really from the North. It was whaling that brought him to the Coast. He came on the boat whaling, and something went wrong, and he was the only one that got ashore. Some of the people wanted to belt him up and send him back home, but the others felt sorry for him and said,

"Oh no, it's not fair to do that. He was saved, the rest died, so we should feel sorry for this Nga Puhi."

Then the old kaumatuas said,

"Leave him. Pai ana tena, we'll see if he's telling us the truth. Take him out and see if he can kill a whale."

So they took him out fishing, and all of a sudden something caught on the line, and he was the man that pulled up the fish. In the end they thought a lot of him, because every time he went out on the boat, he was bound to catch something. That's how he caught the woman too, I suppose. It ended up he married my grandmother.

They had three daughters — Hera; Heni Hautao, Peta Awatere's mother; and my mother Ani. The two eldest girls married at home, but then Wiremu Parata asked the Ngati Porou people to let Ani marry in the North. He wanted to be buried in Tuparoa where his wife was, but his daughter could take his spirit home for him.

East Coast whaling 1900s — at Te Kaha.

That's how Ani was taken North; Wiremu himself took her there, and gave her to Kawhi Kena of Poutou. She had two daughters by him, Ani and Te O; and that's how we were all a bit from the North.

Anyhow, after all that they started to tangi for the death that we had brought, and there was another big fight. Hakopa Haerewa started it. He said that her own people had makutu'd that woman because she went to Omaio. When she got to Omaio she took very sick and died, and that's why he said,

"You people must have killed her."

The local people got wild and told him off, who the devil does he think he is, who is his mother and who is his father? They told him to get out.

"You don't belong here — go home to where you came from!"

Then they stood up as if they were going to kill us. I got frightened; I think it was in the old days, we'd have been finished. Lucky there was a man from Tauranga in our group who was married to a Bay of Plenty woman, and he stood up and told his people not to treat us like that. Although Hakopa Haerewa is a Ngati Porou, still he came with his love to bring this tangi back home, and it makes this chap feel terrible, to have his own people talking like this to the Bay of Plenty people. How can he go back and live with them after this? He told them off, and finally they apologised.

That night there was a dance at the marae and another fight started. Somebody said it was over me. I don't even know, from that day to this, how that fight started — I didn't go out with anybody. In the end I was glad to get away from

49

there. It even put me off going to Auckland. I thought, we've had enough fighting, I want to go home.

So we went back to Raukokore. When we got there they made a big fuss of us, and it's nice to be fussed over instead of having all those fights, so I felt happy.

But when Kareti and I went to our bedroom, I noticed everything was different in this room. There were two single beds for us girls before, but now there was only one big bed in it. I thought, oh well, they might be putting us all in one bed, and that's less trouble for the old lady . . .

That afternoon there was a service. The old man Duncan Stirling always held his service, whether there was anybody around or not. I give the old man credit for that,

Duncan Stirling.

50

even if the family didn't want his service, and they all ran away to a dance or something as soon as they heard the old man bang! bang! on the wall, well, he'd stand in the sitting-room all by himself and hold his service. I used to like it though, because I was brought up that way when I lived with the Williams, there was always a service in that house. . . . And I still respect service before everything.

After service, the old man Hakopa stood up and started talking to me.

"Amiria, Mihi Kotukutuku is chieftainess here. And remember the taumau you agreed to in Ruatoria? Well, Eruera Kawhia is her son. Mihi doesn't agree with the pakeha way, the engagement. What we want is for you to sleep with your cousin tonight."

That shocked me, of course. I thought, now what's this!

"No!" I said. I couldn't make it out — I thought he was still at Te Aute. I was getting very funny in my head, with all the trouble we'd had, all the fights and everything. We had lost the trip to Auckland, and now they were starting about this match marriage again.

"What?" said Hakopa.

"No! Kaore! He's only young, and I'm older than him. Give him two years to grow up."

Then Mihi stood up and she started to talk to me.

"Listen, e hine . . . you are in my house! On your marae, all right, you're the boss, but this is my marae and I'm chief here . . . so listen. Everyone has agreed to have a taumau marriage between you and your cousin Eruera Kawhia. And I'm telling you, this is a better way than the pakeha engagement — that's too long! Who's to know that you could stay as good as you are? You might look at somebody else and that. So this is the Maori way. Tonight you and your cousin will sleep together. The room is ready for you, everything is prepared . . . the people have arranged it all."

Ah . . . then that time I started to shiver! I started to shiver, and I stood up and I thought, no, I'm not! I'm not going to give in to them.

Hakopa shouted at me,

"Don't you stand up, girl, sit down! You heard what the old lady said. This is her marae and she's the chief. Don't be above yourself — sit down!"

I started to cry, and I sat down.

"Why don't you listen — we're not degrading you or anything, we are making you a chiefly woman."

"I don't want to be a chief, I want to go home!"

Mihi said, "That's enough. Stop crying, and don't say any more. We are honouring you."

She grabbed hold of my hand and took me to the bedroom.

"I want to go to the toilet!" I said. I was only pretending. So I got out and I ran outside to the toilet, and I sat there and started to cry. They were watching me, you know. I heard Kareti calling,

"Amy! Amy! Come on. We want you back here. You've been there long enough."

"All right, I'm coming."

You know what I was doing? I was looking round for my horse. It was tied under a pohutukawa tree at the back of the house before, but now I couldn't see it. I thought, if only I knew where my horse was, and the saddle and bridle, I'd get on that horse and go back home to Ruatoria. Then I saw the housemaid Susan, standing on the back porch looking at me. She turned around and went into the house. I thought, perhaps I could ask Susan to go and get the horse, and take it into the quicks. She could tie it there and then whistle. When I heard her whistle, I'd know the horse was saddled and everything, and I'd just run there and nobody could catch me. So when Kareti went to the dining-room, I ran inside, and I found Susan was hanging on to a post there and crying. I put my arms around her.

"Susan! What's wrong? Are you sick?"

"No."

"What's the matter then?"

"It's that beggar!"

"Who's that?" I said.

"That blasted Dick! He's been playing around with me . . . him and I have been — you know. And now you're going to marry him."

"But he's at Te Aute."

"No he's not, he's here! I know, I'm telling you. Do you want to see him?"

"Yes."

She bent over and opened the door a bit, he was sleeping on the bed.

"There," she said, "that's the brute!"

And I looked at him — oh, he was only a young boy. And I saw his hair, yes, he had that stick-up hair — the other brothers had got curls. Later they used to tease me about it. Tai would come and say,

Eruera Stirling as a young man (back left), with his brother Wahawaha (back right) and Tom Collier (front).

"So this is the fellow you're going to marry, eh? That kina! That sea-egg!" and he'd show me all his curls. Then Waha would say,

"Yeah, what about *my* curls? Look here!" They were showing their curls to me, and they were right, they had nice curls all right.

I said to Susan,

"Look Susan, I tell you something now. You've been courting with this man, eh."

"Yes, the beggar!"

"That's all right, now you listen to me, you can *have* him, I don't want him. I tell you what. You go and get my horse for me, and saddle it up. . . . See that bush of thick quicks down there? Take the horse there and when you're ready, blow a strong whistle. I tell you Susan, once I get on that horse, I'll get out of this place, they'll never catch me. Will you do that?"

"Yes."

"Don't go in the daytime though, they'll see you. Wait till it's dark."

"All right Amy."

"Well, I'll wait for you and listen."

It was getting dark, so I went to my room and started to pack my bag. I looked round for Kareti and Areta, but they'd disappeared. It was the first time they had left me. I felt lost, there was nobody around to talk to. I got my bag ready, then I opened the window and I thought as soon as I hear the whistle, I'll jump out and run down the road, straight to that bush of quicks. I was waiting for the whistle — no whistle, no whistle . . .

Hakopa came in.

"All right Amiria, you've got to sleep with your cousin tonight. Go on — get ready for bed. You can't wear a coat in bed."

I started to cry. He took my coat off, gave me my nightgown and made me put it on. Oh, Susan . . . you're a long time to whistle! When the old man left, I sat by the window holding my coat.

The next thing, Dick walked in the room. He had his pyjamas on.

"Come on in the bed!"

He started to pull me to the bed.

"You keep your hands to yourself! You're not my husband yet . . . "

"I am though . . . "

So I jumped out of the window and started running. I was so hurt, I thought, I'm going to drown myself. I ran straight to the reef right out to this very far point. And not a sound of Susan. I ran till I got right to the very end. When I got there, waves were dashing up on the rocks, boom! boom! on the rocks. I called out to my grandmother.

"Nanny, Nanny! I want to go home, I don't want this to happen to me!"

Just then I heard Areta yelling,

"Amiria, Amiria, Amy. Don't do that, Amy, don't, don't, don't! It's all right we're going home . . . stop it . . . "

She pulled me back flat on the stones, and she grabbed hold of me. We sat there crying to one another, she was holding me.

"No, don't do that. Come on home. We're going back to Ruatoria. It's got to stop, this; it's no good, it's no good."

Then Kareti arrived too, and they took me right home. I asked them if they heard someone whistling.

"Did you hear anybody whistling, Addie?"

"No."

"Nobody?"

And I asked Kareti;

"No."

I thought to myself, poor old Susan must have got caught.

They took me inside, and the old people had a good lecture at me. When the old lady came in — she was the one I got frightened of because of the way she talked — I just looked at her.

"Now stop being so stupid! Do you think we're trying to belittle you, to make you a slave? No. You know we are honouring you. And yet you behave like this. You're a *bad* girl. None of the old people want you now, you'll have no relations, nothing! You are making fools of us all. Now you must promise me to stop it — give me your hand . . . "

I shook hands with her.

"You've agreed now. So stop it!"

Kareti, Areta and I went to bed together, but I fell off to sleep and they got up and walked away. He came in and slept with me.

It had to be that way. The next day it was something great to them. Everyone came to visit, to greet us and so on. But the thing that worried me — from that day to this day, I didn't know what happened to that horse. Someone told me that Susan got caught, and she got thrashed for it. And I think they took that horse Waitere back to K. S. Williams at Ruatoria.

The wedding was quite a while afterwards. As soon as the people at home heard it was all settled, they sent a telegram to say that they were bringing the stuff for the wedding. The kai, the kumara, the meat, everything. Mihi started to fight about it.

"Oh! There's that Ngati Porou people again. They think I've got nothing here, and they want to bring everything. No! I've got *tons* to eat, plenty kai, plenty of everything. All they've got to do is to come themselves."

So she told them to keep their kai and not to bring any kai. But it was too late. They already had a ton of potatoes and a ton of kumara, and boxes of biscuits, tins of fruit and all sorts on the *Mako*.[10] They even tried to shift the date of the wedding, but Mihi wouldn't agree.

Once the date was fixed the old lady told me to go to Opotiki to get my dress measured. Course in those days it was all on horseback, but that was all right, girls in those days loved going on horseback. I went down there, got my dress ready and the bridesmaids all set. The dress was beautiful too, beautiful white silk.

It was just a few days before the wedding when old Meri, Mika Eruera's mother, came to our place. She came to ask if Mihi would agree for Mika and Eva to be married on our day of marriage because, oh well, they were already together. Mihi

---

[10] The *Mako* was a surf-boat with passenger accommodation, part of a service run by the Union Steamship Co. until 1912 and after that by Richardson & Co. There was a fortnightly visit to 25 landing-places between Torere and Gisborne.

called me over to hear what the old lady had to say, then we all agreed about it. The only thing that worried Mihi was the cake. It was only a week from the wedding day and our cake was all ready, but it wasn't long for the icing on a new cake to set. Meri didn't know what to do. She said,

"Ah, Mihi . . . I'll leave those things to you."

In the end Eruera went down to Opotiki, and brought this cake up. We did have trouble with it too. The icing was too soft, and it slipped. When Eva saw it, she nearly cried.

"Never mind, Eva," I said, "I tell you what. We'll go to Waihau Store and buy the biggest white ribbon they've got. We can fix it so nobody will know."

Amiria (front right) with Eva Eruera (back) in later years — at the opening of Tukaki meeting-house.

We did too. We tied this white ribbon right round, and the cake was beautiful.

In the end, everything was ready for the wedding. That night, the Ngati Porou people landed at Te Hau Ki Tikirau marae. It isn't there now, it used to be round by the church. I was busy getting my things ready so I didn't go down. Very late that night, Mihi came back home to ask me to go and see my people at the meeting-house, they're having a fight there. Oh dear, I thought, *now* what's the trouble!

"It's your people again, they're starting up more trouble. You've got your dress ready, everything . . . and now they've brought their own frock, they don't want mine. I've got a good mind to tell the whole lot of them to go back — I'm sick of talking to them!" Mihi was furious. Anyhow, I had to go and see them.

When Mihi and I walked into the house, they were still fighting about this, but when we walked in they all sat down.

"Haramai ra mokopuna, haramai e hine . . . ", you know, greeting me. There was my uncle Tamati, he was still on the floor talking, so I went over and shook hands with him. And there was Areta and Kareti and the old man Hakopa . . . they put their arms around me.

"How are you, Amiria — is everything all right?"

"Yes, it's all right."

I sat down, and my uncle Tamati Kaiwai started talking again. It was all about this frock. There was a mat on the floor, and there was a frock there, and the shoes, and the veil. Tamati said,

"We agree to this marriage . . . but we want our grandchild to be married in our own clothes. This marriage was made by the tribe, and we won't let her go to you naked. Now Mihi, you've had a dress made for this woman — that's all right. But until the ring is placed on her finger, you don't own her, she is ours. So we want to dress her and everything."

So of course, the old lady stood up.

"A tena! Why should there be two dresses — are there two women? This dress of ours has been fitted on Amiria, it's hers. Now suppose your dress doesn't fit this woman, what are you going to do about it? Don't ask me to give my frock — I won't give it! If that frock doesn't fit her, right, you can tie that on her neck and send her to church. You're a stuck-up lot, Ngati Porou, to do this to me. First the food and now this!"

Then Tamati spoke again,

"These clothes are your people's, Amiria. The final choice is yours. Will you wear our clothes to church? It's the last thing we can do for you . . . "

I thought, oh, now what! I know the other dress is all right because it was fitted on me, but what about this one? And Mihi has said that if it doesn't fit me, they can tie it around my neck. I looked at the dress, then I saw Kareti talking to me with her eyes, sitting there and looking at me. She went like *this* to show me that the frock was fitted on her, because she and I were the same size. Whenever we used to go to dances, if I hadn't got a nice dress, I'd borrow one from her. Well, then I knew that dress'd fit me.

"It's your choice, Amiria. Which dress will you wear tomorrow? Your people's dress, or the dress of your mother-in-law Mihi and your husband Eruera Kawhia?"

I stood up on the floor. I went over, and picked their frock up from the mat and held it. When they saw that they all jumped up and started to sing:

Koa, koa, koa, hari taku ngakau!   *Happy, happy, happy, my heart is glad*
Koa, koa, koa, i nga wa katoa;   *Happy, happy, happy, all the time*
Mana taku tono, tika taku tono,   *I've got what I wanted, I was right*
Ki tonu au i te koa, koa, koa!   *So now I'm full of joy!*

Everybody, even the men were singing "Koa koa" on the floor, and when I looked at them I felt happy to see my people, they were so happy, and dancing around.

Then Mihi got up.

"I've had enough! You be happy then," and she walked out. They didn't take any notice.

Kareti came over and put her arms around me.

"That dress'll fit you perfect. *Beautiful!*"

They had brought everything, even the pair of shoes and the veil. I tried the shoes on, everything fitted. I took it all home and when I tried the dress on, it was beautiful. I wondered what to do with the other wedding frock and I tried to tell Dick's sister Kate to wear it, but she took a while to think about this changing over then she said,

"I wonder if it's all right."

"Well, I've given that dress to you, you're my chief bridesmaid, so why not?"

"Oh, it's a bit too long."

"Well, you can lift the tail up and carry it . . . "

But I could see she didn't want to wear it, it wasn't a nice omen or something like that.

"Oh well, I'll leave it to you, Kate."

She went and told her mother, and I heard Mihi telling her off about it, she's going to be the bride for the day or what. But I didn't chip in, I thought, I'm not going to step in any more. Even today I'm not sure whether she wore that dress. I felt so funny about it I didn't want to look to see.

When I woke up next morning luckily it was a nice day, a fine day. I could hear the people talking about it, because to the Maoris, well, everything is fine if its a fine day. If it's a rainy day — no good. I had to get my bridesmaids' frocks ready, there were some little things we had to fix up about these. Kate was running around doing her bit, and we made sure the bridesmaids had their little bouquets and everything. Then the bell rang. It wasn't even 11 o'clock and the wedding was supposed to be at one o'clock. I thought, it can't be the bell! I ran out to see, I thought it might be the children are banging something . . . gee, it was the bell all right.

The old lady came into my room.

"By . . . this woman! Ka *mau* te wehi. Are you asleep or what?" She was growling at me in Maori, telling me off because I'm not ready. I told her the time and she cursed back at me.

"You hear the bell ringing! You should have been on the move now and there you are, not ready. Come *on!* And where's the groom?"

Then I started to panic too, to get myself ready. I yelled out to Dick to get ready, because there's the church bell ringing. He tried to tell me it wasn't time yet.

"Look, no use talking about the time . . . there's the bell going, the old lady's quite right, it's . . . it's ringing now!"

I managed to get my dress on, and then I just rushed the bridesmaids and little flower girls into their frocks, and Kate was doing her share . . . What with the old lady driving behind, I could hear her voice *yelling* at everybody. We got out of the house, walked onto the road and started to go to church. Tai, Dick's eldest brother, went past on a horse, and I called out to him to go and see who's ringing that bell. He took off on his horse and when he got to the church, it was Te Waena.

He went over to her, grabbed hold of her and pulled her away. She was hanging onto the bell and wouldn't let go.

"What are you trying to do?!"

She turned round to tell him that she was the one who nursed Eruera, and looked after him and washed his clothes right up to his wedding day. She wanted to be the one to ring that bell and nobody else.

And Tai said,

"Look, you let go or else I'll give you this!"

He had to give her a hard knock to get her away from the bell, and that's how it was. When he got her away, somebody else grabbed her and took her to comfort her somewhere, then he came back to tell us.

We started to move again, and then this other trouble started. My uncle Tamati was taking me, and I had the chief bridesmaid with me and the two flower girls. We were about halfway to the church when I heard a voice; I thought it was a pohiri, you know . . . a sort of Maori welcome. We stopped to listen. Oh, no! It was my mother, lamenting. She was right on the hill there overlooking the church, and she was calling out a farewell:—

"Haere atu ra e hine, goodbye, my daughter! . . . These cursed men Hakopa Haerewa and Tamati Kaiwai are taking you to make you a dog, a slave . . . haere atu ra, haere atu . . . !" As soon as Uncle Tamati heard her he said,

"Gah! I'll break her bloody neck for her!"

I tried to stop him, but he just threw me down like that.

"You heard her cursing us . . . I'll break her neck for her!"

He went running up the hill, and I stood there and started to cry. There was nobody to take me to church. Tai came galloping past again and I yelled out to him,

"Tai! Tai! Wait a minute . . . you go to the church and see if you can get Hakopa Haerewa. Ask him to come back here to take me to church, because Tamati Kaiwai has gone up the hill. You do that, Tai, right now."

"Right, I'll do that, sis," Tai said, and he galloped off to the church.

We stood there, and Kate looked at me.

"Now, what are we going to do?"

"I don't know . . . " I said.

So we stood around, waiting. The next thing we saw the old man Hakopa coming behind Tai on the horse. Tai dropped him off, and he came over and put his arm round me. By that time, we looked round, we couldn't find the little flower girls. They were lost.

"Mary! Mary! Hine! Hine!"

Nobody.

"Well, we'll have to go and look for them. Kate, you go behind those quicks and have a look, they might be down there."

Tai went somewhere else, and I went down to the beach. We couldn't find them.

Church of Jesus Christ, Raukokore-Taumata-o-Urunga hill in front, where Ani wailed for her daughter.

We stood there and started calling. The next thing I heard a voice, but I couldn't work out where it came from. There was a culvert, running out to sea, and they were down in this little hole playing stones.

"Hine, come on Mere! Come on up here! Haramai!"

They still had these stones in their hands so I took the stones and threw them away.

When that trouble was over, well, we went to the church. Just as we were going to step inside, someone grabbed hold of me.

"No . . . your part is over now, Hakopa. Ngati Porou have had their share. It's not right — I'll take her in now."

Then these two had a bit of an argument. I belong to Tauranga too in one part of my whakapapa, so they wanted this man Eria to take me into church. Hakopa got wild because he was pushed out, but he had to stand aside.

All right, we got up to the altar, and there were Mika and Eva, and they were married first. When it came to us, and the minister came to the part about the ring,

"Ka mau au i tenei mohiti . . . I place this ring . . . " — Nothing. No ring.

The minister looked at Eruera,

"Where's the ring?"

Eruera was feeling around in all his pockets.

"Oh, I must have left it at home."

The minister scratched his head. He looked at me and then he said,

"Well, that's all right, we can marry you with the key of the church."

I just about collapsed on the floor, I thought, now what next! If it's ending up with the key of the church, we might as well forget about it. The minister said to me,

"It'll be all right, though. After the service, he can go home and get the ring, then you two can come back again and we'll bless the ring in church and put it on."

Somehow or other, a ring was passed over. Somebody must have known what happened, so they passed it forward. It was a band ring, really for a middle finger, and when they put the ring on I had to hold onto it with my thumb. I felt better about it then.

So that was all right. We walked out into all the confettis, and all the screaming and everything. The next thing, we had to go to the dining-hall where the tables were set out.

When we walked in, there was Wikitoria, Mika's cousin. She was at the entrance to the dining-hall and she pointed out our table to us, and the other table to Mika and Eva. When we walked to the table I noticed the cake, I knew that cake was not ours. It had the big white ribbon on it with a bow. I looked up to Dick and he said to Wikitoria,

"Wikitoria, this is not our table. Our cake is on the other table."

"But that's how they placed it."

"I'm telling you, Wikitoria, this cake is not ours! You'll have to change these cakes."

"Oh, I can't do that."

So, I had to chip in.

"You go and ask Eva. She'll tell you we had to fix this cake with the white ribbon, the icing was too soft."

She went over and she asked. Eva wasn't taking any notice of the cake you see, they just sat down. She had a shock.

"Oh! ka tika! That's right. We're at the wrong table."

So they came over and we sat at the other table. She looked at me and she smiled, and that was all right.

But then I got a bit worried. I saw everybody around but my mother, and I wondered if Tamati had really belted her up. I said to Eruera,

"I can't eat. I'm worried about my mother. Might be that fulla has hurt her. . . . I want to go and see what's happened to her."

"Where are you going? Are you going up the hill?"

"I'm going to find out where she is. This is not right. We're having the wedding breakfast, and my mother is not here. I want her to sit with us," I said.

"Oh well, if you want to go and see we'd better both go then, and look for her."

So we got up and started walking out, then somebody came and stopped us.

"Where are you going?"

"I can't eat without my mother being here," I said.

"Oh, she's somewhere."

"That's all right, but I'm going to get her."

I walked out, and saw Kareti.

"Have you seen Mum?"

"Yeah."

"Where is she?"

"You go behind those quicks."

I went straight out there. When I got there I saw her lying on the ground, crying her heart out. Wihana Tatai, her husband at the time, was sitting beside her.

I went over to her and put my arms around her.

"Mum? I want you to be at the table with us — please, Mum."

She got up, and hit me, and told me to get away, she didn't want to have anything to do with me.

"Go away, you're a slave now, you've made yourself a slave . . . "

"Mum, I only wanted to come and ask you to sit at the table with us. We've had enough of all this, haven't we Mum? It's too late now . . . I know I'm wrong . . . "

"No," she pushed me away, and my veil flew up and got caught on the quicks, and a piece of it was torn off. I had to run away from her. So I left her there, it was no use, she wouldn't come. That was one of the saddest things in my life. I didn't see any more of her, I think she must have gone home. They told me afterwards that she took her money to the minister, she wouldn't put her money with the people's gift. She cursed the Ngati Porou for what they had been doing, and told the minister he was to keep that money.

"I'm by myself from that day to this day, and I remain like that! What I've got I'll give to the minister himself, not to you people . . . "

Anyhow, we went back and sat at the table. Then they had all the speeches and there was so much to say, with all the big chiefs of different places; Te Kaha, Omaio, and so on. . . . And the presents they were putting out, and the *money!* There were piles of notes there, they must have been thousands, every tribe put something down. I don't know what happened to that money though, they must have shared it to the people.

That night there was a big dance at the meeting-house, and more speeches.

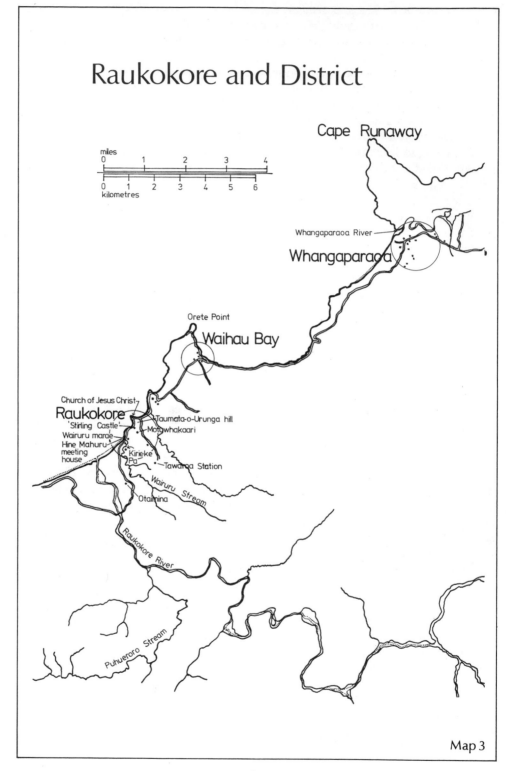

Raukokore and District

Cape Runaway

miles
0   1   2   3   4

kilometres
0   1   2   3   4   5   6

Whangaparaoa River

Whangaparaoa

Orete Point

Waihau Bay

Church of Jesus Christ
Raukokore
'Stirling Castle'
Wairuru marae
Hine Mahuru
meeting
house

Taumata-o-Urunga hill
Motuwhakaari

Kirieke
Pa

Tawaroa Station

Otaimina

Wairuru Stream

Raukokore River

Puhueroro Stream

Map 3

Before the people went back, they had a talk at the marae. They said that when everything is finished we had to go back to my marae, to Tuparoa, to take me back home to Ngati Porou. The Whanau-a-Apanui people must promise they'd do that, because they want to welcome us at all the individual maraes — first Whare Kahika, then Te Araroa and so on, before we get back right home to Tuparoa. So it was agreed.

That last night at Raukokore, during the speeches I heard Kareti and Areta playing the piano. But when I came to listen to the words, they'd stop singing, they'd just vamp the tune. It was only recently I got the words from their sister, and it was a farewell song for me:

He wawata i nga ra nei	*A yearning in these days*
I nga po roa nei	*And these long nights*
I kite au i a koe	*I saw you*
Amiria e kua wehea nei	*Amiria, who has left us.*
Ma nga tai e haruru nei	*The sea's murmuring*
Mau atu te aroha	*Carries my love,*
He moemoea	*A dream*
He wawata	*A hope*
He tohu aroha . . .	*A sign of love . . .*

There are quite a few verses to it. I was told when they left Raukokore, they were cantering on their horse and singing this. And they'd stop and look at the sea as if, oh well, they've left me behind and now they're going home. . . .

I think it was about three days after when all the food from Ngati Porou arrived on the *Mako*. It happened to be bad weather that week so the *Mako* couldn't call in at Raukokore, it had to go on to Auckland. But then afterwards, they came back when the weather had settled and dropped all this stuff. *Tons* of potatoes, kumaras, sweet drinks, boxes of biscuits, tinned meat and all. Mihi got a lot of people to go down and collect it.

"You take your lot, so-and-so take your lot," giving it to different sub-tribes of the Whanau-a-Apanui. She was still growling about it.

"That's that Ngati Porou people, I told them there's plenty here. No! There you are!"

Some of it had to be thrown away, but they didn't mind, as long as it was accepted.

A few days later, Wihana Tatai came to pick us up on the buggy, but the rest of the people went on horseback. We called in to Whare Kahika and had a night there, and then a night at Te Araroa, Kiwikiwi, Tikitiki, Reporua, all those maraes. At Whareponga, Materoa Reedy announced to the Whanau-a-Apanui people that my family were giving us five hundred sheep to start us off in farming. And when we got to Tuparoa, that was one of the greatest nights, all the people from Ruatoria were there. In my mind now, it's a sad memory when I think of those people — they're all gone. But they were the people that made a fuss about me. I don't know why they made such a lot of fuss about me, I've often wondered. . . . Perhaps that's why I'm still here. I had three sisters, and a brother from the other marriages — they're all gone. It's only the mokopuna pakeha that is left.

CHAPTER FIVE

Getting On Our Feet

After we came back from travelling around Ngati Porou, we settled down at Raukokore in Stirling Castle. It *was* a castle in those days, there wasn't another house like it in the district. There was a long verandah around the house, and a passage right through, with a big kitchen, dining-room, sitting-room and about six bedrooms — it was a huge place.

The old man Stirling was a builder, he built all the churches from Whangara to Ruatoria to Torere, and when he married Mihi Kotukutuku he built his own house. He was a very fine man, and a Church of England man too. That was how the Whanau-a-Apanui people turned to the Anglican Church. They were all Ringatus before, I believe, even Mihi herself, but when she married Duncan they all changed. Duncan Stirling wasn't a local man though, he was a half-caste from the South Island.

You see, Mihi was the youngest of three girls, the daughters of Maaka Te Ehutu and Ruiha Rahuta, who were both senior people in their own lines. Their eldest girl Te Wharau was drowned when she was just a little child. One day Maaka crossed the river to feed his pigs up in the bush at the back of their farm, and his daughter saw him and came trotting along behind. He didn't know she was there. When he got back to the house his wife said,

"Where's Te Wharau?"

"She hasn't been with me."

"Oh!"

They started looking, and then all the people round joined in. It was three days later when they found her on the beach at the mouth of the river. She was lying on a flat rock with her arms stretched out, and a kotukutuku tree was hanging over her with all its flowers. It was the tree that gave the last mihi to this little girl. They had a big tangi, and people came from all over the place for the funeral.

The next daughter was named "Keita Horowai", for her sister who was lost in the water, and the last daughter they called "Mihi Kotukutuku", for the farewell from the kotukutuku tree. When Keita came to a marrying age the people wanted her to marry one of their chiefs, so they started to match her. While this was going on, something struck her and she took very sick. All of a sudden, she died.

Then the people started to worry, they said someone had put a makutu[11] on these girls because they were senior in their line. Someone must want to get rid of them, because to the Maori the man is the rangatira, the woman is of lower rank,[12]

---

11 Makutu is black magic — in the early contact period practitioners were often punished by tribal councils or *runanga*.

12 Although in most areas chiefs were almost invariably men, in the East Coast area there was a long-established tradition of women wielding great influence in the tribal group.

Maaka Te Ehutu (far right) and Duncan Stirling (left, with horse) at Orete Point Native Telephone System Office. The carved pole has a representation of Paikea at its head; it was supposed to bring down a tapu upon those who didn't pay their dues.

and this person must want a man to rule the Bay of Plenty and right around. So they decided to send Mihi out of the area while she was still in her teens, it might be safer that way.

Mihi went to live at Reporua with some Ngati Porou relations on her mother's side, and while she was there, she took very sick. They took her to a tohunga, and the tohunga told the people about a waterfall near her own marae where the makutu had been laid. He took his followers there to Raukokore and lifted the tapu, and blessed Mihi in the water, then she got well again. Her people said it would be better for her to stay in Ngati Porou and not to come back to Raukokore until she was married.

When Mihi started courting around, her relatives said,

"She'll be better to marry a pakeha, it might protect her from this Maori business."

St Barnabas Anglican Church at Hicks Bay, built by Duncan Stirling.

Duncan Stirling was staying at Ruatoria at the time; Williams had brought him there to start building the East Coast churches. The people went to Duncan and said,

"There's a nice girl here for you."

He looked at her.

"Yes."

So they got to know one another, and in the end there was a big wedding. After a while the people from Torere called him to build a church there, and he took his wife home to Raukokore. Anyhow, Mihi got quite a big family from Duncan Stirling over the years. The Whanau-a-Apanui people liked him in one way because of the churches; he built his own home and the church at Raukokore and they admired him for that. But the trouble was, he didn't understand Maori much, so the people always talked to Mihi, they didn't bother with him. He had a lot of pigs and cows on the farm, but if the people wanted some meat for the tangi, they went to his wife.

"E Mihi, we want some meat for the marae."

"Oh yes, yes."

It was all O.K. to her. She'd just tell the old man to kill some meat, and because it was the Maori way, he had to do it. Their house was always open too, and a lot of the families in Raukokore grew up in Stirling Castle, because Mihi was a wonderful woman to her people. They would come to her for every little thing, and if anyone was stuck for a place to live, Mihi would say,

"Oh, haramai, there's plenty of room here!"

So they came with their families and lived there.

She couldn't bear to see people going past her home, they had to call in. Even if you were going by yourself on horseback, she'd stand on the verandah and wave you in to have a cup of tea. When I was living there, Kate and I had to rush round cooking for them. If there was no bread, Mihi didn't worry; she was always calling people to the house. Kate used to say,

"Oh, listen to Mum! She's called those people in and we haven't got enough bread."

"You know what she's like, Kate. We'd better fry some."

So we'd rush around and make up the dough, and get the fat in the frying-pan ready. Mihi would growl at us if she knew there was no bread.

"What's the matter with you girls? Why didn't you make some more? Now *hurry* up and cook something."

In the end, whenever I saw the bread was getting low, Kate and I would do some baking before we went to bed. We'd sit there by the stove, and sometimes Kate would play the piano just to keep us going. You had to take about three or four mugs of flour, and mix it with the yeast and water so it's not too thick, then you roll it and give that dough a press, and spread it out in a round slab. The stove had to be hot but not too hot. Manuka is a good wood, it keeps the heat so it's best for baking. If you haven't got any manuka, the tawhao from the beach is all right, but the heat quickly goes and you have to keep putting more wood in. Once the dough has risen about a third, you stoke the stove up and put the heat on. There you are; and it's beautiful bread. That was the only way, otherwise we'd get caught with no bread.

The Whanau-a-Apanui people respected the old lady because she was the

Mihi Kotukutuku wearing the tiki Mahu-tai-te-Rangi.

tuakana, the eldest in the senior family, and she was senior in everything, even the speeches on the marae. On the home marae it didn't matter if the men were there, Mihi had to finalise everything. When the men went out fishing for moki, they'd always bring her the first fish, te ika a Pou; if that first fish didn't go to Pou, the god of the sea, they'd never catch any more.

She was very strict too, in making sure that everything was done in the right way. One time when we went to a tangi at Ruatoria, the Whanau-a-Apanui group was so big that the local people laid out all the kai on mats in the meeting-house, because they knew they couldn't get all those people in their little kitchen. After the speeches on the marae were over they called out.

"Mihi, bring your people in to eat."

Mihi stood up and started marching off to the kitchen. Someone said,

"No, not there — in the meeting-house."

Mihi walked into the meeting house, and when she saw all the food laid out she just stood there. It wasn't the custom in those days to eat in the meeting-house; that was the place to sleep. She said,

"Ngati Porou! I thought you were the great people for marae custom. And now you tell me to eat in the meeting-house. . .!"[13]

She grabbed one of the cloths, dragged it to the back window of the house and started throwing everything out of the window. Then she took the other cloth and emptied that one too. The Ngati Porou people just stood there and watched everything, flying out of the window. Mihi called to the chieftainess of that marae.

"Rahera! Is this how your people respect their ancestors? Serving kai in the meeting-house!"

The local people had to collect what was left in the meeting-house and take it to the kitchen. I heard them say,

"Mihi was right, you know."

That was the first and last time food was served in any meeting-house in the area; no more food went into East Coast meeting-houses after that.

Mihi would never allow anyone to override her, either. When Apirana Ngata died in 1950, the old lady was still alive. After the tangi the people had to travel from one place to another, taking his death to the different tribes. They wanted to start from Waiomatatini and go to Te Kaha the first day, then on to Waikato, because they thought Raukokore was too close to Ngati Porou. The people of Te Kaha told Mihi that Ngati Porou had asked to stay the night at Tukaki, and she was furious about it. . .

"I am their senior, and Ngati Porou are not going to overstep me. They can stay here at Wairuru marae, they're not going to step over *my* head!"

Mihi was like a man the way she ruled her people. Whatever she says, that was it, whether it was right or wrong. And the people knew it was no use arguing; if she says *no*, it's no.

"It wasn't our idea, Mihi, it was Ngati Porou's."

"Never mind. There's no marae at Te Kaha for them; the marae will be Wairuru!"

Even though the marae at Te Kaha was all ready, the people thought well, they'd better get to work at Wairuru.

The first cars that came from Waiomatatini shot past Wairuru marae, they didn't call in. When they got to Te Kaha there was no marae there, and they had to stay at Whakatane in the pub. When the main group with the chiefs, Hamana Mahuika and all those people came on the bus, Mihi stood out on the road and called them in. The bus pulled on to the marae and there was a big tangi at Wairuru. The Ngati Porou people brought Apirana's portrait and put it on the verandah where all the people could see him. When the speeches were finished, the chiefs told Mihi they were going to Te Kaha to stay there for the night, and the old lady stood up and *told* them off.

"This marae is the first marae of Whanau-a-Apanui, and it's not right for you people to go over my head, to trample me by taking Apirana to Te Kaha! If you came the other way, from Opotiki, then all right, but you can't go above me like this. Those of you who must go, go; but Apirana is staying here with me."

She grabbed the picture and took it right inside the house.

---

[13] Food is *noa* (profane), and should not be taken into the *tapu* (sacred) meeting-house.

"Api, you stay here. Your people can go, but you, e Api, will sleep one night on my marae."

The people didn't know what to do. In the end they had to stay there the night because she wouldn't give them the photo.[14] The next day she was glad, and she thanked the people for accepting her wish. She reminded them never to try and overstep her.

"I am chief, and you people are not strong enough to tread upon my head!"

Then she spoke to Apirana's portrait.

"E Api, it was right for you to sleep one night in your ancestral house, Hine Mahuru," and she gave the genealogy. "Go now with your people to Waikato."

They travelled on to Waikato. There was a great talk in those days about the cars that passed Wairuru and were stranded, and had to stay at Whakatane.

The greatest talk that Mihi ever started though, was when one of the Anarus died in Rotorua, and Mihi and her people went to the tangi. After the first Arawa speaker stood to welcome them, the visitors had to put somebody up to reply. The menfolk looked at one another, they weren't willing to stand while Mihi was there.[15] One of the local elders called out,

"Well, it's time for you people to reply."

The Whanau-a-Apanui men said,

"If the old lady isn't going to stand, I suppose one of us had better speak."

When Mihi heard that, she stood up and began to farewell the dead. She was just like a man, the way she talked and moved on the marae. Mita Taupopoki jumped up from the Te Arawa side.

"E hoa . . . Mihi Kotukutuku, you sit down! No woman has ever stood to speak on this marae. . . . Sit down! E tau ki raro!"

Mihi took no notice, she kept on talking. Mita yelled,

"Taurekareka! Slave! Sit down!"

Then Mihi got wild. She said,

"*You* sit down. Who do you think you are, Mita Taupopoki, telling me what to do? You say, no woman has ever stood on this marae. Well, I tell you this. If it wasn't for a woman, you wouldn't be here today. . . . This is where your grey hairs come from!"

She turned round, bent over and threw up her skirts, and showed her backside to him.[16]

"Anei! See your pathway into this world. . . ."

Mita Taupopoki was so hurt he just sat down, he couldn't reply, and Mihi kept on with her speech. Afterwards when all the chiefs were talking about it, someone told them,

"She's just like that in her own area, she does all the talking before the men."

Well, when Mihi died Te Arawa remembered this. Kepa Ehau said to his people,

---

14 When a death is carried to other areas (*kawe mate*), the photo is treated as the dead body was at the *tangi*, and is therefore of key importance in the ceremonial.
15 Whereas on the East Coast, high ranking women are traditionally allowed speaking rights on the *marae*, in Te Arawa, no women may stand to speak. This is because men and the *marae* are both *tapu* (sacred) but women are *noa* (profane).
16 The custom of a woman exposing herself in derision (*whakapohane*), is the ultimate Maori insult — it expresses the opinion that the victim is as *noa* as her genitals, which are very *noa* indeed.

"We're all going to go to this tangi. No matter how that woman treated us, she was a real chief and a leader of her people. And now is our time to answer her back — the tangi is the right time for such things. We can't leave her insult lying on the grave of Mita Taupopoki. . . ."

Two busloads of Te Arawa came to the tangi. The local women called them and welcomed them on to the marae, and the Whanau-a-Apanui elders gave their speeches of welcome praising Mihi Kotukutuku. When it was time for the visitors to reply, Kepa Ehau stood up and started jumping around the marae.

"Taurekareka, Mihi Kotukutuku! Slave! You were the woman who exposed herself to Te Arawa . . . good job you died! So goodbye, you terrible woman, slave, big-headed. . . ."

Mark, Dick's brother, was in the kitchen and somebody said,

"Hey, Mark, come out and listen to what Kepa Ehau is saying about your mother."

When he heard it, Mark ran out to the front of the marae.

"Kepa Ehau! You *get* off this marae! Coming here and cursing my mother on her own marae. You've got a damned cheek. . . . You get out or I'll get something and bash you on the head!"

Kepa Ehau kept talking, telling Mark what Mihi had done to them, but Mark didn't listen. In the end Eruera had to stop his brother.

"Mark, that's enough. . . ."

"That's all right for you; I'm not going to let them come here and curse our mother!"

"Mark, you don't know why these people are doing this. She hurt those people, and now it's her tangi, they've come here to settle it. They are making chiefs out of us. . . ."

"Agh! You're just letting Te Arawa trample all over us, you're letting us down. That's you — not me!"

After a while he settled down. Then Eruera said to Te Arawa,

"All right, Te Arawa, we've had our battle — now it's over. You have held on to your pain all these years and now you've hit back, we're even now. That's enough!"

He went over and shook hands and rubbed noses to Kepa Ehau.

"Kepa, she's dead now. So forget your hurt, and look back at all the good things she did while she was alive. Whenever the people needed her, Mihi was there."

Then all the people stood and started to tell Te Arawa about the good works of Mihi Kotukutuku.

I was quite happy at Stirling Castle, but I wanted a home of my own; I was funny like that. I felt that married life is a house where you can care for your own children, not staying with the old people and looking after all the tribe. I talked to Eruera about it.

"It's not right for us to stay here all the time and live on your parents. We'll have to shift away and get ourselves a house, even a little kauta, before we have our family."

He told his mother about it and she got wild.

"With this big house! There's plenty of room here for all your family. What's wrong with staying here? That woman of yours is always saying something."

He came back and we had a bit of a row over it. I said,

"Well, I can't help it. You're at home and you're quite comfortable, but I can't feel that's *our* home. We can't depend on the old people all the time. . . we've got our own life to battle, and we've got to be on our feet in our own way, whether it's in a toetoe hut or whatever. I'd rather be that way; I want a place I can call our own."

Mihi came to talk to me.

"If this is how you feel Amiria, well, we've got a big house here. There's the passageway, you can have all the rooms there and live on that side of the house. . . . What's the matter with you?"

"Mum. It's not that I'm against you or anything. I just want a little house of our own, for me and my children. That's all."

"Why do you have to go and leave? There's everything here."

She was right, it was comfortable at Stirling Castle and we didn't have to pay for anything.

"You're only trying to drag Dick away where he's got to shoulder everything, buy this and buy that. Let his father do those things."

But I still wanted a little bach. She thought, au! this woman! And I felt that I wasn't happy, so I'd go back home for a while to my grandmother.

After we had been married a while, the sheep arrived from Ruatoria. We didn't have any land of our own, so Eruera put them to run with his father's stock on the farm. Neither of us knew much about sheep-farming, how to shear, crutch and dag, all that work, so Eruera said to me,

"I think I'm going to Pakihiroa station to learn how to look after these sheep."[17]

We went and stayed with my mother at Tuparoa, and started work on the Williams station. Eruera was shearing and wool-pressing in the shearing season, and cutting manuka, fencing and doing stock-work the rest of the time, and I was a fleece-o in the shearing shed. We enjoyed that work.

It was around about that time when my mother's third husband, Watene Campbell died. He was scrub-cutting at Pakihiroa station and he wanted to come home to see his daughter Kuatau. The people told him not to go because the Waiapu River was in flood, but he wouldn't listen and he was carried away and drowned. You see, it was that year that they had the great flu epidemic,[17a] Kuatau had got sick. She had gone away to Queen Victoria College and when she came home for a holiday, she caught the fever on the boat. By the time she got home she was delirious, and my mother had to rush her to the hospital. I was shocked to see my mother crying there.

"How did she get this, Mum?"

"Well, I don't know. She got sick when she was coming home on the *Mako*."

Kuatau didn't even know me. She was only in the hospital a couple of days, and she passed on. It just about knocked me out. Just before she died, she turned to our mother and said,

---

[17] T. S. Williams trained a number of young Maoris under a Farm Training Scheme; several of these men later went on to win the Ahuwhenua Cup for Agricultural Excellence.

[17a] 1918.

Pakihiroa Station 1915.

Wool being carted from Pakihiroa across the Waiapu River c. 1903.

"Mum, if I pass on, would you put my school badge on my photo?"

That was her last wish, because she was so disappointed that she couldn't complete her time at Queen Vic. Mum did that for her, and the badge is still on her photo today.

Well, about two years after that I started carrying Lucy and when I got a bit heavy I stopped work.

I was at my grandmother's place when the pains started, so I asked her to ring up Heni Pokino, the local nurse. Heni came, and she had a job too; the baby wouldn't come the right way, she always seemed to come feet first. Heni said,

"By Jove, this is a hard baby!"

She kept trying to turn the baby but no, it was always feet first. I heard her growling in Maori to the baby, telling her that she'll pinch her toes; in the end she said,

"It's no use, the child will not come the right way. We'll just have to pray to God that he will help to bring the baby away, because it's been too long, we can't hang on."

She told me she was hoping that the baby's arms are by her sides, because if the baby has her arms up they'll have to rush me to Te Puia Hospital. The old lady was sitting there praying in her Maori way, and Heni was trying to catch the baby's hands. In the end she caught the fingers.

"Oh, I've got the baby! Now, put all the force and bring her out."

The next thing, the baby was born. Heni said,

"Well, tena hoki koe!" and she clapped her bottom. "Stubborn brat!"

All the people in the pa were calling out,

"Hey, the baby is born."

"What is it?"

"A girl."

"Agh! It would be!"

I didn't mind though, I was happy the baby was born.

We spent three years altogether at Tuparoa, and when the baby was off the breast I went back to work with Dick at Pakihiroa. It was all right, because I could leave her at home with my grandmother. I worked as a fleece-o, roll-up and all those sort of jobs. I was keen to learn, because I knew we would have to be farmers one day. There was no other way of living in those times, just corn-cropping, dairying and sheep-farming. After I was a fleece-o for a while, I got to be a roll-up. You had to grab the two ends of the fleece, fold one end and then flip it over and roll it, so the back of the fleece was right on top. I enjoyed it, and while I was doing my own job I used to watch the wool-classer and ask him questions. He showed me how the short fleece has crinkles in it and other sorts have long fibres; how some wool is soft and silky while other wool is thready. You learned all that with your hands — the feeling of the wool.

One day he took sick, and somebody had to do the work, so I offered. In the end I was pretty good. I wasn't satisfied with that though, I wanted to know about cooking too, and I ended up as a cook for the whole gang of about 70, cooking in the big boilers and making bread in the camp oven. I had a man to help me with all the heavy lifting, I just organised the cooking and made the bread. I enjoyed every bit of it, and I thought, now I've got that part, I can run a gang myself. I was very happy.

All this time we were shifting between Tuparoa and Raukokore. Dick had to go home sometimes to help his father with the farm, and it was at one of our stops at Stirling Castle that I had the last trouble with this wedding ring of mine. Lucy must have been about two then because she was walking around, but she loved this ring, she always wanted to play with it. Sometimes I'd give it to her and she'd drop it on the floor, and if it rang she'd laugh. If it rolled she'd crawl along behind it and put it in her mouth. I slapped her hand.

"Don't put it in your mouth, you might swallow it!"

"Mm."

So I let her play with it for a while. The next thing, I couldn't find the ring.

"Where is it? Where's that ring?"

"Ah", she was looking around for it too, she couldn't find it. In the end we looked all day for that ring, I lifted all the carpet and everything.

"By gosh, now I suppose you've lost that ring!"

I smacked her and she howled.

Kate, the old lady, and all the family were looking for the ring; we even went under the house but we couldn't find it. The old lady said,

"Ah! What a stupid thing to do, to give it to a little baby. Ka mau to wehi!" and she told me off about it.

"Well, that was it."

I think it must have been three or four years later when old Duncan said to Tai and Dick,

"I think, boys, you'd better empty out that chaff box. I want all new chaff there for the working horses."

There was a great big box near the verandah at the back of the house, and he told Tai and Dick to take all the old chaff from there and put it in the boxes on the fence, because each horse had his own box nailed to a fence-post. So Dick and Tai shifted all the chaff.

A few days later I was sitting on the back verandah feeding the baby, when I spotted this horse. He put his head in the chaff box, then had a chew and shook his head around, and I saw something glitter in his mouth. I thought, that's funny! All the other horses are all right, but that one . . . there's something funny in that chaff. I went over to have a look and when I looked down in the box, I saw my ring. I grabbed hold of this horse and kissed him.

"Oh! That was very good of you."

Then I called out to everyone,

"E hika ma! I've got my ring back!"

By Jove, I was glad. I said to Lucy,

"Lucy, you see? You're not going to have this ring anymore. It's going to stay here now!" And that ring has been on my finger from that day to this.

But I just couldn't settle at Stirling Castle somehow, and I had about four years before George was born to romp around on my horse, come to Raukokore, back home again to Taumata-o-mihi and then off to the station, shearing.

In the end my uncle said to Dick,

"You two can't keep on like this. You'll have to decide whether you want to start farming, Eruera, because that's the trouble with your wife. She keeps coming back home, coming back home; she needs a place of her own. You're the man, you'll have to make up your mind. She wants to be with you all the time — why not give her what she wants?"

Eruera had another talk with his mother about it, and one day she came to me.

"Now, what's the matter with you?"

"I want a home, Mum."

"All right then, you'd better go to the top of that big hill there, is that what you want?"

"Yes."

She didn't think I'd agree, she thought I'd refuse it.

"Ka *pai* te wahine nei!"

Then old Duncan heard about it.

"What's the matter with you, Amy? You're worried over something."

"No, I'm not worried, Dad, I'm quite happy here. This is a *beautiful* home. But I just want a little house for my family — you know what I mean?"

"You want a home."

"That's it."

"All right, Amy, we'll build a little house for you."

I was so happy, I kissed him, and he said,

"*I'll* build that house for you."

He started carting things up the hill to Motuwhakari, and the next thing the house was up. It was lovely. It had two rooms and a kitchen, and a little sitting-room; although it wasn't very big, it had everything. I really adored that place when we stayed there. The sea view was beautiful. You could see the White Island and that was its name — Motu Whakari, the White Island, because it was so high up. I planted flowers and everything.

I was happy in my house. The only thing was, we had no living; the old people had to give us everything. I wanted to start farming, like Tai and Margaret on their little place. I said to Eruera.

"We've got to have some sort of a living. Your parents are farmers, they've got the maize, and the stock, and working-horses. . . Why can't we be like them?"

"Well, we don't have any land. The old people have got the run of this place."

I knew I couldn't say anything about the sheep because old Duncan had been looking after them, and there wasn't room for all those animals at Motu-Whakari. I decided to go home and see if my family would give us some cows. When I arrived at Taumata-o-mihi, my grandmother asked me how we were getting on.

"I'm happy in my marriage, grandma, and I'm glad we've got our home. The only thing is, we don't have anything to live on. We have to rely on the old people for all our food, and when we buy anything at the store we have to book it to them. I want us to make our own way."

"What do you need, then, Amiria? Do you want money?"

"No," I said, "But I would like some cows."

"How big is your place? How many acres?"

It was only a little place but I didn't like to tell her that.

"I don't know. But it's quite a big . . ."

76

"You go back and ask your husband first. How are you going to manage if the farm is too small? Run the cows on the road?"

"It's all right, grandma — we only need a few to start us off."

"Well, Amiria, if it's cows you want, Hakopa Haerewa is the man. You go and talk to him."

I went over to the Haerewa home. The old man Hakopa was working in the paddock.

"Oh, hello, Amiria!"

"Hello, koro."

Then I asked him about this milking.

"Is that what you want?"

"Yes, koro."

"All right, Amiria, I'll call Tipu straight away."

Tipu was Kareti's husband. He got on the phone to Tipu, and Tipu agreed.

"I want twelve milking cows, Tipu, and a bull. Nice young cows, too."

"I'll have them ready, Dad."

Hakopa came back to me and said,

"It's all fixed up, Amiria, your cows are ready. Who's going to take them to Raukokore for you?"

"I think my husband will come and get them."

The next day I went back to Raukokore and told Eruera. He couldn't believe it. And when he told the old lady, she was stunned, she said,

"Hika! How many?"

"Twelve cows and a bull."

"Au — i! Look at that. But I don't think you people have enough room at Motuwhakari, you'd better shift to Kapongaro. There's more room there."

That's how we came to live at Kapongaro. We had to leave our little house at Motuwhakari; we leased it to the postmaster and somehow it got burned down, I don't know how that happened. There was a little bach already at Kapongaro, and we managed to fix that up for ourselves and the baby. All the grazing was there for the cows but there wasn't a cowshed, and we had to milk the cows tied up to the fence. It was hard in the beginning, but we managed.

Milking cows tied to a fence, East Coast.

77

CHAPTER SIX

Life On The Farm

Not long after we settled at Kapongaro farm, Lucy took sick. It was colder there, because Kapongaro was away in the hills, not near the sea like Motuwhakari, and that's how Lucy caught this pneumonia. The district nurse knew that I had been nursing so she thought I could manage. We tried to get her to come but there was always some excuse, she was too busy or something, and she wouldn't come.

In the end it was too much for me. Handling a baby is not like handling grown-ups, and if it's your own child, you know that if you make the slightest mistake, well. . . . Her temperature was very high, and nobody around was any help at all. I was crying and all that sort of thing, so I decided that I'd be happier if I sent Lucy to Opotiki Hospital, and if we can't get anybody to take the child, to get the *Waihau* to call in at Raukokore. There was no transport in those days, only the launch owned by the Walkers who kept the shop at Waihau Bay, to take the stuff from Raukokore to Opotiki.

The district nurse saw the launch go past Te Kaha, and somebody told her it was coming to pick up our baby and take her to hospital. She sent a telegram to tell me not to take the baby to Opotiki, then she got on her horse and started riding to Raukokore. Someone brought the telegram to our farm, and when I read it I thought, yes, that nurse knew all the time our baby has been sick, and she wouldn't come! Now she's trying to stop me, and the *Waihau* is half-way to Raukokore.

In those years it cost twenty pounds to get the *Waihau*, and that was a big lot of money. I thought, no, I won't listen to her this time, I'm taking my baby to the hospital. I got everything ready and we started down to the old lady's home. The launch was going to pull up right in front of Stirling Castle. We were just going out of the gate when I saw this person tearing up the road and yelling out to us. It was the nurse. She pulled up and said,

"Look, that baby will never last, she'll never get there! She's been running this high temperature too long. Leave your baby at home here, she's too far gone to go. She won't reach Opotiki Hospital, she'll be dead before you get there."

"Yes, sister, why didn't you come? I've been asking for you and . . ."

"Oh well, I've been busy with this and that."

Anyhow, she stopped. We put the baby to bed, took her temperature and sponged her. She sat up with me all that night. I will say this for her, she did wonders for that baby, she saved her life all right. Otherwise Lucy would have been dead.

I started carrying another baby when Lucy was about four. My grandmother called me to come home to have the baby, because Heni Pokino was there at Kariaka to look after me. I thought I'd rather go there than to Opotiki Hospital, so I came back to Taumata-o-mihi.

Well, this baby played up with me too. I kept getting pains and then they would go away again; the baby didn't seem to want to come. After a while Heni started talking about Te Puia hospital, but I said,

"What's the difference? You're a nurse, you can deliver the baby."

The pains came and Heni got prepared, then the pains would go. After a while, Heni got wild with me.

"By . . . gosh!" She grabbed hold of me and shook me.

"I think it's you! You're holding that baby. Come on, let go! What's wrong with you?"

"It's not me, Heni."

"Oh yes it is. And if the baby's not born tomorrow, you'll have to go to Te Puia. Do you know what's the matter?"

"No — I don't. . . ."

"You ought to know by now." She was growling at me. "Give that force! You're not giving that force. You're scared, that's what's wrong."

But I knew it wasn't me. The baby had been playing up like that; I kept getting pains and then they'd disappear.

In the end, Heni got tired of waiting. She said to me,

"I've got a family too, you know. If you're going to play up like this with me, I'm going to leave you, I'll go home to get tea for my husband."

Then she turned to the old lady,

"Tell your mokopuna to bring the baby. She's scared, that's what's the matter."

Mereana came and told me off.

"I'm telling you, Amiria, *bring* that baby. Go on! While Heni is still here. Hurry up!"

She took me and put me down on the floor on a mat, then she put her knee against my belly and just *hit* me there.

"Wait on, Heni, wait. The baby's coming now!"

I heard the baby coming. Heni came running back, and the baby was born. Oh, I was glad. I was just resting back with relief, I was glad it was finished. The next thing I heard them crying.

"Heni! What's the matter? Is the baby dead?"

She looked around and shook her head.

"Why are you crying?"

She shook the baby and the baby started to cry.

"Oh, grandma . . . why are you crying? The baby's born and you're crying. . . ."

My grandmother took the afterbirth and said to me.

"You must wash this and look after it."

"Why? All that has to be buried, doesn't it?"

"No," she said. "This baby was born with a cap on his head, and this is the cap. You must look after that cap, so the baby will be all right. Otherwise, something terrible will happen to this child."

I got sick of all this Maori talk.

"Look, the baby is born, he's all right! Never mind about all that — those days are finished."

Heni came and kissed me, and Mereana took the baby and washed him. I didn't know she kept that afterbirth until years after; I went back one time and she showed it to me, it was like silk. I don't know what happened to it when she died.

That child was our son George. When I think back now and remember what happened to that boy, I can see it all. If only I had listened to her, he would still be alive today. But I was like a lot of young people, I couldn't be bothered with the old Maori ways.

Amiria at Otaimina 1976.

We didn't stay long at Kapongaro, only about a year. We grew one crop of maize there, and then we shifted to Otaimina. We had a mixed farm at Otaimina, milking and sheep-farming and later on, cropping. All our other children were born there; Wahawaha, Mokikiwa, Lily, Tama, Marama and Te Kepa the last. And I had all my babies at home except Tama; he was a floating baby and he didn't seem to bother about coming away. The time was up and he should have been born, but he wasn't worried, he was still there. Dr Scott was the doctor then, and he said,

"I think you'd better go to Opotiki Hospital, Mrs Stirling, because a lot of things can happen, you'd better have that baby there."

When I told Dick he agreed, and he said,

"If you go to Opotiki, go to Motoi's place, she lives close to the hospital. Just stay there the night, and we'll book you into hospital for the next day."

He arranged everything, and when I got to Opotiki, Motoi was waiting for me at the bus-stop. She took me home and she had a nice little place. She said to me,

"Never mind about going to the hospital — you stay here. If anything happens and I can't manage, it's all right, I'll just ring the doctor and he can come."

That night the pains started.

"Look Motoi, I think I'd better go to the hospital. . . ."

"Don't worry, it's all right!"

She wouldn't ring the doctor. I kept asking her but she said,

"No, *don't* worry about it. Come on, you have the baby and I'll look after you."

In the end she was the one that helped me to give birth all right. The funny thing was, when the baby was born we heard all the rockets go off, it was Guy Fawkes night. I heard the crackers and the next thing, *bang!* Tama was born.

At Otaimina we had the Maori Affairs house. Eruera went and had a talk to Apirana about it, and after a while Maori Affairs built us a place.

With all the children and paying the Maori Affairs, it got pretty hard on the cream cheque, so we used to go out and pick seaweed, leave it on the beach to dry and then send it up to the Internal Marketing in Auckland, and that brought us a bit of extra money for the family at home.

A few years later, Eruera heard that some other people on the coast were cropping kumaras and potatoes, so he thought he might try it. He said,

"Gee, I think Mum, I'll plough up a patch of paddock here and put in a few kumaras and potatoes."

There were people in Te Araroa growing these and selling them to Lou Gow, the Chinaman who came round in a truck between Gisborne and Opotiki, buying for the market. I said,

"Do you think they'll allow us to do that? Maori Affairs is the boss of this ground now they've built the house."

"Oh, *blow* them. It's my own land! I think that I'll give it a go."

It was a lot of work getting the ground ready for cropping. The puriri stumps were the worst, and once the trees were all out, the soil had to be ploughed. One old chap called Marama Brown said to Eruera,

"Eru — the horse is no good for ploughing, that's the trouble. They drag too fast, and if the plough gets stuck, they keep pulling until it's all smashed up. The bullock is the best. You try and train a couple of bullocks. Although it takes months

Marama Brown with his team of bullocks.

and months, once they're trained, they're the best; if the plough gets caught, the bullock will just stand, not like the horse."

Eruera started training steers, and the old man helped him. He was right, too; the bullocks were very good. Then Eruera got the kumara plants from his mother. She had a patch of kumaras, what they called the whakaika kumara, down at Stirling Castle. After that season she showed me how to do it; you put the kumaras down in a big bed and bury them, and when the shoots start to come up, you pick them, bundle them up in kits and plant them in the ground.

That year, we did very well. The next year we thought we'd like a really big batch, tons of kumaras, because it's an extra cheque to come in. Dick said,

"Oh blow the Maori Affairs, we'll plough Otaimina up," and he did.

That's how we got on; we had the cream cheque, and the kumaras and potatoes, and we felt we were on our feet. We could pay for the house and the children's clothes and everything, we were doing very well. Then Eruera was in Auckland one time, and he went to see the people at Turners and Growers. They offered to buy all his kumaras and potatoes, and told him to contact them about prices, not to bother with Lou Gow. In the end Eruera thought he could handle the other people's crops as well. He waited until Lou Gow went past in his truck, then he went up to Te Araroa and Ruatoria and asked the people how much Lou Gow had offered them for their kumaras. He wrote to Auckland, and Turners and Growers told him to buy all those kumaras, they'll give a better price than Lou Gow's. When Lou Gow came back the people told him,

"Oh no! Our kumaras have gone, Dick Stirling has bought them."

"What?"

"Dick Stirling — he gave us more money."

"Oh . . ."

He got so wild he came to see Dick, and told him not to chip into his business, to leave his customers alone.

"Well, those people deserve a better price."

"Look here, you mind your own business!"

"If they agree to sell their kumaras to you, that's all right; and if they agree to give them to me, I'll take them."

They had a bit of trouble over that.

Every now and then when we saw Lou Gow go past, Dick would take the bus and find out what the price was.

"Oh well, I'll give you this. . . ."

When Lou Gow came back to collect the kumaras, they'd say,

"No, Dick Stirling's got my lot."

Lou Gow bumped his price up, and that's how he went broke. Dick wrote to Turners and Growers about this price, and they told him to leave it, the prices in Auckland had dropped. So Lou Gow went broke, and the Chinese people in Gisborne put him back in the market gardens.

We had geese and fowls and ducks at Otaimina too, to give us plenty of eggs. In those days you had to bake all the time, it wasn't like the town where the bread is ready for you and everything is at your finger-tips. I'd boil up a big pot of eggs for the children to take to school with their bread, and they used to take the bread down to the cowshed for a feed. There was a big patch of strawberries near the shed, and they'd eat strawberries and cream and bread for breakfast. For a while our cream kept coming back from the factory, Second Grade. Dick couldn't work it out until one day he emptied out the can and it had breadcrusts and bits of strawberry in the bottom, so we had to stop the strawberries then.

After that the first of the children who got up in the morning to get the cows would collect all the eggs. The next thing you'd hear them yelling, fighting in the paddock over these eggs. I'd open the window and call out to them,

"What's the matter?"

"Oh . . . so and so's got my eggs, I found the eggs and they took them off me!"

"You should be in bed! Come on back home."

Another thing the children liked was keeping pets. I remember when the boys went pig-hunting one time, they shot a pig, and when they started skinning the carcass a little suckling pig came squeaking out of the bush. That was Porky. They caught it and brought it home, then they came inside and asked me for the baby's bottle.

"What do you want it for?"

"Oh, we've got a little orphant pig out there."

"You mean to say you're going to give the baby's bottle to a pig?"

"Mum, come and have a look, it's a dear little fella."

When I saw the pig, it was white, pure white, and grunting along as though it was starved. It had its mouth open, ready to grab onto anything.

"Well, you'll have to ride down to Waihau first and get the baby a new bottle."

"We'll go soon, Mum, but this pig needs a drink now."

I had to give them the bottle. That poor little pig sucked away, it was grateful to have a drink. The children looked after it like a mother looking after her baby; they always remembered to feed it and it grew into a great, fat animal. If strangers came to the gate, all the pig's hairs would stand up on end, and you could hear it growling away, telling them not to come in. It was so tame the children even used to ride it to school, and it would follow Eruera when he went riding off to Waihau on his horse. One time when the pig went up with the cows to the top of the hill, though, somebody shot it and took it home to eat.

We had two pet horses on the farm too, Des and Hokey-Pokey. Des was George's pet, and whenever George went to catch him, Des would run and dodge as if he was playing football. George would say,

"Don't run away, Des — just stay there, won't you?"

But Des always backed off and as soon as he saw a gap, he'd slide out and run that way.

"Watch out, Des, I'll knock your blooming head off!"

The horse would duck back, and run off in another direction. So George picked up a stick.

"All right, you do that again and I'll have your head off." And when Des tried to dodge, bang! on his head. After that he seemed to understand, he'd just stop there and let George catch him.

Hokey Pokey was another one. Once when one of the horses was ready to foal, the children came in one morning to have a look and found her dead in the hay, with the little foal sucking away — no milk. They brought it back to the house, and that was another bottle the baby lost. The kids made a bed with an old blanket under the cowshed, and they fed the foal themselves. I didn't think it would live, it looked so weak; but when Dick told the children it would be kinder to shoot the animal, they all sat down and howled, so he let them keep it. In the end Hokey Pokey grew into quite a healthy pony, except that his back wasn't quite straight. I said to George,

"You people shouldn't be riding that horse, it's only a pony. See, its back is getting crooked. . . ."

"I can't stop the kids, Mum, they ride him when I'm not looking."

Hokey Pokey seemed to understand everything. When Waha and George went to get the cows, he'd trot along behind them, and if anyone was late for school after milking, they could hop on Hokey Pokey and he'd take them to school. There was no need for a saddle and bridle, he knew which way to go, and then he'd come back home by himself.

Just before three o'clock in the afternoon, I'd hear Hokey Pokey at the gate, pushing at the latch. When I opened the gate, he'd trot off as fast as he could go to fetch the children from school. Sometimes Porky the pig would go too, running along behind him. The first children to come out would say,

"Hey! Here's Hokey Pokey! We'll get him to take us to Waihau!"

"What about us?"

"Oh, you can ride the pig!"

So they hopped on Hokey Pokey's back and rode off to Waihau, pulling his ears so he wouldn't go home. When he'd get back to Otaimina, the children would say,

"Yeah! Where have you been, Hokey Pokey? You're supposed to bring *us* back, not cart those other kids to Waihau."

Their other pet was a sheep. Its mother died, so the children looked after it, and it grew very big. One day when some people came to ask Dick for meat for a hui, he didn't have any animals ready, and they said,

"Well, what about that big fat sheep?"

"No, that's the children's pet."

"We've got to have meat for the marae you know, there's a lot of people there and there's no meat."

So he said all right. They took the sheep to the marae and killed it. When the children came home they were looking for their pet sheep, and we had to tell them in the end. Then there was a big tangi at Otaimina. They said,

"We're not going to milk *your* cows anymore, Dad — you killed our sheep!"

"Well, what could I do — let those people starve?"

"Why don't they get their own meat? There's meat at the shop in Waihau."

For a whole week none of them would eat meat, they were frightened it might be their sheep. That's how bad it was, life on the farm. . . .

CHAPTER SEVEN

Life In The Bay Of Plenty

We did a lot of work on different maraes around the Coast in those years, and it was all because of Apirana Ngata. If it wasn't for him, none of those meeting-houses would be here today — Porourangi, Tukaki, Ruakapanga, Te Hono-ki-Rarotonga and all the rest. That's why I have so much respect for that man; he started as a solicitor in the first part of it, but then he thought somebody had better come home to work with the people, so he dropped it and came home. He talked to the people about the maraes, the carving and the tukutuku.

"We are going to lose all these wonderful things; we have to bring them back to life!"

But the old people couldn't do much, so he had to make his own way. He went to all the different places, talking to the people,

"If we let these things go, maoritanga will die, and we'll be a lost people. We must keep our own language and study our arts! Once the genealogies are forgotten, you'll lose the last piece of land under your feet, you won't be able to claim it any more. . . . We'll be mongrels — not Maori, not pakeha — wandering around this country looking for a place to sleep. By all means get a pakeha education — but hold fast to your maoritanga!"

He didn't just work in his own area; he helped the Waikato people get on their feet as well. Princess Te Puea brought her people to the Coast,[18] and Api promised to help find her the money for a new meeting-house at Turangawaewae. Te Puea's group stayed for one whole week giving concerts around the place, and besides that Apirana collected money from all the different tribes.

"Te Puea has come here in the way of chiefs to ask us to show aroha for the treasures of our ancestors. If Waikato want a marae, surely we can help them. . . ."

They collected several thousand pounds that time, just from Ngati Porou.

Later on when Hine Tapora meeting-house at Mangahanea was renovated, I was one of the women doing the tukutuku work there. In those days it took months and months to do the carving, and during that time the women did the tukutuku and cooked for the carvers. This time the carvers were taking so long that the women all started to worry about their families; we'd been on the marae for months, and we didn't know how far the carvers had gone because no women were allowed inside the meeting-house. Some of my mates started to growl about it.

"You never know, they might be sleeping in there. I bet those men are having a good time in there, while we're cooking all their kai!"

Someone else said,

"Hey, Amiria, you go and have a look. . . . Take them a cup of tea and make sure they're working, not playing cards or something."

---

18 In 1927 (Michael King, private communication).

I thought, yeah, that's right, they have been there a long time. We got the tea ready and I carried it over to the house, then I stepped on the verandah to have a look through the window. I called out,

"Hey, you men! I've got your tea here, it's all ready!"

Hika! Before I'd finished, someone jumped out from inside the house and *threw* me right off the verandah; I crashed to the ground.

"What . . . *why* did you do that?"

"You women keep out of the house!"

"All right! If that's how you feel, we're not going to stay here and cook for you fellas — who knows if you're doing any work! Cook your own kai, I'm going home to do my washing and look after the children. . . ."

"You know women are not allowed in and that's that!"[19]

"Yeah. Well, we're packing up now, we're going home!"

I went back and told my mates.

"Oh! Tino kino! Those men nearly killed me . . . they tossed me right off the verandah, onto the ground."

So Mania said,

"Well in that case we're going home, they can cook for themselves. We'll do our tukutuku at home."

Someone else said,

"Yeah, we'll pack up now!"

I got my horse and we were just packing up when Apirana arrived.

"Hey, Apirana is coming!"

"Where?"

"There, by the gate."

I said,

"You'd better tell him we're packing up."

"No, *you* tell him. Go on, Amiria, go and tell him we're leaving — before he goes into the house."

He was tying his horse on the fence when I walked over to him.

"Hello, Apirana."

"Kia ora, Amiria. . . ."

Then I started to tell him what had happened.

"I went to the meeting-house, Api, to take those men their cup of tea, and I thought I'd just peep in through the window to see how they're getting on. When they spotted me, they grabbed me and threw me off the verandah! So now we think we're going home, we're not going to do any more cooking for them. We've got our children at home — those men can cook for themselves!"

Apirana looked at me and said,

"Amiria! No, no . . . you don't understand. You come here and sit down with me."

So we went and sat down on the little seat near the meeting-house, and he started to tell me.

"Listen to me, Amiria — this is the Maori custom. When a man is chosen to carve, he has a blessing put on him so that he can carry on the work of his ancestors.

---

[19] A meeting-house under construction and carvings being completed are both highly *tapu*; and women, being *noa* (common) should keep away from them.

It makes him clean so he can use all of his heart and his hands in the carving. All these men have been blessed like that and washed in the sacred water, and while they're tapu they have to keep right away from women. If you had gone in there, Amiria, *everything* would go wrong. They've been away from their wives for months now, and if they started to think, now there's a fine-looking woman, all sorts of funny thoughts would come into their minds and the grace of the Maori would be gone. Then they wouldn't be able to work. They don't draw their carvings first, you know, it all comes out of the mind. . . . I'll go in there and see how far they've got, and then I'll come and tell you."

He went into the house to have a look, and I went back to the kitchen and told the women,

"Hey, put all your things back."

"Why? Do we *still* have to cook for them?"

"Yeah! And you listen to me."

So I started to tell them what Apirana had said to me. One woman protested, she wanted to go home to her family.

"Do we have to stay?"

"Yes, otherwise this house will never be finished."

We carried on until all the work was done. And you should see that beautiful house now, Hine Tapora at Mangahanea — it was worth all that.

Another thing we were very keen on in the Bay of Plenty was hockey. I used to play in Ruatoria, so after I came to Raukokore I joined the Bay of Plenty team.

Amiria and Eruera outside Hine Tapora meeting-house, Mangahanea 1976.

They called us "Kai-Kanga"[20] after all the maize grown in the district, and we could play hockey all right.

One time our team was invited to a match at Waioeka, and that turned out to be a funny sort of a trip. Mrs Manaehu Waititi and I were in charge of the bus because we were the senior players — I must have been getting on for forty then, and I was the goalie in the team. We won the match at Waioeka, and we were so excited about it that we thought we might stay for the dance on the marae that night. It was a marae belonging to the Ringatu church, and after the speeches the elders started to explain the Ringatu custom to us.

"All right, Kai-Kanga, this is a Ringatu marae, and tomorrow is the 12th, it's like a Sunday to us. At 12 o'clock tonight we close the gates of the marae; no-one can leave the marae after that until the service finishes. If you want to stay for the dance, you'll have to leave before midnight."[21]

As soon as Manaehu and I knew there was going to be a special service we weren't too keen on staying, but all the girls wanted to go to the dance and so did the drivers. They said,

"You don't have to worry. There are two of us, so if one goes to sleep, the other can take over the driving. It's all right — we'll be out of here before midnight."

"By Joves, you people have to make sure you pack up in time!"

"Oh yes, Amiria, we'll do that."

So we let them have a dance and Manaehu and I kept looking at the clock. While we were sitting in the meeting-house a woman came in and threw down all the clothes we'd hung up in there onto the floor. I asked her why, and she told us that if we hung our coats on the wall, they'd be up there above the men's heads and that wasn't right. That was another thing I learned at that marae.[22]

The next time we looked at the clock it was nearly midnight. I said,

"Manaehu, you'd better start rounding up those girls, we've got to get them out of this marae before the twelfth."

"All right — but you'll have to get the driver to take the bus out of the marae."

We managed to get the driver to take the bus out to the gate of the marae, then we started to chase those girls. Some of them had disappeared, gone off with a boyfriend I suppose, and we had a job to find them. In the end we got the driver to start tooting the horn, and the old man of the marae came out.

"Hurry up, Kai-Kanga! Go on! I want you out of that gate right now — it's after 12 o'clock already."

We got out in the end, but it was just one o'clock by the time we left. Once we started going I thought, that's all right . . . the girls were singing away and I fell off to sleep. I don't know what woke me up, it was the yelling and screaming I think. Huh! When I came to myself and looked around, I couldn't make out where I was.

---

20 "Maize Eaters' — the Whanau-a-Apanui nickname. The maize-cropping industry on the East Coast was already well-established by 1850, and the Bay of Plenty was renowned for its excellent crops.

21 The Ringatu faith was founded by Te Kooti in the late 1860s, and his followers (particularly in the Tuhoe area) still meet on their maraes on the twelfth of each month. Visitors to a Ringatu gathering are enjoined by a *tapu* law to arrive before sunset on the day before, and they may not leave until after sunset the next day.

22 This is again a *tapu* law. The clothes of women are *noa*, and should not be hung above the highly *tapu* heads of their menfolk.

The bus had turned over and was lying on its side. The window was next to me, and when I looked down I saw the river just below . . . the bus had fallen into the river! The back of the bus was caught on the bank, and the rest of the bus was just hanging there.

I looked around, and all the seats were over to one side; there were about half a dozen girls groaning on the floor. I felt something wet, and I realised I was all covered in blood. A girl had been thrown onto me from the other side of the bus, and she'd hit the glass window and the blood was dripping down on my clothes. I grabbed her and pulled her back, and I saw her face was all cut to pieces. The next thing, I heard a man's voice outside. It was Mark Munroe, he had spotted the light in the river and thought it was someone eeling, but when he pulled up to have a look he saw the bus hanging by its back wheels over the bank. It had crashed off the side of the bridge. I started to crawl, and he yelled out,

"Don't go to the front! The bus is just hanging by its back wheels, you might push it over. Crawl out the back. . . ."

I crawled back, but the way was blocked by a heap of people with seats all over them, so I crawled out of a broken window into the mud. Mark Munroe had already called the ambulance, and in the end we got everyone out of the bus and the ambulance took eight people to Opotiki Hospital. I was all right, I was just covered with blood from that other woman.

Somebody had rung Raukokore and told them that the bus had crashed into the river; all the men went to the marae and had a big tangi there, they thought their wives and daughters were dead. It wasn't until we arrived that they knew it wasn't so bad, only eight girls had been taken to hospital and none of them was seriously injured, they'd be out soon.

Then the elders stood on the marae and told us off. If we hadn't trampled the day of the Ringatu church, that bus would never have crashed into the river. I quite believe that. The young people of today don't take these things very seriously, but from that day to this day, I believe in the Ringatu twelfth; you must respect that day whatever you do, because it's their Sunday and our Sunday too.

Another year our hockey team played in a competition for all of the Coast. We beat all the local teams, so Apirana picked us to go to Taranaki to play for the Lady Ngata Cup. We got to the finals and that was a *great* game. I got hit on my back that time; I was the goalie, and I had to go right down on my two knees to stop this ball, and a girl came up and crashed her hockey-stick down on my back. I still have that trouble today; my back aches every now and again, especially in this sort of weather. Anyhow, all the time we were playing, old Taite te Tomo was barracking for us.

"Come on, Kai Kanga! Come on, Kai Kanga!"

Matemoana was carrying the ball and he called out,

"Come on, Kai Kanga!"

She dodged this way and that, then passed the ball to somebody else and they picked it up, and the next thing bang! into the goal. Everybody screamed,

"Oh! Ka mau te wehi! Kai Corn, Kai Corn, Kai Corn!"

Ae . . . in the end, we won it too.

That evening there was a big do at Manukorihi marae, and during the night the people asked Apirana to recite his poem "The Scenes of the Past".

"Api — we've only seen it written. We want to see the man himself acting 'The Scenes of the Past'; this is our request to you."

"Is that what you want?"

"Yes, Api."

"Well then, where is your korowai?"

"Oh?"

"Your korowai. I've only got pakeha clothes on — fetch me the cloak of our ancestors."

Then they realised they had to go. Someone shot off on a horse to get a korowai from an old woman who lived near the marae. Before long he came back with a beautiful kiwi cloak, and he ran up to the stage where Api was sitting and placed it around his shoulders. Then Api stood up.

"Ae . . . kia ora. That's better."

Well look, that's something I'll never forget, it's stuck in my memory, how beautifully Apirana acted that poem. The most gorgeous sight in my memory is that "Scenes of the Past". He started walking around the stage in his cloak with a mere in his hand, and he began,

"*There* the old pa stands today,
Where the mountain clad in koukas,
Bends with gentle slope and fondly
Showers kisses on the stream!
Rippling, laughing, winding, moaning,
Hies she on to join the ocean,
Emblem of a race that's speeding
Sadly onwards to oblivion.

Day is breaking on that pa;
All within is bustle, stir.
'Tis the hour of dedication,
Te Kawanga, solemn consecration,
When our whare in its beauty,
Tukutuku, pukana, e korirari!
Duly to the gods in Heaven
With our war-dance must be given.

All day long from far and near,
The crowds pour in to see and hear.
Amid this group are chieftains bold,
Rewi, Taonui — names of old.
Yonder Kahungunu, mere in hand,
   (he jumped up with his mere in his hand)
Frowning marshals forth his band —
Te Arawa, Tainui me te Whakatohea
Whakaata, Taupare, Tuwhakairiora!
   (and he *jumped* up and went like this with his taiaha! Beautiful . . .)

A noble sight th' intruding band.
But grander yet unfolds itself.
Yonder, massed, one sea of forms,
Maids with warriors alternating.
In the van are maidens lovely,
Dressed in mats of finest fibre,
Cheeks with takou gaily hued,
Plumed with quills of rarest huia.
Beyond — but no; no more is seen,
Though hundreds lie to shout 'Haere mai!'
The maids must first display their graces,
Then we'll gaze on warriors' faces.

Softly and gently and chanting most sweetly,
Uplift they their welcome, 'Haere mai! Haere mai!'
With knees bent gracefully, with slow step and gesture,
As soft as the panther,
   (he walks like a panther)
Yet queenly and stately.
Hark! now it is changing, in chorus they're joining;
It swells and it rings, it bursts forth *triumphant*!"

"Triumphant" — and he jumped! Even with the girls, he was trying to show how they moved their hips . . . Gee, it was lovely. And then the house was clapping! But I liked that part about Tuwhakairiora best, he had his tongue out and his taiaha flashing — I'll never forget that. Everyone was calling out,
"Oh, ka *rawe*, Apirana — lovely!"
So we came back and we brought the Lady Ngata Cup home to the Coast. All the people from the Bay came to welcome us at the marae, because that was a great name for the Bay of Plenty and it covered the whole of Ngati Porou too, when we won the Lady Ngata Cup at Waitara.

I did a lot of nursing in the Bay in those years. Once the people found out I'd been nursing before, they didn't bother about the District Nurse, they'd just ring up a taxi and come to my place. It was hard to get the District Nurse then because she was always busy. She had to cover from Omaio to Te Kaha and all about the country there, including Raukokore and Cape Runaway, and it was a big area, so they'd turn up at my place and say,
"Oh, Amiria . . . my wife is having a baby."
"By Joves — why don't you get the nurse?"
"Well, look at all the miles she has to come, she mightn't get here in time."
Then they'd start to cry and beg me to go, and I had to go with them.
One time I went to help a woman called Te Huinga to have her baby. When I arrived at her place I saw a woman hanging onto the verandah post of the house and I thought, good gracious, is that Te Huinga? When I got closer I realised it was her Aunty Hariata.
"Hariata, what's the matter?"

"Oh! Huinga is having the baby."

It looked as though she was having the baby herself, the way she was hanging onto that post. I said,

"Look, it'd be more help if you hold Huinga instead of that post, she needs you."

She just couldn't manage that sort of thing. I went inside, and there was poor Huinga on the floor in pain. I felt the baby and I knew it wasn't coming the right way, so I tried to turn the child so that it could come away. In the end I got the baby right, and I grabbed Huinga with my knees and pulled her towards me, and the baby was born. The blooming baby howled like anything, and I said,

"Good job . . . hurting your mother like that!"

I called to Hariata to help me and I saw her shaking, poor soul, just about in tears. I said,

"It's all right, Hariata, the baby is all right now. You can just help me clean up."

I put the baby down on the sheets and turned to tie up the cord. When I was finished, I couldn't see the baby anywhere.

"Hariata! Hariata!"

No answer. I went outside, and there she was putting the sheets on the rubbish pile to burn.

"Hariata! Where's the baby?"

She was still shaking, she couldn't tell me. I looked in the sheets and there you are, the baby was right in the middle. I rushed the child inside and washed it in a basin of water, it was all right. Poor old Hariata, she just couldn't stand it I suppose.

Another one of my patients was Nap Brown, Parekura Brown's boy. He took very sick one time and the District Nurse was away, so Parekura got a taxi and came to Otaimina to fetch me. I said,

"Parekura, who's going to look after *my* family?"

"Look here, Amiria, you've got all those children. As for me, I've only got one son, and if that boy dies I'm going to die too!"

Lucy was quite a grown-up girl then, and she said to me,

"You go, Mum — I'll look after the children."

"Come *on*, Amiria, there's a taxi waiting!"

I had to go with him. When we got there I found Nap running a very high temperature, he was delirious. I sponged and sponged him, trying to bring the temperature down, but I couldn't manage it. In the end Parekura said to me,

"You know Amiria, I think that boy needs a tohunga, the way he's talking."

"Don't tell me that — he's running a very high temperature, and that's why he's imagining all those things — he's delirious!"

Parekura went away, and after a while three or four men turned up; one of them was the tohunga. They started up their prayers, and I asked Parekura,

"What are these people doing?"

"Well . . . we think the tohunga can help Nap."

"If you want the tohunga, Parekura. I'm going home to my family. I don't know what to do when he's there too, doing his side. . . . I'd better let him take over. But I think Nap needs the doctor."

"Oh, the tohunga will do it."

I didn't take any notice, I went straight away and rang Opotiki Hospital to make an appointment for Nap. I knew something was wrong inside, but I didn't know what it was. When I came back, the tohunga had finished his service. I said,

"Well, that's done now, but this young man still has to be sent to Opotiki Hospital. There's something very wrong with him, but it's not for me to judge — the doctor will tell you what it is."

Everything was already set, so Nap was sent to Opotiki. When he got there they found out it was gall-stones, and they operated. After that he recovered, and Pare-kura had a big celebration for his son on Christmas Day. He sent Nap over to ask us to the hakari, and I asked him,

"Will the minister be there, Nap?"

"I don't know . . ."

So I rang up Parekura to find out.

"No, Hakaraia isn't coming."

"What's going on, then?"

"Just a celebration because Nap has recovered."

"Well, Parekura, if you want to celebrate your son's recovery you should have a thanksgiving service first, and then I'll come. . . . But if you just want to get drunk, I'm not coming for that."

"That's your trouble, Amiria, you've had too much education. All you can do is lecture us. . . . You can stay there then!"

I came back to Nap and said,

"I'm not going. If you want to have a good booze-up about your life, all right, you carry on your way. I won't be there."

Nap was all right though, and he lived for years and years after that.

I think it was about 1937 when we finally got the road through Otaimina, and this is how it happened.

One day, Eruera and the boys finished milking a bit late, and there was a big rush to get the cream can down to the stand in time for the milk-truck. George hopped on his horse and hoisted the cream can up in front, and away he went. It was a long way to the cream stand in those days, you had to come right from the back of Otaimina to the main road, and our cream stand was next to the cemetery there. George was well on his way when a wild stallion came charging up and tried to mount his mare. George didn't want to lose all that cream, so he kicked his horse, but the faster they went the faster the stallion galloped along behind. In the end he was just about on top of them, so George jumped off and the cream can went rolling down the hill. George started bowling the stallion with rocks and cursing him, he was so wild. He said,

"Yeah — I'm going to *kill* you now, you beggar!"

After a while the stallion ran away. George got on his horse again, and there was the can lying by the cream-stand, with the lid still on. He said,

"Good on you, Dad! Just as well you hammered the lid on tight, otherwise . . . no cream."

He put the can onto the creamstand and came rushing back home to tell his father what happened. Eruera got a big shock, and he made up his mind right then to get a road through Otaimina somehow. He said to me,

"You know, Mum, we need a road here. We're the only farmers in the district that don't have a road — it's no use carting the cream every day down that pig-track! I'm going to ask the Government for a right-of-way."

He went round to see some of the people about a petition for this road, but they only laughed at him.

"What's wrong with the road down here?"

"It's no good for me, my family has to cart the cream all the way down from the farm."

"We're all right here, Dick — that road is just for yourself. You want us all to sign to have a road just for Mr Stirling, Mr Eruera Kawhia Stirling . . . e hoa! No, we're not worried about any road for Otaimina."

So Eruera thought, it was no use. He wrote to the National Government and they wouldn't give him a road, even though he had been the organiser for all of Apirana's campaigns. Then he thought, perhaps Labour will help me. He talked to some of the Labour people and they said,

"We will help you, Eruera, but only if you turn Labour. If you turn Labour, you can have your road."

In the end he got so fed up with all the people laughing at him that he turned Labour, and that was a big talk in Raukokore.

"Fancy Dick Stirling changing to Labour! He's been preaching all over for Apirana, and now he's a Labour man. . . ."

When Apirana heard about it he rang Dick's mother, and told her to hold a

Mihi Kotukutuku and Duncan Stirling outside Hine Mahuru meeting-house, Raukokore.

95

meeting at Raukokore marae, he was coming down. Of course, Dick had to hold the meeting, and when Apirana stood up he said,

"This is my first question to you, Eruera. Everyone tells me that you've changed to Labour — I want to hear it from your own mouth — Are you a Labour man now?"

"Ae — yes, Api."

"Now I want to know why? Why are you doing this to me?"

Then Eruera stood up and told him why. He told how this stallion just about killed his own son when he was taking the cream down to the road, and how he decided that was enough, he couldn't carry on milking like that. He just had to have a road.

"I tried the National people, Api, and they refused, they wouldn't give me a road through Otaimina. None of these people would help either, they just laughed at me about it. So in the end I turned to Labour, they said they would give me my road. I think a lot of you, Api, but I have to think of my family too and our livelihood, and that's my reason — I want a road through Otaimina."

Apirana replied,

"Kei te pai, e tama. All right, Eruera. You deserve your road. If it wasn't for that road there'd be no use turning Labour, but as it is, never mind."

By Joves, in the end we did get our road too. Labour won the election, and the next thing the surveyors got to work at Otaimina and at Tawaroa station, setting up their pegs. The manager of Tawaroa was very upset, and he came to see Dick.

"Listen Dick, I'm not going to have those fellas surveying through my property. If they put a road through, the pig-hunters will be up there and you don't know what they might do. You've got to stop it!"

"Mr Neilson — Tawaroa is not your property, you know, it's mine. If I want to put a road through, that's my business. You've got a lease on that place, but when it expires the land comes back to me. . . . If I don't want to put you back there, I don't have to."

"But if you put gates in, the pig-hunters will go right through my place!"

"This is my property! I'm going to have a gate there, and a gate here, and another gate down there. . . ."

That was the end of that. The next thing, some of those people who wouldn't sign the petition came asking for gates, and Eruera said,

"You were the people that said you were all right, you didn't need a road. Well, I'm going to take you at your word on that."

Not long afterwards, the Raukokore bridge was washed away. It was placed down by the cemetery, and that was the third time the bridge had gone. Eruera contacted the Labour people again and they shifted the bridge back to the new road, and ever since then it's been quite safe, the banks are much higher up there. So after all that, the Otaimina road was a big help to the people; and at the next elections Eruera went back to National again.

Soon after that, our eldest son George sat a special examination at Raukokore Maori School and won four years' schooling at St. Stephen's College in Auckland. He was a wonderful boy, a very clever fella, and we wanted him to be really educated. He was the eldest of the family so he had to be the farmer and take over

Kingi Hori Te Ariki Tapu ki Waho — George Stirling.

the farm, and our way of farming was just the ordinary Maori way. . . . We wanted him to get all the pakeha knowledge and run the farm in the pakeha way. We got his uniform and everything all set, and he went to St. Stephen's, and we missed the chief cowboy of the farm.

All the work fell back to Waha, and Waha was a good boy when he set his mind to it, but he was a little daring fella. He was hard to control, Waha! He loved to be on horseback, and when he was herding up the cows you'd hear him *singing* at the top of his voice, then tearing down the road to his grandmother's place, or if he wasn't satisfied with that he'd go to Waihau. Everybody could hear the horse galloping, and the voice on top singing, and the people round the pa said,

"Bet you that's Wahawaha Stirling singing away!"

George was very happy at St. Stephens, but the one thing that bothered him was the boxing. At home his father would never let him hit his brothers, and they used to play up with him. They knew that if Eruera saw George hitting them, he'd get a thrashing. Eruera told him,

"You're the oldest of the family, George. You're supposed to look *after* your brothers and sisters, not belt them up. If they don't listen to you, you let me know and I'll take care of them."

George got so used to that way of handling the children, he'd just growl at them, and he never put a hand on his brothers.

At St. Stephens they had a boxing class, so George thought he'd put his name down because he didn't know anything about that. On the night of the boxing class the teacher called out all their names.

"George Stirling?"

"Yes sir."

"Oh well, here's your partner."

It happened that this boy was the teacher's son himself, and he was much younger than George. When they walked into the ring, all the other boys laughed.

"Look at that fella, he's a big boy to fight a little chap like that!"

Of course George didn't know how to box and he was just hitting away, but the other boy knew how to duck and George couldn't land a punch on him. The other boy kept landing them on George, though, and the next thing — George was flat out.

All the boys laughed.

"Oh! Look at that big waster!"

George was a very big-built chap, but this young boy belted him up every time. This went on for a while, and George just could not hit that boy. Every time he thought, I'll get you this time, the little chap would jump back and give him a blow. In the end he got wild at his father for not teaching him how to box.

"You know Mum, it was Dad's fault — he should have taught us how to look after ourselves . . . now look, I'm just useless. They call me 'Useless' and 'Fat Lump' at school — oh, they've got all the funny names for me! And they always like to go and watch this young boy hitting me because he's only a little weenie fella, and sure enough he'll knock me out!"

In the end, George got really boiling inside and he thought, I'm *not* going in there to be made fun of, I'm going to learn how to box. The next time the teacher came round with his list he called out,

"George Stirling!"

"No sir!"

"Did you say no?"

"Yes sir."

"You're not going to fight tonight?"

"No sir!"

"Oh!"

All the boys laughed and said,

"You know that big gooby — he's given up, he's not going to fight tonight!"

Then they teased him.

"George! Aren't you going to fight?"

"No. And mind your own business."

"Oh, you're a big fat no-good!"

They started to give him all the funny names.

The next time he was in town, he saw a notice about evening classes in boxing, so he decided to go there. He wrote home and asked for some money for football boots and a jersey and something else, and he started boxing classes. At school the boys were still teasing him; if he was watching football someone would kick him on the behind and then run away and pull faces at him.

"Yeahh! You big fat useless, you're frightened of that young fella — waster!"

In the end, George got very good at it and he won the Lightweight Championship at the boxing school. He entered himself as "Te Ariki Stirling" so that no one at school would know. He'd been taking classes for months and months, and all the time Eruera was growling at home,

"You know, I think that boy's doing something. He must have a business or something . . . the way he's *always* writing for money, money, money!"

I said,

"Never mind. When George comes back from school you make him work, he'll pay back all that money."

One night the teacher came round again to ask all the different boys about boxing, and when it was George's turn he said,

"Oh well George Stirling, I suppose you're not interested in boxing any more."

George said,

"Yessir."

"Was that you, George? Did you say 'yes sir'?"

"Yessir!"

The whole school started to laugh. They said,

"Ey, that big fat gooby has come back again!"

Someone said,

"Are you going to fight tonight, George?"

"Yeah . . . well, I thought I might give it another try."

"Oh! and the same fulla?"

"Oh well . . . I suppose so."

"Oh! We're going to come and see you. . . . If you're going to box, we're coming to see you!"

That night all the boys came to have a look, and they were laughing about it.

"You know. George is going to box tonight."

"Is he?"

"Yes . . . I heard him say 'yes'."

When it was George's turn the teacher called out,

"George Stirling."

"Yessir."

"All right — you know your partner. Go into the ring."

George walked into the ring, and at first he pretended that he didn't know much about it. After a while he landed a blow on this fella, and then he really went wild. He told me later,

"Mum, as soon as I landed one on that boy I kept on punching him and he yelled 'oh, oh, oh, oh!' — I was so *wild* with all the insults they'd been giving me."

His partner was down on the floor and the teacher yelled out,

"Look here, George Stirling, what are you trying to do? That boy is only sixteen. If you want to do that, try it on me, not him!"

The next thing, George landed a punch on him and they had a fight. In the end another teacher had to come and pull George away.

"Listen, George Stirling! What's the matter with you? Are you trying to kill someone? Now stop it . . . if you want to be a sporting man, do it the sporting way. You hear that?"

"Yes sir."

George told me,

"But after that, Mum, they found out . . . oh! I had got the art all right. They didn't kick my backside any more."

We only found out about it when he came home for the holidays; he had a parcel with his suitcase, and he gave it to me.

"Here Mum, that's for you."

"For me?" I said. "Is that how you spend your money, George? We don't need presents, we just want you to get on with your schooling."

"Oh Mum, open it up and have a look!"

"Well . . . all right."

When I opened the parcel there was a silver cup inside, and it had written on it, "George Stirling, Lightweight Boxing Champion, St. Stephen's College".

"Oh George, did . . . did you win this?"

"Yes, Mum."

He was allowed to keep the cup for a year, so Eruera took it to Opotiki and put it in the bank window. Then we had all the rings, everyone was ringing us about it.

The children were always very excited when George came home for his holidays. That was one thing about him, he liked to bring something home for his brothers and sisters. When the bus pulled up they'd yell out,

"There's George! I'm going to take his bag home to the house. . . . You stay and finish the cows!"

Then they would all go racing down to the bus-stop.

"I'll take your suitcase, George." . . . "No, *me!*"

They'd run home with the suitcases, and as soon as they got home they'd open them to see what was inside.

"Oer! There's nothing in this one!"

One holiday, George brought some ice-cream home. He saw it in Opotiki and he thought he'd bring some home for his brothers and sisters, because he knew they'd be excited about it. But instead of putting it in a bag or something, the silly fool stuck it in the pocket of his brand new overcoat. When the children met him at the bus-stop he said,

"Who got the cows this morning?"

"I did, George."

"All right, you're going to have a holiday now that I'm home. For the week that I'm home, I'll do that work for you."

Then he asked,

"Who took the cream can down?"

"I did that!"

"Well, I've got something for you, too."

He put his hand in his pocket to pull out the ice-cream, and there you are — it was all melted. What a mess! When I told him off about it he said,

"I just wanted to give my brothers and sisters some ice-cream, because there's ice-cream in town, Mum."

"But you've spoiled your new best coat. . . ."

George loved the garden, too; any new flower that I had blooming, he wanted to know what it was. Gardening has always been my big weakness, and I had all sorts of things growing around the house at Otaimina. When you came to the house along the track, there was a wooden bridge over the little creek leading to the pond by the cowshed. I filled up the pond with water-lilies, all different colours to make the place look nice, and I had big rows of daffodils and freesias planted on both sides of the path so that when the daffodils finished, the freesias came out.

In front of the house my garden was laid out like a pack of cards, with a diamond here and a club there, and a spade and a heart. I had violets and freesias for the borders, with other flowers in the middle. When I saw a plant I liked in the catalogue, a nice rose or something, I'd send away for it. So when George came home for the holidays, the violets and freesias were out in masses, and they were beautiful. He'd stand there and admire them, looking down at the water-lilies and smelling the flowers. I remember one time I was waiting up at the house for him, and I asked the children,

"Where's that boy? Where's George?"

"Oh, he's down there somewhere."

I went out on the verandah and called,

"George — hurry up, come home! You must be hungry!"

"I'm here, Mum. I'm here."

He came up with a few violets and freesias in his hand and he said,

"Look Mum, I've been admiring your beautiful flowers. . . . I love the way you've grown them all the way up to the house."

"Well you like flowers and I like flowers too."

"Oh yes, Mum," and he came and put his arms around me.

Waha always tried to be smart when George came home; he liked to show off for his big brother. We had a great big working steer on the place called Judge,

and whenever the cows came to the shed, this steer would rush down to the gate
and start judging them. He had his favourite cows, and if he noticed one that he
didn't like he'd start butting it out of the road until the right cow came along, then
he'd let her through and the rest could follow. One time Waha thought, well if
you're as clever as that, Judge, I'm going to try and ride on you. I was sitting on
the verandah up at the house and I saw Waha come round the back of the cowshed
and start pushing Judge towards the fence, but I didn't know what he was doing.
The next thing huh! Waha got on the fence and in a minute he was on the steer's
back. I shouted,

"Waha! Waha! Get *off* that steer. You'll break your neck!"

The steer started to butt, his forelegs were down and his back shot way up in the
air. I called to Eruera,

"Dad! That boy, Dad — he'll be killed! Aue, Waha . . . Waha!"

The steer bolted down to the gully with Waha hanging on to his horns, and the
next thing he dived right down among the rocks. I thought, oh, my son is dead.

"Aue, taku tamaiti kua mate . . . aue!"

I raced down to the gully and Waha came running up the hill, whistling as
though nothing had happened. I *told* him off.

"You . . . blooming. . . . Look, Waha, you're lucky you didn't break your neck!
Don't you ever do that again."

I still can't understand how he escaped, he must have fallen onto a toetoe bush
among the rocks. He just looked at me and kept on whistling.

George was very keen on pig-hunting, that was one of his great sports. There
was a man around the pa, Barney Crawford, and whenever he went pig-hunting
he'd come to our place and whistle out for George.

"Hey, where's George?"

"He's milking."

"Well, tell him he can come pig-hunting if he likes. . . ."

The boys would rush off to George, and George'd ask his father,

"Oh Dad, can I go pig-hunting with Barney?"

"All right, go and catch a horse — you can go."

In the end George got so keen on pig-hunting that even if none of the boys would
go with him, he'd go off by himself. This particular Christmas holidays he decided
to go out, and it happened that a young boy called Basil Richardson had gone
missing from Raukokore at that time. His mother was not quite in her proper mind
so her brother Kahu controlled her family, but I think he was giving Basil far too
much work to do. He had to clean up the shed and wash it out before school, and
by the time he had finished the other children had eaten all the food and gone.
One day he was so hungry that he went to a neighbour's place and stole a piece of
bread from the kitchen, and he got caught. His uncle Kahu grabbed hold of him
and thrashed him, and they called the police to come and arrest him for it.

When Basil heard that he ran away in the bush, right to the back of Raukokore
in the Puhueroro hills. When George came home for his holidays we told him about
it, and he said,

"Where is Basil now?"

"Well, we don't know. He might be up the Coast, in Opotiki or somewhere.

The police are still looking for him."

"Ahh, poor Basil."

Anyhow, George decided to go pig-hunting one day, and he went right up the Raukokore River into the hills. When he got into the bush he saw some smoke, and he thought somebody must have killed a pig, so he decided to go and see this fella. He tied up his horse and walked over, and when he got quite close, he spotted Basil. The poor fella had been down to the river and caught some eels, and he was roasting them over the fire.

"Basil! Is that you Basil? *Basil*!"

When Basil heard that he jumped up and ran into the bush. George ran after him.

"Basil! It's only George — you know, George Stirling. Come back, don't run away. You come with me, Basil — I'll take you home to Mum."

"They'll go and get the police!"

"No. Mum and Dad wouldn't do that, Basil. You come with me."

"But they might find me at your place."

"No they won't, they won't know about it."

In the end Basil came over to him. Before they set out for home they tracked down a pig and shot it, and put it into two sacks then rode out of the bush with the sacks strung over the horse and Basil sitting on top.

When they came to Otaimina, George ran into the house and called me.

"Mum! Mum — I've got Basil here, Basil Richardson! I've brought him home."

When I heard that I thought of all the stories about Basil's stealing, and I just looked at him.

"Mum, please keep him here. Don't let the policeman know he's here — poor fulla, he's hungry."

" . . . All right George, bring him in."

But Basil stayed outside, he wanted to make sure we would accept him I suppose. I called to him,

"Basil, come on in! Come here. Nobody will know you're here, we won't tell them."

I looked at him and his clothes were all torn, he was a hungry-looking fella. I served them both tea, and from that time on, Basil lived with us. When George had to go back to college he said,

"Look, Basil — you stay here with Mum and Dad, don't go back to Kahu. You help Dad on the farm, and I'll come back again in the holidays."

"All right . . . as long as Mum won't let the police know I'm here."

I said,

"No, I won't, Basil."

Basil stayed with us and helped on the farm, but one day somebody spotted him. This man was riding along the public highway through our farm, and he saw Basil go up the hill to take the cows to the shed.

"Hey . . . that's not George, George has gone back to school. That fella is Basil Richardson!"

He rode straight back to Kahu's place and told him.

"You know, Kahu, I saw Basil today."

"What?"

"I saw Basil. And do you know where he is? All the time you've been looking for that boy, Eruera and Amiria Stirling have been hiding him at Otaimina!"

"E . . . hoa!"

"It's Basil all right. He's been milking their cows all these months, and Dick's been coming to our meetings and he didn't even let us know."

"I'll fix them up, I'm going to Otaimina to see them!"

The next thing, I saw Kahu coming through the gate. Eruera and Basil were away in the hills fencing, so I went out on the verandah, and Kahu called out,

"Ah . . . kia ora, Amiria!"

"Hello, Kahu."

"Well, pae kare! Fancy — all these months you two have been hiding Basil, and we've been looking for him everywhere. . . . To think that you would *do* this to us! And Dick has not been genuine enough to tell me about it. It's all right now, though, I've rung the police and they're coming here to pick him up."

Then I hoed into him.

"Kahu! Don't come here and talk to me like that — haven't you got any love in your heart for your sister's child? He's your own nephew. Basil has told me why he stole that bread, because you didn't leave him anything to eat; he was just your working bullock, that fella, you worked him to death and you don't even feed him. So don't you talk to me!"

"Well, it's too late now, the police are after him."

"You leave that to me. I'm going to tell the police why Basil did it. It should be *you* to go to jail, because you starved that boy."

"Don't you say that!" — he wanted to come and hit me.

"All right Kahu, you hit me and you'll see where you land."

Kahu went away, and then the police came. We told them all about it, how Kahu starved the boy and that was why he stole that bread. The policeman said,

"What do you intend to do with the boy?"

"Well, we feel sorry for him. Our son George brought him here and he was all cut and scratched, he'd been living on eels. He's all right now though, and if you'll allow us to have him, he can stay here."

The policeman asked Basil,

"Now — will you stay with Mrs Stirling and her family, and promise not to steal any more?"

"Yes. . . . All the days I've been here, I've had more than enough to eat, and they have given me the best of everything — George has given me all his old clothes, and I feel happy here with them."

"All right, we'll try you out. But if you get caught again you won't get another chance, you'll go to prison."

From that day on, that boy was the best. He always called me Mum:

"Mum, do you need anything before I go?"

If he was going out ploughing or fencing, he'd always come home to ask me if I needed any wood cut or anything, and if I wanted something that I didn't have at home, Basil would go down to Waihau on the horse. He was such a good boy, and he stayed with us right until the war broke out.

CHAPTER EIGHT

The War Years

When the war broke out, Eruera was appointed the Recruiting Officer for all of the Whanau-a-Apanui district. George was still in his first year at St. Stephen's, and his father wouldn't let him go to war because he wanted him to go through the proper channels of farming, so when George came home for his holidays he felt ashamed of himself; the young fullas round the district teased him and said,

"Well George, we have to go and fight for you, eh? What about doing your share? There's Dick Stirling recruiting all the soldiers, but his own sons are sitting around at home — e hoa!"

George felt ashamed and he said to his brothers,

"You know, those boys are quite right — we should be doing our share in the war. I think I'm going to run away to war. It's no use here, Dad won't enlist me, he won't!"

Waha said to him,

"No boy, you stay home. You've got the brains and I haven't, so I'll do our share."

"You? Ha! You're not twenty-one yet, how can you go?"

"Oh . . . I know I can go."

"No, Waha. I'm going to give up this school life, I can't bear seeing those fellas coming here to enlist. They're quite right when they talk about Dick Stirling's sons not going to fight — one of us has to go."

So Waha started to plan something out, and every time some boys came to our place to enlist, Waha would leave the cows and run into the house. The next thing he'd be standing behind his father, looking over his shoulder to see how he signed the forms. When Dick noticed him he'd say,

"Look! What the devil is this fulla doing here? Why aren't you at the shed, Waha?"

"Yes, yes Dad," and he'd run back again.

"By Jove, that's an inquisitive beggar!"

One day when we went to a tangi and Lucy was outside doing the washing, Waha broke into his father's cabinet and took out all the papers. He filled in the forms exactly the way he'd seen his father do them, and signed his age twenty-one, then he got a ride on a milk-truck to Opotiki and went to the office there. He gave his name.

"Wahawaha Stirling?"

"Yes."

"Are you Dick Stirling's son?"

"Yes."

They looked at him and started talking to one another.

"Gosh, this boy's not twenty-one."

"Dick Stirling should send this boy to camp first . . . "

"Oh well, his father must know about it."

One of the men asked him,

"Do you really want to go to battle?"

"Yes."

"And does your father agree?"

"Yes sir."

They examined him and they knew he wasn't twenty-one — he was sixteen at the time; but they OK'd it and he came back home. A few weeks later they sent him a letter telling him to report to Opotiki that weekend, he was going to Papakura Military Camp. Lucy was washing the clothes and she found this letter in the pocket of his pants, so she took it out and read it. She came to me and said,

"D'you know, Mum, Waha is going to camp in the weekend?"

"Who told you that?"

"Well, I've got the letter here, I found it in his pocket."

I showed the letter to Eruera and he had a look.

"Heck!"

He called Waha,

"Waha — come here! How the devil did you get to Opotiki and enlist yourself at your age? You know you're not twenty-one yet. Now how did you do this?"

"I didn't do anything, Dad . . . "

"Look here's the letter — it was in the pocket of your pants. You're only a boy, you can't go to war! You must have stolen my papers out of the writing bureau and signed them."

"Well, because Dad, Mum, ah . . . my brother George said he was going to run away to war. So I thought, he's got more brains than me, he'd better stay and keep going to college and let me go to war."

"Look here Waha, do you think those people are stupid? They know you're not twenty-one yet, the doctors can tell. You can't go there and fool them like that."

"Oh well, they have agreed . . . the letter says here, I can go."

They started to have a fight about it, and Waha said,

"If you won't let me go, I'm going to run away!"

So I chipped in, I said,

"Waha, why don't you go to the Territorials? If you really want to go to war, they can train you there until you're twenty-one. You can't go to war at your age."

"But I want to go over . . . "

His father said,

"You can't! I'll let you go to the Territorials, but that's all!"

"Well, at least that's better than staying at home and milking cows. All the boys tease us, you know. They say, "Oer! Dick Stirling's boys don't go to war, we have to fight for them.""

Waha joined up with the Territorials. After that poor old Basil got lonely, and one day he came home and said to me,

"Mum, I'd like to go to war too."

"Basil!"

"Well, Waha's gone."

"Oh — you'd better have a talk to the old man."

Wahawaha Stirling (right) in the Territorials.

When Eruera came in I said,

"Well Dad, this son of ours Basil wants to go to war; seeing that Waha's gone he feels lonely, and he thinks he wants to go too."

Eruera turned to Basil.

"Is that right?"

"Yes, Dad."

"All right, Basil, if you want to go. Your uncle wants you to go to prison, so perhaps it's better if you go and fight for your country. We can be proud of you that way."

The next thing Basil landed at the Territorials, and Waha was excited to see him; but before he went to camp he came to me and said,

"Here Mum, I've got a letter for you — you hold on to that."

When I read it I found that he'd made over his money to me.

"Basil — why did you do that?"

"Well, what else could I do? You've been my mother all these years . . . "

Not long afterwards we heard an announcement over the air that all the Maori boys in the Territorials were going to be shifted into the Maori Battalion. Apirana wanted the Battalion to fight overseas, so he thought it would be better to get all the Maoris together, instead of some here and some there. When the boys came home for their final leave, we had a big night for them at Wairuru marae. We invited all the boys from the other maraes to come to this farewell, and we held a great big dance and presented each one of them with a gold watch.

When it came time for the speeches, the chiefs of all the maraes stood up to greet the boys, but when Brian's uncle Kahu gave his mihi, he farewelled all the soldiers and he didn't even mention his own nephew Basil. It happened that Eruera was the last speaker, and after he mihi'd the soldiers he had a talk to our son Waha, then he turned to Basil.

"Goodbye, Basil. I'm happy to see that you're in the Maori Battalion — your family should be proud of you. All the people are proud of you, especially myself and my family, because you are going to fight for us. But as for your uncle Kahu, after all his greetings to the other soldiers he didn't even mention your name! He should be proud that he has a nephew in the Maori Battalion. As for me, I'll give you all the blessings from my family and the tribe — goodbye. And I'll say this — it would be a honourable death, to die over there; better than rotting in prison according to your uncle's wish. So die there, Basil! Better for you to die there, instead of being locked up in a prison . . . "

He said all that because he was furious with Kahu for speaking to the soldiers, without even a word of farewell to his own nephew. I thought oh! — fancy talking like that to Basil. Eruera finished his speech but no one spoke, not even Kahu, and after that we presented the soldiers with their gold watches. I said to Basil,

"You're a rich man now — look at you wearing a gold watch!"

"Gee, that's right . . . "

"Well, make sure you come back with it, eh."

"Yes Mum, I will."

It was years afterwards when I saw Basil again. When all the boys came back from the war, sure enough, Basil came back too, but he didn't come straight home to Raukokore. It was a year or two later when he turned up at home.

"Oh! Hello Basil! By . . . Jove, where have you been touring?"

"I've been all over, down to Tauranga and everywhere. . . . And Mum, I'm going to get married!"

"You're going to get married?"

"Yeah. I've brought my wife — here she is."

"You mean you're married already?"

"No, but we will be soon."

"By Joves. . . . Does that woman know everything, Basil?"

"Oh — she doesn't need all that. She only wants me."

I said,

"No, you be fair to that woman, you tell her everything."

"Oh Mum, never mind, never mind. I've got a house for her, everything. So we'll leave that; what is past, is past. I'm a different man now, not that porangi fella — I've got money put away and all that."

"Is that true, Basil?"

"Yes," and he pulled out his bankbook to show me. "I thought when I left New Zealand, I had nobody, only you and Dad, so I saved my money. Now I can spray that money, I've got plenty in the bank."

"Good on you, then."

I went into my room and came back,

"Basil, I've got something to show you too. D'you remember before you left, you signed all your money to me? Here it is, it's all down in this bankbook — this money is yours. You take it and go and cash it, draw that money out."

"Oh no, Mum! I've got my own money, that money is yours!"

"Listen, Basil. When I look at that fine-looking girl there, I don't want her to have a hard life, a sad life. You take the money and buy her everything she wants for the house."

He still wouldn't take it, so I threw the bankbook over to the girl and said,

"If you're going to marry Basil, that money is yours."

She put it in her pocket.

"You see, Basil? She's put it in her pocket, so that woman is going to marry you. Now you be fair and straight and be a good husband to her, and she'll make you a good wife for you."

He didn't argue any more. They stayed at home for a while then they left, and from this day to that day, I haven't seen them.

When we heard that the Maori Battalion was going overseas we started up the Young People's Club in Raukokore, and later on we split it into the Tribal Committee and the Maori Women's Welfare League. Eruera was Chairman of the Tribal Committee and I was the first President of our League branch.

We raised a lot of money for the boys in those years; we held hockey tournaments,

War-time fund raising at Wairuru marae, Amiria and Mrs Callaghan at front.

sports days, dances and bazaars, and when one marae had a day they'd send word to all the other maraes around the Coast to see if they could come. That's how we managed to buy each one of our soldiers a gold watch, and when the Battalion went overseas we got together and collected all sorts of Maori kai for them. We used to bag up dried fish, dried pauas and kumara kao, and the men went out pig-hunting and we'd boil the wild pork at the marae and seal it up in its own fat in great big drums, then send it all off overseas.

Sir Apirana appealing for funds outside Porourangi meeting-house, World War II.

Wairuru marae 1976.

We sent food parcels and Christmas parcels too, because in that time it was easy to get money. We were wealthy in those days, we had a lot of money to fix up the maraes and buy things for the schools — but now, there's no money on the Coast.

It wasn't just the war effort, we did a lot of work in the district too. Wairuru had the name of being the best-kept marae for miles, and one year we won a photo of the King and Queen for having the best marae in the area.

At first we had no mattresses or linen for the meeting-house; we needed twenty or thirty beds, and mattresses cost about £10 each then. I decided that was too much money for us, so I wrote to Farmer's in Auckland and asked them for quotes on a bale of kapok and about 150 yards of ticking. It turned out to be much cheaper that way so I ordered all the stuff, then I told the women of the marae about it. They groaned at me because they thought it was too much work, but I had my mind made up, and before long a great big parcel arrived at the marae. I rang up the other ladies and told them to come down and get started.

"Ha! What do we have to do?"

"You have to tease the kapok."

"Oh!"

Anyhow, they all turned up and set to work, then I got in my gig to go home.

"Hey — where are you going? Are you leaving us to do all the work?"

"No . . . I've got to sew up the ticking for the mattresses. When you've teased all that kapok, I'll bring a scale down to the marae so we can weigh it, and put the right measure in each mattress."

"Oh — all right, Duchess."

I went back to Otaimina and started sewing the mattresses, and by the time I'd finished, the women had teased the kapok, so all we had to do was to stuff it in and sew up the end of each mattress. The next thing, I decided we should have fancy-work pillowcases for our marae, so I asked every family to supply a pair of pillow-cases embroidered by the women of the house. I made sure they put "Wairuru marae" on each pillowslip so that if I saw one on another marae I could just pick it up and take it back home. The sheets and pillowcases are still there at the marae in a big iron box, as good as the day I left.

So that was this Amiria Manutahi — I might be a nuisance but if I wanted my way I'd have my way, and that was it. I suppose that's why Hine Te Ra and Mrs Ben Callaghan and all the others used to call me "Duchess"; they even called my horse "Duchess" too. That was the horse that pulled my gig, and she was a hard-case pony. One time when I was at a meeting she thought, this is too long for me, I'm going home, so she rubbed at the bridle until it fell off, then she pushed the gate open and trotted off down the road. When the bus came along, there was Duchess trotting away as good as anything, without any driver in the gig. All the passengers began to laugh, and the bus-driver said,

"I know that horse, it belongs to Mrs Stirling . . . it must be going home!"

The driver tooted his horn but Duchess wouldn't shift over, she just kept on trotting down the middle of the road until she came to Otaimina, and the bus had to follow on behind.

It wasn't just the women who worked for the marae, the Tribal Committee did a lot of work as well. They made everyone choose one bull-calf from their farm and marked it, and after that it couldn't be sold because it belonged to the Tribal

Committee. If there was a death or a hui at the marae, Dick might ring up Moana Waititi and say,

"Oh Moana, how's your beast — is it big enough for meat yet?"

"E hoa, no, it's not ready."

So they'd both ring around until they found someone who had a marked steer that was ready to kill. That was the beauty of those days, there was always plenty of meat for the marae, you didn't have to worry.

After the war had been going for a while they had to close St Stephens' down and they shifted some of the boys to Paerata; and after Paerata, George had a year at Feilding Agricultural College. He used to come home and teach us all sorts of tricks for farming. One year we were planting out the kumaras and George said,

"Hey, Dad, you should try planting them with the rows quite at a distance apart, about three feet . . . "

"Why, George?"

"Well, then you can grow potatoes in between."

"Potatoes?"

"Yeah. And when you dig up all the kumaras, the potatoes can get away."

"That's a good idea."

We mounded up the kumaras and then planted potatoes in between, and while the kumaras were there you couldn't see the potatoes, they were all covered over by the leaves. When we dug up the kumaras, though, the people had a shock to see potatoes growing. One fella was riding past that paddock and he just about fell off his horse; he had to stop to have another look.

"What the . . . devil is this? There were kumaras there the other day, and now it's potatoes!"

He thought it was a real nanakia, so he hurried off to our place.

"Pae kare! Eruera, where did those potatoes come from? It was all kumaras the other day, and when I came past just now, potatoes were growing . . . "

We had to tell him in the end, and the old man sat down and scratched his head.

"By. . . . That's a smart boy all right!"

After the kumaras George taught me how to grow great big cabbages.

"D'you know Mum, you can grow *huge* cabbages, with great big hearts?"

"How?"

"Well, I'll tell you. First you cut off the outside leaves, only leave about four to keep the heart clean, then you bury them near the roots. After that, get some skimmed milk and feed it to those cabbages."

"Skimmed milk?"

It sounded pretty funny to me but I thought I'd try it, and you wouldn't believe the size those cabbages grew! That year when we took the sheep to Tawaroa station for shearing, I only took one cabbage to feed all the shearers; the cook couldn't believe it.

"Good gracious! That's a cabbage?"

"That's right."

"Where did you get it from?"

"From Otaimina of course, where else?"

"Nah!"

That was a big story, it went all round the station and a lot of them came over to the house to see those cabbages. When they couldn't find them in the garden they said,

"Agh, it was only lies."

One day when Mika came, though, he asked to see my cabbages and I said,

"All right Mika, but they're not in this garden."

"Where are they?"

"Behind the cowshed. But please don't tell Dick, or he'll growl at me for feeding all his milk to the cabbages!"

The next trick I learned from George was how to grow peanuts. He came home one holidays and told me about it.

"Hika ma! Real peanuts?"

"Yes — I've got the plants here. You feed them at the roots, Mum, and when the plant has dried off you'll find the peanuts under the ground; that way you'll always have nuts for the children."

Next time he came home he asked,

"How are the peanuts, Mum?"

"Well, George, I dunno — there's nothing underneath them."

"That's funny, we've got peanuts now at College."

He went to have a look and he started to laugh — there were the shells all sitting by the plants.

"Look Mum — those kids have been getting your peanuts! They know what to do all right; they pulled off all the nuts then they buried the roots again, so the plant is still growing!"

We had a good laugh about that.

I managed to grow great big melons too, with George's help — other people never had melons that big. One time when the Ngati Porou people came through on a bus they saw those melons hanging down our bank. Apirana was with them and he said,

"By Joves! Whose place is that?"

"That's Dick Stirling's place, Amiria's husband."

"If that's the case, we're going to get some of those melons."

All my relations got off the bus and picked the melons, then they took them back home to Ruatoria for their sports day. When we got home, all our melons were gone. The next year I decided to bury our melons before they got too big, and when Ngati Porou came past on their bus they couldn't find any. One man was hunting around on the bank and he tripped over, he'd caught his foot on the runner of one of these melons. He said,

"Ha! Look at this!"

He pulled the runner and the melon popped out of the ground.

"Oh . . . *cunning*, eh. Amiria's buried all her melons!"

They dug up all the melons and loaded them on the bus. Unfortunately we weren't home that day, Eruera was up on the hill fencing and I'd gone to a women's Welfare League meeting at the marae; only Kiwa was at home minding the baby. She saw all the people through the window, carting all our melons away, and she heard them say,

"Kia ora, Amiria — we're taking your melons home for Ngati Porou to eat!"

When I came home that afternoon I saw some rinds and pips left by the cream-stand and I thought, those blooming children must have had a feed of melons there, they're always getting up to something. I got to the house and Kiwa ran out,

"Mum, Mum! You know what happened?"

"No."

"All the melons are gone! A big bus pulled up and took all the melons!"

"Huh! What bus was that?"

"I think it was a bus from Ruatoria, they said that Ngati Porou would eat those melons."

I looked around the melon patch and sure enough they'd taken all the ones that were buried, but left behind all the ones that were on the ground.

Now the next year that I grew those melons, one morning I got up and heck! — all the melons in the patch had gone white, the skins had been chewed away. Eruera came back from the shed and I told him about it, so he went down to the patch.

"There you are . . . it's the blooming hares done it!"

"The hares?"

"Yes — once they get into them there'll be no more melons, they chew off all the rind."

I decided not to grow any more melons after that, it wasn't worth it, and we told the people at the pa that Otaimina wouldn't be supplying watermelons for the sports days any more.

"Oh — why not?"

"The hares keep eating off the rinds."

"Well . . . what about putting netting-wire over them?"

"If you people pay for it, we will."

Not long after that I was in Opotiki, and I saw these white melons in the shop. I went in and asked the chap,

"Are those pie melons?"

"No, they're watermelons."

"But they're white."

"That's right, but they're watermelons all right, and they're good keepers too."

I started to think that perhaps if I grew those watermelons, the hares would see that they're already white and they might not eat them. I thought . . . yes, I'll try this out. I asked the man,

"Have you got any seeds?"

"Yes, you can buy seeds here — they grow the same as ordinary watermelons."

The next year, I grew those melons and the hares left them right alone. And when Ngati Porou went past on the bus they said,

"Hika! You know what? Amiria's growing pie melons now, she must be getting mean. What's the use of pie melons, only to make jam — agh!"

Even Eva and some of the women around the pa spoke to me about it:

"You're mean, you know; growing pie melons."

"Oh well, they're good for jam. If you want any for jam-making, you come and get some."

One day Eva was at our place, and she said how much she missed those melons.

"Eh . . . you miss the watermelons, Eva?"

"Yeah."

I went out to the whata where we stored all the melons and brought one inside and cut it up.

"Here, Eva, have a taste."

Eva took a bite and it was very sweet.

"Oh, Amy! You mean they were watermelons all the time?"

"Yes."

"By Joves, you're cunning all right. You've been growing white melons so we wouldn't bother you," and she laughed.

"It wasn't that, Eva; it was the hares that were the trouble."

With all my gardening, I had lots of fruit trees on the place — a walnut tree and a million-dollar peach, pawpaws, apples and even two pear trees.

Whenever we went on a trip to play hockey or something, I'd always end up in the gardening shop or the nurseries, because I liked to take home a fruit tree or a shrub to remind me of that place. When we went to Waitara they had a plant there just like a manuka, but it had red and white flowers and a *beautiful* perfume. I brought one home and if you came there when it was in bloom, you could smell it as soon as you came into the place. George used to try out all his grafting on my fruit trees but I didn't like it much. I had a big Golden Delicious peach there, and I told him,

"George, don't touch that peach, you leave it alone. I don't want a plum or something else on the other end."

The next season though, it had about three different kinds of fruit on it.

We had an old pear tree on the farm too, and George reckoned he could make it fruit.

"Oh, nemmine George, don't touch it; the old lady might get annoyed. It's an old pear tree and she reckons it's older than she is, about 100 years old."

But somehow or other he did graft that pear tree, because the next year I saw some fruit on it. I showed Eruera and he said,

"There you are, I'm sure that boy did it."

When George came home I asked about it and he laughed.

"Yes Mum, I did it."

"You little devil. By Joves, if you kill that tree the old lady'll go mad."

"No, you tell grandma to come and have a look. She can have some of the fruit."

When George finished his year at Feilding he went to Massey, in 1944 I think. He did very well there — he won the Agriculture Cup, and towards the end of his last year he captained the Massey team for the Premiership Cup. They played the final in Auckland, and he wanted me to come to Auckland to see him play, but I couldn't come away because of the baby. We listened to the match on the radio, though; they were playing against Auckland University and in the beginning Auckland were having all the success. At half-time Auckland were ahead, so they did a haka as if to tell Massey that they didn't have a chance. After the break Massey started to catch up, but they couldn't quite make it, and in the end the match was just about over, there were only a few minutes left to play. Then we

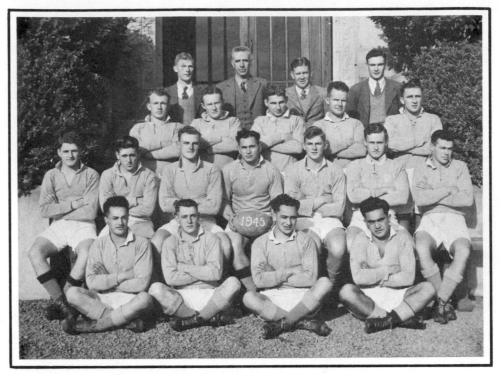

George (holding the ball) — captain of the Massey College 1st XV 1945.

heard the announcer start to talk about George.

"Here's George Stirling coming up, he's a dangerous man, he's after the man with the ball — *watch out!* He's got him!!"

George tackled this chap and picked up the ball and started to run.

"Now George Stirling is heading for the touch-line with two Auckland men chasing him . . . they've got him . . . no, he's still going! He's carrying two men on his back — it's a *try!*"

The whistle went and time was up; George placed the ball for a kick and booted it straight over the goal posts — 9-8 to Massey. We heard all the yelling and cheering on the radio and everyone was talking about it — it was great. George told us later that after the game in all the excitement, someone threw his shoes down the gully and he couldn't find them anywhere. He wanted to go to the dance that night but his shoes were gone, and he had to walk home to his uncle's place barefoot. His uncle Herbert said,

"Never mind about those shoes, boy — I'll lend you a pair of mine for tonight."

Poor old George went to the social but he kept tripping over because his shoes were far too big. Anyhow we were so pleased with him that we sent him the money for another pair.

George had a lot of friends at Massey because he was an easy-going chap, and one of his best friends was a fella called Roy Gallagher. When Roy went overseas to

America he was sorry to leave George, and he said,

"Well George, you'll be staying on the farm I suppose, and I'll be away in America. But I want you to promise me one thing; whichever one of us gets married first must bring his wife to the other one's place. So if I get married first I'll bring my wife to your place, and if you get married first, you'll bring your wife to mine. Is that all right?"

"Yeah."

They shook hands on it, then Roy said,

"George, there's one other thing . . . I'm going to leave my dog Pete with you. He'll be a big help to you on the farm, because you can't go running around barking at the cows! Look after him, and give him a bar of chocolate every week, otherwise he'll miss that."

So George kept Pete at Massey, and when he came home at the end of that year the dog came too. My word, I've never seen such a dog; he seemed to understand everything, and he was a beautiful-looking animal. Whenever George was going out, Pete would look at his shoes and start wagging his tail.

"All right, Pete, that's right, I've polished my shoes. Do you want to come too?"

Pete would start to bark. But if George said,

"No Pete, you stay here with Mum — I have to go to Waihau," the dog would put down his head and howl.

Pete was a great help in the mornings. If George slept in, the dog would scratch away at his door until he woke up.

"Oh, hello Pete. You go and get the cows, eh? Make sure you bring them all in, don't miss any . . . "

Pete would shoot off over the hill and we'd hear him barking away at the cows, then I'd look out of the window and see the cows coming to the shed. George and the other boys would have to get their clothes on and go to the shed to start milking.

1945 was George's last year at Massey, and that year the war ended and all the boys started to come home. The Army put the East Coast soldiers on a bus and they spent a month touring along the Coast from one marae to another. After that Apirana rang Eruera and asked him to take Colonel Awatere around the North Island maraes, to carry the deaths of all those soldiers who were left behind. Eruera couldn't come for the first part of it, he was too busy milking cows, so he said to me,

"I think Mum, you'd better go with your cousin Peta. I can't manage it, so you and Kahupuha go, leave the baby at home."

I thought oh good, I can have a little holiday at last, so I got ready. Peta came to the marae, then we left to go to Waikato. There was a big hui at Turangawaewae marae because they all knew that Colonel Peta Awatere was coming to tangi for the soldiers who'd been lost in the fighting. They made a great lament for the soldiers; there were hakas and speeches, and that night after tea we settled down in the meeting-house and the speeches started again. I must have dozed off because when I woke up, one our men was having an argument with another elder about the paua eyes in one particular tekoteko by the name of Kahungunu. The East Coast chap said that the pauas in those eyes came from Tolaga Bay, he even knew which rock they came from, but the other elder didn't agree with him and they started to fight about it. After a while I sang out,

"Oh, never mind! We didn't come here to fight about these things, the fighting is over — we came to tangi for the soldiers."

The East Coast fella said,

"You shut up, Amiria! Go to sleep . . . don't you try and talk!"

So I thought, oh well, I'd better let him have his fight. I turned over and pulled my blanket over my face, and went off to sleep. The next thing, hah! I had a dream. I thought the tekoteko above me had come to life, he was bending over, and he grabbed my neck and started to choke me — uh! uh! uh! . . . I started screaming! I woke up and Peta said,

"What's wrong, Amiria?"

When I told him he said,

"That's your own fault! You were sleeping under the wrong ancestor — there's Porourangi over *there*. You should have been sleeping under him instead of sleeping under someone else's ancestor; that's why you got choked in the neck like that."

"Oh, that's right . . . that tekoteko looked like he was alive!"

I looked up at the carving and it was only a tekoteko after all, but I gathered my blankets and shifted my bed under Porourangi instead. Now when I go in a meeting-house I try not to sleep under someone else's tekoteko, especially if the names are written up. But if you go to a meeting-house where there are no names written on the tekotekos, you're quite safe, you can sleep under any one of them.

At the end of 1945 George came home from college and he brought the Agriculture Cup with him. He walked into the house, threw everything down and kissed me, and he said,

"Well Mum, at last I'm a free man! Dad's got what he wanted so I'm free now, I can do what I like . . ."

He went over to his father and said,

"There you are Dad, there's your Diploma! Now I can please myself, eh Dad. . ."

That afternoon when his father went off fencing, George said to me,

"I'm off now, Mum, I'm off! I've got a position in the Research Department in Wellington . . ."

"What's the hurry, George? You'd better wait — Dad wants to have a talk to you after tea."

"Oh, Mum — I don't want to listen to any more talk. My mind's made up!"

That night I put a meal in front of him, but George didn't seem to be hungry; after tea his father said,

"You know George, your tipuna Apirana saw the write-up about you in the paper, and he rang our place from Ruatoria to congratulate the family. When he was talking to me, he asked one thing; I want to tell you about it. . . . Your tipuna Apirana has asked you to go to Ruakura for twelve months, because the Maori soldiers are all coming back from the war, and some of them are going onto the land. They need a Maori supervisor to train them, someone who can speak Maori and who has started farming right from the bottom. And George, Apirana said you are the man he's been waiting for all these years. I just couldn't refuse him, so I OK'd it."

Then, well . . . I'd never seen that boy look so . . . the way he spoke to his father!

He said,

"Dad! You know, you're never satisfied Dad, *never!* When I wanted to go to war, you wouldn't let me go, and that's why my brother went. You went as a scrutineer for other people's sons to go to the war, and we had to take all the shame. And now you've got something else! This time Dad, I'm not going to listen to you; I've got everything in my hand and I know where I'm going — I'm *not* going to blooming old Ruakura! I'm going to the Research Department in Wellington, they've offered me a position — see, here's the letter . . ."

Eruera looked at the letter and said,

"And where will you go after that, George?"

"I can see my way as clear as anything. Once I've been through the Research Department, Dad, I can go anywhere in the world. I can travel overseas and earn big money — I'll be on top of the world."

"George, look — listen to me! Apirana has told me they need a Maori to help the soldiers, someone who can tell them in their own language what to do. The returned soldiers will be hard to handle, and they have to be helped in the right way, otherwise there'll be trouble. Just go to Ruakura for twelve months, then . . ."

"No! You've been on my back all this time, Dad, this time I'm *not* going to listen to you."

He got up and went into his room, and slammed the door. I said,

"Look Dad, I think that boy is right — he's given in to you all the time. Now that he's got his diploma and he thought he was free, here's something else that has cropped up."

"It's Apirana's doing, not mine."

"I don't care about Apirana! He can get someone else to do it. . . . I'm going to pack my son's things and he's going to Wellington."

I went to George's room and tried the door, it was locked. I called to him,

"George, open the door, George. Look, I'm going to pack all your gear, you're going to that job in Wellington."

He wouldn't open the door so I knocked again.

"George."

After a while I heard the key turn, but he didn't open the door, he threw himself back on the bed.

"George — oh son, don't get too depressed about this. You're right, you should go . . ."

Then I saw all his papers on the floor.

"George! What have you been doing?"

"I wanted to show Dad where all his money went — there it is! And I thought I could go to America and catch up with Roy, but at Ruakura I'll be down at the bottom again, digging in the mud . . ."

"Don't go then, George, you go to Wellington."

"Oh Mum, it's no use . . ."

When he left to go to Ruakura he said to me,

"Well, I won't be able to take Pete to Ruakura, I'll have to leave him with you. You look after him, eh — and try to give him a bar of chocolate every week."

"George, what an expensive dog you've got! I can't even get chocolates for the children, let alone a dog."

"But he seems to look forward to that chocolate . . . "

"Oh well, I'll try."

When George went down to the bus, Pete was running around looking at his shoes and wagging his tail as if to say,

"Oh, we're going now, eh George?"

George turned around to rub his head and said,

"No Pete — you've got to stay with Mum this time."

Then that dog started to howl.

"I'll come back at the holidays and we can go pig-hunting . . . "

"Oer, oer, oer . . . !"

George tied the dog at the corner of the hedge, and he picked up his bag and went to the bus-stop. Pete was jumping up and howling away; I felt sorry for that dog. When the bus came and George got in, the dog pulled at the chain and put his paws up, and howled his heart out.

George did very well at Ruakura, but he was always thinking about coming home and that's why he bought this motor-bike. He thought he wouldn't have to spend his money on bus-fares, he could just hop on his bike and come home. One time he wrote to me and asked me to come to Auckland for a holiday, because he was planning to spend a weekend there and he wanted to see me. I went to stay with my brother-in-law Herbert Wright at Remuera — he'd been married to Ani, my half sister, before she died; and George came up on his bike. I wanted to go home after that but George asked me to stay another week, he'd be back the next weekend.

When he got back to Ruakura he went one night that week to an indoor basketball match, and he took one of his mates behind him on the motorbike. It happened to be raining and misty that evening, it was wintertime. They came to a bridge near Hamilton and that's where it happened. They couldn't see very well with all the mist, and a truck was parked on the wrong side of the road just beyond the bridge with no lights on. . . . They crashed into it, and George was killed.

Afterwards we sued the man who owned the truck for doing that to our son. He said in court that he'd just gone a little way from his own place when he realised he'd left his wallet at home, so he thought he might as well leave the truck there and rush home and get it. He left that truck on the wrong side of the road with no lights on, and that slight mistake of his caused our son's death. The boys crashed into it, and George was killed.

A policeman came to Herbert's place in Remuera soon afterwards and told him about the accident; then Herbert woke me up and told me that George was dead. From that day, everything changed with me. . . . . .

We took the body home from Hamilton and the people from Ruatoria came with us. A man called George Grace who used to live with us on the farm made up a beautiful lament for our son:

Nga iwi, karanga ra!	*Call, the tribes!*
Mo taku mate, taukuri e	*For my dead, alas,*
Hinga mai nei i runga o	*Fallen upon*
Nga mania o Hamutana	*The plains of Hamilton.*

Toro atu aku ringa	*I put out my hands*
Hei piriti mai ki ahau	*A bridge for you to come to me*
Aue! Hori e,	*Alas! George,*
Moumou ra koe, i tenei ra	*You are wasted, this day.*
Hori e, e tama e	*George, child*
Hoki kino mai ra ki ahau	*This is a bad home-coming*
Ki te kore koe i Hamutana	*If you hadn't gone to Hamilton*
Ara kei Te Reinga	*You would not now be dead*
Toro atu aku ringa	*I throw out my hands*
Hei piriti mai ki ahau	*A bridge for you to come to me*
Aue! Hori e!	*Alas! George*
Moumou ra koe, i tenei ra	*You are wasted, this day.*

When we arrived at the marae all the women started wailing; it was the most heart-breaking sound I've heard in my life. There was a dog howling in the background and it was Pete, tied up at the back of the marae, jumping at his chain and crying his heart out. The body was put on the porch of the meeting-house, and all the people kept coming to tangi for George. In the end somebody let Pete loose and he came racing to the meeting-house and tried to jump on the coffin — I could hardly bear to see that dog. The people kept coming for days, and then George was buried. They shovelled dirt on to his coffin and I cried out,

"Oh son, the violets and freesias are blooming now — where are you . . . ?"

That night the dog broke loose from his chain. Someone heard him howling in the cemetery, and they found Pete digging at the graveside, trying to find George, so they took him home and tied him up again. Later on the family told me that on the night George was killed, Pete had suddenly started to howl at about midnight and he cried for the rest of the night, they couldn't make him stop. Early the next morning the news about the accident came to Otaimina.

That's how our son George lost his life.

CHAPTER NINE

Getting Low In My Mind

After George died I just couldn't bear the place, everything was too much a memory of him to me. Even the dogs and the horses in the paddock and the fruit trees, they all made me feel sick. I started to get low in my mind and I didn't feel hungry and in the end I grew very weak. One day I collapsed in the house and it started to play up with me like that. They sent me to the doctor in Opotiki and he said that I had TB, I'd have to go to Waipukurau to get better.

Then I started to worry about the family; I knew I'd have to leave them for Eruera to look after and he already had the cows to milk and everything, and that made me feel worse.

One morning I was lying in the bed while the girls were doing the housework, and they must have all gone outside because it was very quiet. I fell off to sleep and I had a funny dream — I dreamt I was on a mountain. When I looked up it looked like Hikurangi with all the snow on top, but when I looked down it was black, as though it was floating in mid-air. I was about half-way down that mountain and I was slipping, you could see the marks where I'd been. I knew that if I wasn't careful I'd fall right off and that would be death, because it was black all around and the mountain was just standing there in the middle of a great big hole. I slipped a little way and I prayed to God in my heart that he'd give me strength to climb up again, but the grass was slippery and every time I put my foot on it I'd slide down again. I struggled to get back to the top of that mountain but I kept on slipping, and in the end I fell off. When I was falling I knew I was dead, so I called out,

"Dear Lord, help me to get back, I want to stay with my family!"

A rock broke my fall, it was protruding from the side of the mountain and I knew that was the Rock of Ages from the song, "Rock of Ages, cleft for me. . . . " I started to sing this in my heart, and there I was, hanging on to this rock. When I looked down — oh, it was jet-black down there. I knew that only Almighty God could save me now; if he wanted me to be saved, that rock would stay firm. I made one last struggle to climb up and the rock fell away. I thought, well I'm gone. I had a tangi to my family and I could feel myself going, I was lost and finished.

The next thing I heard the birds twittering, and that brought me back to myself. When I looked around I could see these birds singing in the air, and they seemed to be following me. I was flying too, I had big wings and I was flying in the air beneath the mountain. I looked up and saw the snow on the mountain, and I knew it was this world of ours; when I looked down I could see the sun shining onto dried grass, and that was the other world.

I still wanted to stay with my family so I tried to fly back, but the harder I flew the further the mountain went from me, and in the end I got tired of trying. I thought, well it's no use Amiria, you're for the other world now; you'd better fold your wings and start to walk. As soon as I folded my wings, I landed in a tree; I could see the other birds still flying around, and when I looked down I saw this beach — I'd never seen a beach like that before! The sand was like iron-sand and it was all mixed in with the water, so that when the waves dashed up there was more sand in them than water. I said to myself,

"E hika! Where am I now? I've never seen a beach like this before, even in Ruatoria, Tuparoa or the Bay of Plenty, I've never seen a beach like this."

"Ko te kainga tuturu tenei . . . "

I heard this voice talking and I looked up.

"What was that?"

"This is the last home; the place where people truly love one another. This is the final resting-place."

"The final resting-place?"

"Yes."

"Oh. . . . Do you know an old lady called Mereana Mokikiwa?"

"I know her well."

"And what about my mother Ani — how is she?"

"She's well, we are all well here."

"Where is this place?"

"This is the Rerenga Wairua."[23]

I thought, I'm going to get out of here! I tried to fly but I could only go around in circles so I thought, it's no use, I'll have to go down there on the ground. When I put my wings together, huh! I was on the ground, walking. I could hear people talking but I couldn't see them, and just then a pakeha woman called out to some children and I felt one of them brush past my legs.

"Hurry up, dears — come along!"

I looked around but I still couldn't see them, so I followed the sound of their voices and the next thing I saw this tiny little gate. Every now and again the gate would slam — bang! and after a while — bang! I thought I might as well go through that gate but when I tried it was too small for me.

I kept on trying, and in the end I turned sideways and managed to slip through. I heard these people still in front of me, and then I saw the church. I thought oh! — this is the first thing you've got to do, you've got to go to church; I must be really there now. The people were going in so I started to climb up the steps, and just as I was about to put my head inside I heard the minister start up a hymn. When I heard his voice I knew it was Te Aperahama Tatai Koko, a minister who used to be in Tuparoa — he had such a beautiful singing voice. I wanted to go in and listen, but the next thing,

"Moo . . . oo . . . oo!!"

One of our working steers made a big noise and he woke me up. I looked out of the window and it was Reddy, he was leaning over the fence crying out to the cows in the milking-shed; he couldn't get to them because the gate was shut. I thought, oh Reddy, good on you, you've brought me back! If you hadn't called out, I might have been stuck in that other world forever.

---

[23] It is a widely accepted Maori tradition that the spirit of the dead leaves the body after burial and travels to Cape Reinga, where it leaps over a cliff at the place called Te Rerenga Wairua (the leaping of Spirits), there to pass into the Underworld, or Po.

After that dream of mine I got very low down, I couldn't eat and I couldn't sleep at night — cough, cough, cough, cough! I thought I'd have to go to the sanatorium in Waipukurau, but one day Eruera said,

"No Mum, I want you to go to Auckland first."

"Auckland?"

"Yes, you'd better see a specialist up there."

I came to Auckland and stayed with my brother-in-law Herbert Wright. He said,

"Amy, I'm going to take you to see Dr Richard. He's the best doctor we've got here in Remuera — I'll take you there tomorrow."

The next day Dr Richard examined me.

"What did the doctor tell you in Opotiki, Mrs Stirling?"

"He said I had TB, so I had to go to the TB hospital in Waipukurau."

"Have you got any TB in your family?"

"No, nothing."

"Well . . . I don't know. You'd better go to Auckland Hospital and have an X-ray."

I went there and had an X-ray, and a few days later Dr Richard rang me. When I went back to his office he examined me again.

"You haven't got TB, Mrs Stirling — there's your X-ray, look at it! Your trouble is you've strained your heart, and that's why you're coughing. Every time you cough it relieves the heart a bit, but that's not the real trouble. . . . Now tell me — what is it that's been worrying you?"

I had to tell him the whole story.

"All right Mrs Stirling, you listen to me. From now on you have to try and forget what's happened. I'll give you some pills for three months, and in three months I can cure you, but you have to keep away from tangis, anything that depresses your mind. Keep that weight down and do the things that you enjoy, and I can make you better."

He made me shake hands with him and promise.

I came away and I tried, but I just couldn't manage it. I kept worrying about my family at home, and how Dad was getting on, and how we could get Tama to College, and Kepa, and Kiwa and Lily. . . . When I went back for another check Dr Richard said,

"No . . . no, you haven't kept your promise, Mrs Stirling."

I decided that the only thing to do was to go home and ask my husband to lease Otaimina, so we could bring the family to Auckland; because if I went home and looked at hills and started thinking about George, it would all come back to me again.

When I asked Eruera to leave the farm, he agreed, but he said,

"What about our son? We'd better get his stone finished, then we can leave everything behind us."

That's how we hurried the unveiling of George's stone, and it was at the unveiling that I had my last black-out. We started to get the meeting-house ready, and when I looked at the mattresses they were all dirty, so I went to get some ticking from Waihau. On the way home I stopped in at the marae and told the girls to get on with our work, while I went home to sew up the ticking. They didn't like the idea much because we had fifteen fowls to stuff, but I said,

"You don't have to worry about that. Just get the stuffing ready and when I get back, I'll fix it all up."

I went back home and cut up the ticking, then I put the machine on and I must have collapsed. When I came to myself I was lying on the floor, and when I looked at the clock it was four in the afternoon — I'd started to sew at eleven. I couldn't stand up so I crawled out onto the verandah, and the cream-truck came along. Maani Waititi was driving, so I called out to him to send one of my kids from the marae to catch my horse, it was running around in the paddock with the saddle on and everything. He thought I was just sitting there and having a rest.

"Why don't you go and catch it yourself, Amiria?"

"Maani, please send . . . "

"Oh! Get on your feet!"

After a while he realised I wasn't well, so he went to the marae and sent the kids home to Otaimina. I managed to finish my sewing, then I got on my horse and went back to the marae. When I arrived they told me off.

"Oh — Good gracious! Fancy, you went home and had a sleep, I suppose."

I told them I'd had a black-out but they didn't believe me, so I thought never mind about that. When I looked at the chickens, none of them were done although it was getting quite late. I said to them,

Unveiling George's gravestone at Raukokore Church.

"You could have done these chickens yourselves — see. It's simple, you don't have to sew them up; you just put the stuffing in then fold the top through the point of the tail like this . . . '"

They'd never seen that before; I suppose in the country they didn't know how to cut chickens that way, but I'd learned it all in Auckland. In the end we managed to get everything ready, and the unveiling turned out very well. All the people came from Ruakura, it was one of the biggest unveilings at Raukokore in those years. One of George's professors, Dr McMeekan, came out from England to unveil the stone, and afterwards we had a big evening at the marae.

It was two or three years later when Roy Gallagher arrived at Raukokore. He had come back from America with his wife, and the first thing he wanted to do was to come and see George. When his parents told him that George had passed on he couldn't believe it, so he found out where Raukokore was and came there in his car. It just happened that we were staying at the old people's place, and I was in the kitchen looking out of the window when this couple came walking up the path — I'd never seen them before. The old lady was sitting on the verandah and they talked to her, then she called out to me,

"Amiria, te pakeha nei e pirangi ana ki te kite i a korua — this pakeha wants to see you . . . "

I stepped out on the verandah, and when I shook hands with this man, he was crying. He said,

"Mrs Stirling, I'm Roy Gallagher, and I was one of George's best friends at college — but I've been away in America."

He told me how he and George had shook hands and promised each other that whichever one of them got married first had to bring his wife to the other one's place. When I told him that George was dead he said that he had heard that, but he didn't want to believe it; anyway, he wanted to keep his vow. The old lady and I took them down to the cemetery, and we've still got a photo at home of Roy Gallagher and his wife standing beside George's grave.

Before we came away to Auckland, our youngest son Kingi came to live with us at Otaimina. You see, when George was killed and I was sitting beside his body at the tangi, one of the women told me that my sister-in-law Edie had given birth to a baby the day before George's accident. I asked her,

"What is the baby?"

"It's a boy."

When I heard that I felt that my son George had come back again, and all through the tangi I was hoping that I could get this baby; I knew it would help me to forget what had happened. When Edie came to Stirling Castle with the baby not long after, I asked her to call the baby after George, and she agreed. Then I said,

"I would like to take the baby, Edie — you give that baby to me and I'll look after him."

"Oh no, no! You leave the baby with me, but it's all right, I will name him Kingi George, after George."

Kingi George was the name given to our son by Mrs Williams. He was born on June 3rd, and when Mrs Williams heard about it she said,

"Fancy that—June 3rd is King George's birthday! I'm going to ring Amy up and ask her to call the baby King George."

She rang me up about it and I said,

"I'm very sorry Mrs Williams, but this baby has already been named. The old lady has called him Te Ariki-tapu-ki-waho, after one of her ancestors."

"Well, you can give him this name too, because he was born on King George's birthday."

Just to make her happy I agreed, and our son was christened Kingi George Te Ariki-tapu-ki-waho.

Anyhow, Edie said she would call her son Kingi George too, but she said,

"I want to keep this baby, Amy. Later on maybe, when he's running around and you can feed him on kumara it might be all right, but while he's a baby, I think I'd better look after him."

"It doesn't matter about the feeding, Edie; I fed my own babies with a bottle, I can look after him."

"Oh never mind, Amy, leave it, leave it . . . "

I didn't bother her again while I was sick, but when I came back from Auckland I really started to think about this baby. One day somebody said to me,

"Did you know that Edie's gone to Te Puia?"

"What for?"

"Oh, she's going to have another baby."

"Is she? Who's looking after the baby?"

"Her eldest daughter, Maru."

I thought, here goes, I'm going to get that baby now. I rang Frank Walker and told him that I wanted a taxi to Te Araroa.

"All right Amy — when?"

"Right now, today!"

He came and picked me up, and away we went to Te Araroa. When we got there I walked into Edie's house.

"Hello Maru, how's everybody?"

"Oh, all right auntie. Mum just had her baby the other day you know, she's still in the home."

"Where's Kingi now?"

"There he is, under the table."

The baby was crawling around and trying to stand up under the table so I grabbed hold of him and picked him up.

"Where are his clothes, Maru?"

"In the room. Auntie . . . what are you going to do?"

"I'm going to take this blanket and look after him. Just give me his clothes and a blanket."

She gave me all the baby's clothes and I wrapped him up in the blanket, and got in the taxi and went back to Otaimina.

When Edie came back from Te Puia, she couldn't see Kingi anywhere.

"Maru, where's Kingi?"

"Oh, Auntie Amy came here and took him away."

"Did she now!"

As soon as she was free Edie came to Raukokore and told me off for stealing her baby.

"But I *told* you Edie, I wanted that baby. If you'd had a trouble like mine and lost a dear son, you'd need some comfort too. I feel better now, because I've got someone to talk to when the kids are away at school. . . . So you look after your baby and I'll look after mine, and we'll both be all right."

Edie wasn't very happy about it but she went away, and left Kingi at home with me at Otaimina.

CHAPTER TEN

Auckland

Once George's stone was unveiled and everything was set, we had to shift to Auckland. I went ahead to try and find a home for the family, but Eruera stayed back to sell the cows and lease the farm to somebody.

I got a flat in Vincent Street and started some night-time work at the Post Office; Tama went to Te Aute and Kepa went to Grammar, and Lily and Kiwa both came to the Post Office to work with me. During the day I had a job at Hellaby's, but sometimes when I had a holiday I'd do some different work instead to make a bit of extra money for the family. I worked at Crest's in Parnell and the chocolate factory in Parnell, and even the clothing factories too — I don't know where I didn't work. At first I couldn't sew on the factory machines, but I got a job at Ambler's by asking them for one week's trial without pay, and by the end of the week I could sew all right.

Hats were very expensive then and I thought it might be better if I could make my own, so I got a job at N.K. making hats and ties. That's how I managed, and in the end I got on my feet.

At night I worked at the Central Post Office, just for part-time cleaning. A van used to come round and pick up all the cleaners at about three in the morning, but because I had my job at Hellaby's during the day, I started to think up how I could get started before the rest of the girls. I thought I might walk down each morning from Vincent Street to the Post Office because it wasn't far, and I asked the supervisor to give me the keys to my part of the building. She agreed, but my daughters said,

"Mum! Aren't you frightened of walking down Queen Street at 2 o'clock in the morning, all by yourself?"

"No — it's all right. It's all lights from here right down to the Post Office."

Then Lily said,

"Look Mum, it just came over the radio tonight that Wilder has escaped from jail. You never know, he might be hanging around in town."

"He's not that silly, he'd soon get caught if he came up here. I bet you he's hiding in the bush somewhere."

"Oh Mum, *fancy* walking down by yourself when they've got the van to pick you up!"

I didn't take any notice. I grabbed my bag and started to walk, but when I went past St. Matthew's Church I heard the lily leaves rustling and when I turned around, it looked as though someone was moving behind the church. I thought oh! those girls might be right, I wonder if that's Wilder hiding in there. I started to run down to the bright lights in Wellesley Street and I could hear somebody chasing behind me. I thought oh, that's Wilder all right! Then a voice sang out,

"Stop! Stop, will you? Stop!"

I ran as fast as I could, but the next minute someone grabbed hold of me and swung me around.

"Stop, I say!"

I felt my bag falling and I yelled out,

"I'm going to call the police . . ."

I looked up and it was the police himself. The policeman said to me,

"Now look! What are you doing out at this time of the night?"

He took my bag and had a look inside.

"D'you know what time it is? It's 2 o'clock! What are you doing out?"

I said,

"I'm going to work."

"Going to work? This is not the time to go to work. Come on! You're coming to the police station with me!"

"What for?"

"Well, I want to find out what you're up to."

"I'm telling you, I'm going to work!"

"No fear, this is no time for work. Who works at two in the morning?"

"Me! . . . Look here sir, I've got all the keys to the Chief Post Office here, I'm one of their cleaners."

"But they've got a van to bring the girls to work."

"Yes, but I don't go in the van because I want to start ahead of them. I work at Hellabys during the day."

"Ahh . . ." and he scratched his head. "By Jove! Aren't you frightened to go out at night?"

"No, not until now."

He took my name and the address in Vincent Street, and gave me back the keys. I went off to work and by the time the other girls arrived I was well ahead with my cleaning.

After the flat in Vincent Street we lived in quite a few places, but I noticed that it was hard for Maoris to get rooms in those days, very hard. As soon as the agent or the landlady saw you they'd ask,

"Oh . . . what are you?"

If you said a Maori, oh no, that place was already taken, and yet you'd see in the paper the next morning it was still there. In the end I decided to get a boarding-house, because as the children came up one by one there wasn't enough room for them all, and I had to board some of them with our relations. I thought that a boarding-house might be better, so one day I had a chat to one of my friends. I had a lot of nice pakeha friends that I'd met at my different jobs, and this friend of mine Betty had the lease of Seaview House in Hobson Street. Her lease was almost up and she was going back to Napier to live, so she told me that I could have the first chance at the lease.

"Oh — I'll take it, Betty!"

"Well, get the hundred pounds ready to start off with — or it might be better if you had two hundred . . . or better still if you had three hundred."

"Now Betty, that's enough," and I laughed. "I'll give you the hundred and I'll pay for the stuff you leave behind — how about that?"

"All right then, Amy."

When I took over Seaview House I decided it was going to be a boarding-house for Maoris only; I thought I'd put that back on the pakeha. The only trouble was once I'd filled the place up with Maoris — by gosh, they played up with me. They lived in the place for a while, and when they found somewhere else they'd just walk down the fire-escape with their bags, they didn't pay any board. I had a talk to Betty about it and she told me,

"This is what you have to do, Amy — get a bond, make them pay in advance, and if they take off you've still got your money. But if you wait for them to pay, you'll lose it that way. . . ."

And then she said,

"You know, the best boarders are my people, the Dalmatians. You should try Dalmatians, they're very genuine people."

So I changed to Dalmatians for boarders and I must say, she was right. The Dalmatians are very straight people, and they are fair, and most of the Dalmatian people that are here now stayed at Seaview House in those days.

While I was running the boarding-house Eruera was still at home in Otaimina, because it took quite a while to find the right man to take over the farm. One time when he came up to Auckland he said to me,

"I think, Mum, we'd better look for a house of our own. This boarding-house is too much of a worry to you."

He looked at some places in Parnell but he couldn't find anything, and then he had to go back to Otaimina to settle up about the farm. I decided to get rid of the boarding-house anyway, so I had another talk to Betty.

"You know Betty, a man was round here last week, and he said he was interested in taking over the lease. . . . I think I might give it to him."

"Don't hurry yourself, Amy — get yourself really set first."

"But he said he wanted to start next month, and I can't get settled in a home by then!"

"Listen, you're the boss — you've got the key of the place, he can't take it off you. Ask him for key money and if he's got that ready, you can add a little bit more and so on until you're set."

She put this into my head, and I started working it in that way. The man came to me and said,

"Mrs Stirling, you're supposed to be out of here by the end of the month; that's when the lease expires."

"I'll go when I'm ready, I have to find a place for myself. I've asked you for a hundred pounds key money, but if you give me two hundred, right, I'll shift out."

He went away to think about it, and that afternoon I went down to the GPO to talk to the postmaster about getting a Post Office house. He said to me,

"All right Mrs Stirling — where would you like to live?"

"I'd like to be close to town, Mr Keogh, because I still have to get to work."

"Well, what about Orakei? There's a house going there."

In those days Orakei was like a Maori pa, and I thought that would be a nice place for me.

"All right Mr Keogh, I'd like to live with my own people, I'd be set then."

He arranged everything with the agent, Mr Keys, and the next day Mr Keys drove me out. The house was way up on top of the hill, not down by the church, and when I looked at it I didn't want it. It was one of those big houses with long windows so you can see everything inside, and I just wanted a little private house for my family. I said,

"No Mr Keys, that house is for wealthy people — think of all the flash furniture you'd have to put inside! I only want a little plain house."

The next day another agent picked me up to show me a house in Herne Bay. When he came he said,

"Oh! . . . Oh well, ah — what are you?"

"I'm a Maori."

I could see by the way he looked at me that he didn't like it, but I thought, you're only the agent, I don't care what you think. When we turned into the street I saw the sea and all the boats, and I said,

"Ohh! I'm going to take that house!"

I was looking at the view, not at the house, and he said,

"It's not down there, Mrs Stirling — here it is!"

"Yes, well I'm going to take it."

"Don't you want to go inside?"

"Oh yes, I suppose I'd better."

When I turned to look at the house I saw it was all under a huge willow tree, it must have been about a hundred years old.

"By . . . Joves. Who's going to cut down this tree?"

"That's not my job, Mrs Stirling, I'm only here to sell the house to you. If you take the house, that tree is yours."

We went around the back and oh! the house was wide open, and there was a great pile of rubbish under the willow tree — motorcars, bedsteads, cans and all that. I nearly cried and I thought, if Eruera comes here and finds this that is the house I've bought, he'll have a big row with me. I looked at the house but I kept thinking of that beautiful view. Then I thought, perhaps if I can get someone to cut down the willow tree and cart away all the rubbish, it'll be all right, so I said,

"I'll take this house!"

"All right Mrs Stirling — what about your deposit?"

"Come down to the GPO tomorrow morning and I'll get the money out for you.'

The next morning I paid him the deposit, then I made arrangements for all our stuff to be transported from the boarding-house. It didn't arrive that day, and Lucy and I had to sleep on the floor in our clothes. Over the next few days I cleaned the place out and moved our furniture in, then one evening Eruera turned up. Someone had told his sister May that I'd left the boarding-house, and when she told Eruera about it he started to panic, so he got on a bus and came to Auckland. He arrived after dark and luckily he didn't go outside so he didn't see the willow tree. The next morning when I was walking to Ponsonby past the Catholic Home, I saw a man in there cutting down the pine trees so I thought to myself, this might be the man to get rid of that willow tree for me. I went up to him and said,

"Excuse me sir — how much longer are you going to be here?"

"I've just finished. I'm packing up now, I'm going home."

"Well have you got time to do another job? I've got a willow tree I want cut down."

"Where is it?"

"It's not far, it's only about five minutes from here."

"Get in the van then, we'll go and have a look."

When he saw the willow tree he said,

"Oh, that won't take long. It'll be down in a few minutes."

"How much will it cost?"

"Five pounds."

Luckily I had five pounds in my purse, so I told him to go ahead.

"All right — you just tell me where you want it to fall."

I went into the middle of the lawn and marked a place with my foot.

"Wait a minute though — I'd like you to trim off all the branches first in case they hit something."

"Yes, all right."

He took his chain-saw and boom! boom! boom! boom!, all the branches were off, and the next thing — *bang!* The tree came crashing to the ground. Eruera was asleep in the house and when the tree fell down he got such a fright that he rushed outside in his pyjamas. All the neighbours came running out too, they thought a bomb had gone off.

"Oh look! It's that blooming willow tree — it's down!"

"Is it? Hooray!"

I heard them talking about it, all the rows they'd had with the man who owned the house, about the branches and all the leaves falling on their side.

"It's that Maori woman over there—she's cut it down! I think it's Mrs Stirling, that's what Mrs Schultz said."

Then one of them said to me,

"Oh — *good* on you, Mrs Stirling. Thank goodness, we can see daylight now."

I asked this fella to cut up the smaller branches for firewood, and he put the big ones on his truck and took them away. When he came back I gave him another five pounds to cart away all the rubbish and he did it, no trouble.

After all that I went inside and Eruera *told* me off.

"Oh . . . fancy! Is this the sort of home that you've bought, with a great big willow tree like that? And did you ask the Council about cutting down that tree? We're in the town now, you can't just go cutting things down, the Council is the boss."

Anyway, the willow tree was gone, so that was all right.

We had some trouble with one or two of the neighbours when we first moved to Herne Bay, because we were the first Maori family in the area and they didn't like that much. The women said to our neighbours,

"You know, you're going to have a rough spin with that Maori family next door. You'll never have any peace now, there'll be beer bottles from the front gate right to the back door and parties all weekend — you wait and see, there'll be no more rest for you!"

"Oh yes. . . . By Jove, if they're going to do that, we'll soon get somebody on to them."

The first trouble we had was when I started to make my garden. The soil round our place was all hard yellow clay and you couldn't grow anything in it, but there was lovely soil down on the bank by the beach. One of our neighbours had a lot of bricks piled up at the back of her place, so one day I asked her,

"Mrs Nicholls — do you want all those bricks there?"

"No, I've got no use for them, that's why they're piled up like that."

"Can I have some of them?"

"Take the lot if you like, Mrs Stirling."

I shifted the bricks a few at a time and I built some little walls, then I took my trundle down to the bank and began filling between these walls with soil. After a while some of the women started to talk about it at the shop.

"You know that Maori woman in No. 1 there, Mrs Schultz — do you know what she's doing? She goes down to the bank every day and takes the soil from there, and she's been doing it for over a week!"

Mrs Scultz said,

"Oh well, I suppose . . ."

"But she can't do that! It's not her property, it belongs to the Council. We're going to let the Council know what she's doing."

A few days later Mrs Schultz came past my place and she leaned over the fence while I was working in the garden.

"Oh, hello Mrs Stirling! You've been doing a lot of work."

"Yes, I like to see something growing, and the soil is just clay around here."

"Mrs Stirling, would you mind if I told you something?"

"What is it, Mrs Schultz?"

"Well, some of these people are going to report you to the Council, they say you've no right to go and get that soil and bring it to your garden. . . ."

"Oh."

"And one woman said there'll be beer bottles at the front gate right to the back door. So I'm just letting you know what they're saying — be careful, that's all."

"All right Mrs Schultz, thank you very much for telling me. We don't drink, we're not drinkers — that's for the first one, for the beer bottles. You'll never see beer bottles in this place as long as I'm here. As for the soil — yes, this is my country. Aotearoa is Maori land, and I'm not stealing that soil, it's still here. I'm putting it round my house because it's better to have a few flowers growing than having to look at these grey clay rocks. So you tell those women, Mrs Stirling is going to keep taking that soil until she's finished, and if the Council wants to put me in jail they can — when I come out I'll go and take some more soil until I'm satisfied that I've got enough!"

Mrs Schultz laughed, and she went away. When the women started talking about it again, she said to them,

"I told Mrs Stirling that she'd better be careful and this is what she said — she's not afraid because that's her soil, she'll keep taking that soil until she's got enough."

"Do you mean . . ."

"Yes, she said that's her soil, Aotearoa is Maori land."

Then those people shut up.

When we got settled down in Herne Bay I left the Central Post Office and shifted to the Wellesley Street branch, and another funny business happened there. I was

Amiria in the City.

supposed to do my cleaning when the Post Office opened in the morning and I didn't like that, because the men had to put their legs up and shift their chairs when I came polishing and scrubbing around. I went to the Central Post Office and asked the postmaster to give me the privilege of doing my work after the Post Office closed at night. I could do my three hours and then lock up and come home. He said,

"Why do you want that, Mrs Stirling?"

"Well I feel terrible, when I start to polish and these men are in the way, I have to ask them to move, and I know they don't like it."

"All right, Mrs Stirling."

He gave me the keys and he said,

"Now, there's one thing you must be careful always to remember. When you step inside the Post Office there's an alarm behind the door; switch it off as soon as you get there and be sure to turn it back on when you leave. I'll be watching you, Mrs Stirling — if you don't do this, you're finished."

"Yes, sir."

I went away and that night I cleaned the Post Office; when the people arrived in the morning the place was all clean and tidy, and that was better. This went on for a long time; I'd do my work at night then go home and have a sleep, and at half-past seven I'd go on the bus to my day-time job at Hellaby's.

One day I had a terrible cold and I wasn't feeling well, so I thought I'd ask Lily to do my cleaning that night, she and Claude were living with us then.

"Lily, I've got a very heavy cold and I don't want to go out tonight. Will you clean the Post Office for me?"

"All right Mum, you give me the keys."

I gave her the keys and told her where to empty all the baskets and to clean and polish and scrub. Then I said,

"There's one thing you must remember, Lily — and you too, Claude, you listen to me! When you go in there's an alarm behind the door — you have to turn it off, and when you leave you have to remember to turn it on again."

Lucy said she'd go along to help, so the three of them went down to the Post Office. When they opened the door, they couldn't find the switch.

"Hurry up, Claude!"

"Well — where is it?"

"It's supposed to be behind the door."

"Which door, though?"

There were about three doors there, and by the time they'd turned the lights on and looked around for the switch, they heard the police cars coming.

"Boom . . . boom . . ."

The next minute the police walked in.

"Well — hello! What are you doing here? Come on out!"

Claude said,

"We're cleaning up the Post Office."

"Cleaning up? Why didn't you switch the alarm off?"

"Well, we couldn't find it."

"Oh come on, no."

They pushed Claude into the van, and grabbed hold of Lucy and Lily too. Lily said,

"Look, my mother is the cleaner for this Post Office. She isn't well tonight so she gave us the keys, and we couldn't find the alarm to switch it off, it just kept going and going!"

Then the sergeant walked in.

"Hello — where's Mrs Stirling? Are you her daughter?"

"Yes."

"Well, what's going on here? Why is the alarm going?"

"We were just looking for it, we couldn't find it."

"Ah well . . . who's that?"

"That's my husband Claude."

"I see. All right then, do your cleaning, and as soon as you're finished be *sure* to switch that alarm on again. We'll check on it to make sure you do."

When Lily got home that night she said to me,

"Oh Mum, I'm not going back to that job again! It was *terrible*. We couldn't turn the alarm off and the police cars all came, and there was blooming Claude still looking for the switch!"

They told me what had happened and after a while we had a big laugh about it. The next day I went down to the Post Office and explained to them that I'd been sick, and that was all right.

I worked all those years at Hellaby's too and I enjoyed that, because the girls there were hard case — they used to play all sorts of games with me. I was at the end of the conveyor belt putting tins of meat through the machine, and sometimes the girls who weighed the meat at the top of the belt would hold back all the tins.

"Hey, what's wrong with you girls? You're not putting the tins on the belt . . . there's no tins down here!"

"Who's running this end, you or us? It's not our fault."

After a while I'd doze off, then they'd *pile* all those tins on the belt. When I woke up the tins would be falling around me and I had to jump up to try and get them through the machine. Those girls would scream and start to laugh,

"Good job! You shouldn't go to sleep . . ."

Another time they kept all the tins back and waited until I started to doze, then they put a big ox-tail on the belt. When I automatically put out my hand I grabbed this great big ox-tail, and I nearly fell off my seat — they thought it was great. I just put the tail beside me and put all the tins through, and when the man who was sweeping our room came near me I tied the tail to the back of his apron — it just *swished* away. The girls were laughing so hard that they couldn't do anything, and the foreman came past and spotted this and he said to this fella,

"Put your hand behind you Charlie, and see what the girls have done to you — you've grown a tail!"

Oh, this is it . . . you have to have a bit of something to laugh about while you're working.

Towards the end of my time at Hellaby's they tried to make me a forelady but I refused — that's the trouble with the Maori. One day there was an announcement that I was wanted at the office, and when anyone was called to the office there was always something wrong. The other girls started to laugh and they said to me,

"Hey, Mrs Stirling — they want you at the Office! You must be getting your walking-ticket, eh!"

I walked up the stairs and I wondered, now what have I done. When I went in the office Mr Beech was there, and he said,

"All right, Mrs Stirling, sit down."

"No, I'm not sitting down Mr Beech! If you want to give me my walking-ticket, give it to me now while I'm on my feet so that I can walk straight out. I'm not going to sit down so that you can tell me, 'you've done this, you've done that, you're finished!' "

Mr Beech looked at me and he started to smile.

"Mrs Stirling, I'm not talking about walking-tickets or anything like that. I just want you to sit down and listen to me."

So I sat down.

"Now Mrs Stirling, do you know how long you've been working here?"

"No — you should be the one to know, you've got it all down in the book."

"Well, let me put it another way. You've been here for six years now, Mrs Stirling, and you've worked in all the departments of the factory, so you know your way around. In a few weeks' time Mrs Brown is going to England for a three-month holiday, and we want someone to take over her position while she's away. We looked up the records of all the women, and you've only had four half-days off in the six years you've been here. We want you to be the forelady while Mrs Brown's away in England."

I said,

"Thank you Mr Beech — but I'd rather stay where I am. I'm quite happy with my work."

"Don't you want to be a forelady?"

"No thank you. I'd rather be just the lady I am, I don't want to be a forelady." Mr Beech started to laugh.

"Oh . . . Mrs Stirling, it's only for three months."

"No. I've got all these hard-case mates here, and they'll give me all the hard-case talk if I take this job. You don't know, Mr Beech, but I do."

"By Jove."

That's why I didn't want the job. I knew how these girls treated Mrs Brown; if someone stayed away they'd tell her that the baby was sick or Mum wasn't well, but later another girl would say,

"Oer! You told a lie — you were too drunk last night and you couldn't get up in the morning. I tried to wake you but I couldn't — that's why you didn't make it until now! You blooming liar!"

I thought if I took up that position they'd made a fool of me too and tell me all the lies, so I thought, no, I'll just remain where I am. I stayed in that job until I left Hellaby's, and when I left they gave me a real big send-off and a beautiful tea-set, because of all the years I worked there.

CHAPTER ELEVEN

Later Years

When I got to my pension age, I had to give up work. After that we had more time to go to huis, and we joined up with some of the clubs around Auckland too — the Pioneers', the Founders' Society, and the Old Folks' group down at Coronation Hall.

Once when the Festival was on, our Old Folks' president told me that there was a bus taking all the old people down to the Flower Show at the Town Hall; if I wanted to go I'd have to be down at Gundry Street on time. I wasn't going to miss out on that trip, so I got ready early in the morning and took a bus from Ponsonby to the Old Folks' Hall. When we got to Queen Street there were crowds of people standing outside, waiting to get in. Soon another bus arrived and a whole lot more people got off; the next thing the back row of the queue seemed to start pushing, and somebody shoved me and I banged into the woman in front.

"What did you do that for? It's no use pushing, you know we can't get to the box!"

"It wasn't my fault, somebody shoved me from behind."

"Don't tell me that . . ."

We were growling at each other like that when something *banged* me on the head.

"Ooh! What did you hit me on the head for?"

She looked up, then she started to laugh.

"Don't do that, or I might hit you on the head too . . ."

Another woman called out,

"Mrs Stirling, feel on the top of your head; up there!"

I put my hand up and I felt something move, then this thing dropped down on to my shoulder.

"Heck! What's this?"

When I turned my head, I saw a pigeon sitting on my shoulder. It hopped back on top of my hat, and everybody was so busy looking at me and laughing that they left the box free. I thought here's my chance, so I ran to the box and put my money down, and I bought my ticket. When I went to the doorman he didn't notice the pigeon at first; I think he thought it was a decoration on my hat until I bent over to put away my change and the bird flapped its wings, then he said,

"Hey . . . you can't go in there with your bird — it's not allowed!"

"Well it's not my bird — and anyway I've got my ticket here, you can't put me out."

I walked inside and it was beautiful with all the waterfalls and lilies and ferns and flowers. The only trouble was that the other people thought I must be part of the show, so they followed me around.

"Can I stroke your bird?"

"How do you get it to sit there?"

"Please can I touch it?"
I said,
"Oh no, I don't think you'd better, the bird might fly up and damage something."
I was sure that bird would fly away inside the Town Hall because it's very high up there, but it just sat on top of my hat. In the end I decided to sing a song to shift it, so I started,

Mehe manu rere ahau e	*If I were a flying bird*
Kua rere ki to moenga	*I'd fly to your bed, dear*
Ki te awhi to tinana	*There to embrace you, dear*
E te tau tahuri mai.	*Oh my darling, turn to me.*

The bird just sat up and flapped its wings, and all the people laughed. Then I sang,

Kei te moe to tinana	*Your body is sleeping*
Kei te wake to wairua	*But your spirit wakes*
Kei te hotu te manawa	*You are sighing*
E te tau, tahuri mai.	*Oh love, turn to me.*

It was no use, so I walked around and looked at all the flowers, then I thought if I go outside, that bird is bound to fly away. I went back out to Queen Street and I tried to shake my hat,
"Go on birdie — you'd better go home now!"
No, the bird just sat there. I thought well, if it wants to sit there I suppose it can do that, so I walked down to the Civic to catch the Ponsonby bus. When I climbed on the bird moved, and the driver looked up.
"Hey! You! Wait a minute, you're not allowed in here with that bird!"
"How else am I going to get to Ponsonby? I haven't got any other transport."
I walked to the back of the bus and sat myself down.
"I *mean* it, lady. If your bird flies around in here and something gets damaged, we'll sue you for it."
"Well if you want to do that you can sue the City Council, this is their bird, not mine."
I stayed in my seat and the bird didn't move. The children came to talk to him and they wanted to stroke his back, but I said,
"No, you'd better not do that — you heard what the driver said."
"Oh . . ."
When we got to Ponsonby I climbed out of the bus. Some of the children got smart and they grabbed some little stones and tried to hit the bird. One stone went straight into Lambournes and there were some cups in there; it hit one of those cups and it fell down and smashed. Luckily the woman in there knew me so she said,
"Never mind, Mrs Stirling."
She picked up the cup and put it in the rubbish bin so the manager wouldn't see it. I hurried off to the Building Society to pay for my shares, and when I went in the manager was laughing.
"*What* are you doing with that bird on your hat, Mrs Stirling?"
"Well I don't know — it just flew and sat there."

He laughed like anything. I was filling in my forms and he said,

"Mrs Stirling, you should take this to the *Westend News*."

"Where's that?"

"It's just a few doors down from here. They'll put it in the paper; that's a wonderful thing, that bird! How long has it been sitting there?"

"It flew on my hat at the Town Hall, and it's been there ever since — I came home on the bus and everything."

"That's a great story, because it's a true one."

He took me to the *Westend News* and they took a photo of me with the bird on my hat.

After that I walked on down Ponsonby Road, and the next thing a woman tapped me on my shoulder.

"Excuse me, Madam — is that your bird sitting there?"

"No, it's not mine. It just flew and sat on my hat."

"That's funny. . . . Can you tell me, what does that mean to the Maori?"

"Well — what does it mean to the pakeha?"

"It means news, the bird has brought news."

"I hope it's good news; I don't want *bad* news."

"It can be either good or bad."

"What do I have to do about it, then?"

"Well. . . . Just think of whatever comes into your head. If it's good, that's all right, but if it's bad, try to fix it up."

"Oh! Thank-you."

I started walking back and I was thinking about what she said, then suddenly I remembered this parcel. We'd just flown back to Auckland from the Maori Battalion reunion, and there was a parcel at home that came with my bags from the Airport. I thought maybe that was it. It was a big box with "J. Lowe" written on it, and it must have got mixed in with my bags on the plane. Eruera had already rung the police about it but they hadn't come to pick it up, so I went to the police station and said to the policeman there,

"My name's Mrs Stirling, and my husband rang you a few days ago to come and pick up a parcel; it got mixed in with my bags when I flew home from the South Island. That parcel is still in my house, and I want you to go and get it straight away."

"We can't do that, Mrs Stirling — you'll have to bring it here."

"But you said you were going to pick it up."

"No, you have to bring it here or take it to the NAC depot."

Just then he noticed the bird on my hat, and he started smiling and looking at the other policemen.

"Look here — I'm talking to you! I want that parcel out of my house. Who knows, there might be a bomb in there, it might explode any time!"

"Yes Mrs Stirling, all right."

They weren't interested though, they were just looking at the bird on my hat. In the end they said they'd pay a taxi for me, and when the taxi came the driver took me home to pick up the parcel, then we went to the NAC depot to leave it there. On the way back I told him that the police would pay for the taxi and he said,

"Oh no! You pay or I'll stop — I have to get paid for my work."

Amiria with the pigeon on her head.

So I had to pay him, I just wanted to get it out of my way. I asked him to drop me at the Town Hall because now that everything was all fixed up, it was time to take the bird back to its home. When we stopped I saw a big car parked outside; I put my hat down on the footpath and gave it a good shake, then I ran and hid behind the car so that the bird couldn't see me. When I looked up again, the bird had gone. I caught a bus and came home. The funny thing is my name is Amiria Manutahi, and "Manutahi" means one bird; Eruera told me that bird might have been my ancestor come back to life.

A lot of people saw that photo in the paper, especially after they put it in the *Herald* as well, and one day a teacher from the Blockhouse Bay school rang me up at home. He said that the children had been painting pictures of me with the bird on my head, and he would like me to go there and give the first prize for the best painting. When we got to the school all the paintings were hanging on both sides of the passage, and when I saw the one that won the first prize I couldn't help laughing. The teacher brought the girl that painted that picture up to me, and I congratulated her and put my pearl necklace around her neck, then I said,

"All right dear, you made a good job of the drawing of the bird and myself — good on you. But the only thing is, you see, I didn't have a hot pants on!"

This picture had a little hot pants like that and a big hat with a pigeon on it — it was great.

One time when I was going down Queen Street there was some sort of a meeting going on, so I thought I might sit at the back and listen. This chap was talking about all sorts of things, and then he started having a go at the Maoris and their tangis.

"Now just look at the Maoris, when a man dies they have a tangi for two or three days before the body is buried! What I want to know is this — what's the use of sitting there and howling over that man when he's already dead? I'm looking at the waste of money involved. We've got the Crippled Children and the Blind and all that, so why waste money on a man who's already dead? They should learn to do it the pakeha way, just send a wreath and a card and that's it, then they won't be wasting all that money. . . ."

I got so wild that I couldn't hang on; I thought, right! and I stood up.

"Excuse me sir, I'm a Maori and you're talking about my people. You can't change our way of life, even if you take it to all your big men of the pakeha, you can't change us! The trouble with you pakehas is that you've got no aroha like the Maori, your love is *money*. If someone dies you don't love that person, you just take a flower and give the widow a clip on the cheek and that's all. But that's not the Maori way — we don't care how much we spend! We take our aroha to the tangi, and a little bit of money too, and after we've had our tears we give the money quietly to the relatives, so they can pay their tangi debt. We press noses with them to show that love, and we stay with them so they don't feel lonely. It's not the pakeha way — a clip on the cheek, flowers, finish, it's gone! That's the light and easy way, but our way is too heavy I suppose. So don't you try to change us, because we were in this country first, and nobody asked you to come here and change our ways!"

Then I thought oh, I've gone a bit too far, so I sat down and then I went away.

But now I'm glad to notice that the pakeha is coming to see the Maori way, because not long ago I went to a tangi at Tira Hou for a young Maori chap, and he must have been an orphan because there was a pakeha couple sitting beside the coffin with all their children. They were having a tangi exactly in the Maori way, sitting by the coffin and crying, and the children would go and kiss him. I asked the people,

"Are those his parents?"

"No, but that chap had been living with them for about fifteen years before he died."

I was surprised to see that pakeha woman and her husband. I thought well look, there's that aroha, the pakeha have got it now. I really appreciated it, and I had to go and speak to them in the end. It was blowing very cold that day so I made a bed for them inside the meeting-house, then I asked the woman to take the children and go and have a rest. I said,

"Why don't you go inside? You can leave the coffin on the verandah, it's all right — but it's too cold out here for the children. Sitting on the verandah is all right for the Maoris, but . . ."

She shook her head and said, no!

"Are you going to sleep out here?"

"Yes."

Well look, I nearly howled myself; I thought, the pakeha . . . that's it, that's it! There's that Maori aroha, they've got it at last. And the next day when a group of pakehas came to the marae, they did the same as the Maoris, they put money down on the marae as a gift; I could hardly believe it.

This young fella had been a sailor and he wanted his ashes to be thrown into the Waitemata Harbour, so the people came to ask me what to do with all these wreaths. Somebody had told them to take them to the hospital, but I said,

"Hey, wait a minute. You can't do that!"

"Somebody said it's better to take them there."

"No, it's not right! It might be all right to the pakeha, but it's not right to the Maori way of doing it. Those people in the hospital are there for their health's sake, they want to live a little bit longer; but those wreaths are for the dead. Now you're taking the dead man's wreaths to the living! It's as if you're saying, 'Come on, you come *this* way. You too, come on!' That's not right."

This man just looked at me.

"Listen here, those people are in hospital to gain their lives, they want to live. Why take the property of the dead and give it to them? If you want to give them flowers, well go and get some, but *not* off the coffin here, no! If I had a relative in that hospital I'd go straight there and stop any of these wreaths going into his room."

They must have had a talk about it because they put all the wreaths back on the coffin, and when they took the body away all the wreaths were there in the cars. So that fixed up that. I suppose they were looking at the waste, all those wreaths at $5 or $6 or $10 each, just to be thrown away. It was money again, worrying their minds. But the Maoris don't worry about money for the tangi — everybody brings their donation to the marae, and in the cities, a lot of tribes have formed associations to carry the cost.

Eruera started the Tai Rawhiti Association in Auckland about ten years ago, so that the East Coast people could be buried at home when their time came. We didn't want a marae in Auckland because there's plenty of maraes at home, but the trouble is, there's nobody to look after them any more. The people have to come to the cities because there's no living for them at home. If the milking was still on the young people would still be there, milking cows and all that, but now — nothing. So now we're trying to think about putting trees on the land, and if the young people are interested in it, well and good.

Anyhow, the Tai Rawhiti Association helps us to save up our money for that last day; all the members pay so much, and we hold our socials at the University Cafeteria, $5 a ticket. Some people grumble about the money but I don't think they should grudge it, it's for a good cause. If you pass on you don't have to worry, they can take you right back home to be buried and that's better. The old people call it "Te ukaipo", the place where you fed at your mother's breast, and they say,

"Haere e tama ki te taha i o matua tipuna; haere ki te ukaipo — go child, to lie beside your parents, your ancestors, in the place where you fed at your mother's breast."

When Lady Pomare died; they carried her ashes from Wellington to Manukorihi marae at Waitara so that she could be buried at her husband's side, and Ani Salmond and I went to that tangi. The first time I went to that marae was to play hockey for the Lady Arihia Cup, and the second time was for Maui Pomare's tangi; but I think this last time was the roughest trip I've ever had. It was all right when we left Auckland, that wasn't so bad. The only trouble was that we left pretty late, and when we got to the Taranaki hills, it was already night. Just before we went into the hills we stopped at a bowser, and I thought ka pai, Ani, it's a good job to fill the car up with plenty of hinu, that way we won't get stuck. But when I noticed there wasn't anybody there to work the pumps I started to feel a bit funny. Ani had to do it all herself, and I think she must have left the petrol cap on the bonnet because as we were going up the first hill she said,

"Oh — we've lost the petrol cap, it's gone!"

"Ani! Where is it?"

"I don't know Nan, it must be back at the pump."

She turned the car round and I felt myself shivering inside, but I didn't want Anne to know I was weak like that. I thought, now what's going to happen? The oil might drip out and the car might blow up. All sorts of funny things came into my mind.

When we got back to the pump I saw some young fellas at the side of the road; one group had a girl with them, holding hands and all that, and I thought, if they see that this car's in trouble they might come over here and bash us on the head. In my heart I was praying that Ani could find that cap quickly. We drove around a couple of times and then she jumped off the car and walked around in the street, looking for the cap.

In the end we drove back towards the hill and right at the bottom there, we spotted it. Gee I was glad. But when we got into the hills, I've never seen such a road — I thought we were bad enough in the Bay of Plenty with all our pig-tracks. It was up hill and down dale, and we went right up and then round and round and round, it never seemed to finish. I started to sing anything that came into my head, because it was getting late, and I didn't want my mate to fall asleep — even one little wink and we'd have been over the cliff. I sang all the songs of my young days and even baby songs too, and then I sang the hymn "Marama Pai" over and over again:

Marama pai ahau e kimi nei	*Good light, I am searching*
Me arahi	*Lead me on*
Tu mai te po, e he ai hoki au	*It is night and I am lost*
Me arahi	*Lead me on*
Te ara pai, me tohutohu mai,	*Show me the proper path*
Kia tika ai, te hikoi o oku wae.	*So that I can walk in the right way.*

(*To the tune, "Lead Kindly Light"*)

I'm sure it was that hymn that took us safely to Taranaki. By the time we got to the marae it was about midnight, and we couldn't go in then. I know *my* people wouldn't allow it. We drove past and found a motel and slept there instead, and in the morning we had a good shower and drove to the marae at about 9 o'clock. I think some of the people must have remembered me from the time I came there to play for the Lady Arihia Cup because they gave us a big welcome, and that night I told them all about Taite te Tomo, and Ngata with his "Scenes of the Past". After all that it was a very good hui, and when we drove to Auckland we had an easy trip home.

Not long ago in Auckland, I nearly got myself killed. I went to a Pioneers' meeting at the Ellen Melville Hall, and when I finally looked at the time it was nearly 3 o'clock, my pensioner's ticket was about to run out. I hurried down High Street to Vulcan Lane, and when I got to Queen Street there were two buses pulling up at the bus-stop. One of them was full with a lot of people standing inside so I thought that's no use, I'd rather take the other one and have a seat. When I stepped out of the queue, the woman in front of me asked where I was going.

"I'm not getting on this bus; you won't get a seat, it's too full. I'm going to the second bus because I'd rather sit down."

I turned to go but this woman rushed ahead of me and got there first. I said,

"Just as well you've got young legs to run like that, I couldn't manage it. I'll just wait for you."

She climbed on to the bus, and I hardly had my foot on the bottom step when the bus took off. The next thing I was flying in the air and I thought well, this is the end of me. I could see three lanes of cars coming from down at the bottom of Queen Street and I hadn't a hope in my mind, I knew they'd run me over. But when I came to myself all the cars were stopped, and someone was carrying me off the road. I said,

"Please, just get me a taxi — I want to go home!"

"No, we're rushing you to hospital."

I looked down and saw all that blood, I'd gashed my knee. Luckily I had a lot of clothes on that day, I was wearing my fur-coat and gumboots and everything, and that's what saved me. The doctor said that if I'd landed another way, I would have broken my neck. As it was I fell on my side and bashed my face and that's why I was blind and deaf on that side for quite a while afterwards.

The ambulance came and took me straight to hospital and the doctor there examined me for broken bones, but I was all right. They bound up my knee and left me lying there half-dressed with all these people going past for a while; I didn't like that much.

My knee seemed to heal all right but I still have to use a walking-stick and when it gets cold in winter my knees ache like anything. That's why I always carry around a crocheted blanket or shawl, because as long as my knees are warm, I'm all right.

I had to wait six months for my eye operation, and when that was finished I wanted them to operate on my ear as well, because I was still deaf on that side. They said they couldn't do it, I'd have to wait another six months — I couldn't have two operations at once. So I told the nurse,

"Well, I'm not going to leave my bed until my ear is fixed up too, because I'm still no good, I can't hear on that side. If I have to wait for six months I'll just stay here until then, and if I have to die here that's all right — I'm not going home until I'm all set."

The nurse looked at me and she went away. After a while she came back with a doctor, and the doctor said,

"All right Mrs Stirling, come on now — we're going to fix your ear for you."

Oh, I was glad. They put me onto a trolley and wheeled me to another room, and the doctor had a look in my ear, then he took a needle and quickly jabbed it inside, it was so fast that it hardly hurt.

"There you are Mrs Stirling, that should be a lot better."

I thought to myself, that's not an operation, it's only something to satisfy me, but anyway I suppose I'd better go home. I went home and I'm still pretty deaf, but I must say the Hospital Board has been very good to me. They helped me in every way they could, even with the expense but the ARA did nothing, even though it was their bus that caused the damage.

I tell you one thing, I'm not very easy to get rid of. I had a bad heart attack last Christmas and I thought I was gone, but here I am, still in this world. I keep working in my garden and I travel around to huis, and when I went to Pine Taiapa's unveiling I saw some people that I hadn't seen for years — they used to be the young men of Tikitiki but they're old men now, and they said to me,

"Hello Amiria! We thought you were dead long ago."

"No, not me! I'm a tough guy, you know. I haven't gone yet . . ."

"Hika, you must be, because it's *years* since you were last here."

I suppose I must be eighty now, and when I look back on my young days, the world is not the same; the tapu, the wehi, the maoritanga of those times has all gone. The people of today don't have the dignity of the old chiefs and chieftainesses, they've taken up too many of the pakeha ways. One step they're Maori, the next step they're pakeha, and that's the way they move around.

When I was young there were certain people in each area who were senior in their lines and everybody respected them — Hine Pepi, the lady of Te Araroa; Materoa Reedy at Hiruharama; Rutu Tawhiorangi, the chieftainess of Manga-hanea, and Mihi Kotukutuku for the Whanau-a-Apanui. If any of those old people

Amiria and Eruera at Amiria Salmond's christening.

spoke to you you had to listen, and that's how they managed our taumau marriage—you couldn't do it today.

If a man had a fancy for a girl and the elders tried to tell him he had to marry someone else, he would just refuse; he would rather have the woman he understood than someone chosen for him by the tribe, and the girl would be the same. But in our days the old people had the right to choose, and that's why they had a big battle about it, to see who could win. In the end, with me, Ngati Porou won all right.

As I say, the maoritanga is not so high up in standard today, any old way will do. Just look at the marae — it used to be a tapu place. When there was to be a hui, the senior man would call all the tribes and sub-tribes, and the local people would come to get everything ready.

It was almost like a church sort of place then, and if you took your children they had to go to the back, otherwise they might make too much noise and upset the man that's talking. But now it's so easy to go to the marae, and the children jump around all over the place. And the meeting-house was built to represent the ancestors, so it's very tapu, and that's why the old people never allowed drink inside. But these days oh! they drink like anything. I was shocked to go to Te Poho-o-Rawiri a few years back, it used to be the most gracious meeting-house; but that night, look here! it was full of beer. I can't help saying this because I saw it and I was disgusted. If the old people came back and saw that, I'm sure they'd cause an earthquake to bring that house down.[24]

24 Te Poho-o-Rawiri used to accommodate large-scale social functions in which liquor was served, but since 1974 that has been no longer the case — the marae committee has changed their ruling.

The language is going too, and even the land. The pakeha has put down the Town and Country Act and the Public Works Act, and the Maori didn't know about it. We were just sitting around not knowing what it meant, but now we see it — they can just come and take that piece of land. The Opotiki County Council put ten acres of Eruera's land as a reserve, and when we went past to a tangi one time there were a whole lot of bulldozers and big machines digging up gravel there — we didn't know anything about it. Eruera got out of the car and said to those people,

"I'm the owner of this land — who told you you could come and do this?"

They'd dug long trenches right along the beach and they were taking all the gravel for the roads right from Hicks Bay to Opotiki. In the end I think they had to pay him some royalties, but it was only because he came along and caught them. So that's the way the land goes.

And the young people of today can't speak their own language, but it's not their fault, I feel sorry for them. I remember what Apirana used to say,

"Go to school by all means and get a pakeha education, but never forget you're a Maori. Put your language in your heart and keep it there, and teach it to your children, because the moment Maori is lost, the Maori people will disappear from this earth. Learn your language and your genealogy, and take your pakeha education with you, then you'll have two fists to fight with — a Maori one and a pakeha one. But if you leave your maoritanga behind, you'll just be a swagger and a mongrel, with no place you can call your own."

Now I see they're even taking the name of Waitangi Day away. It was Apirana who told us about that name, he said that when the first canoes came to this island the people went ashore, and that night they heard voices wailing in the bush. They searched around and they couldn't find anyone, but still they heard that wailing up in the air.

In the morning they discovered it was the sea, and the old people said it was the ancestors calling their last farewell to those who had arrived in the new land. So they named that place "Waitangi" — "wailing waters", for the farewell of their ancestors. But now I hear they're changing the name of Waitangi Day to "New Zealand" Day, the name that was given to this country hundreds of years later by Tasman. *We* are the people who discovered this country first, and when Tasman came our ancestors were already here. Why should we pass the name of this country over as a memory to him, instead of to our own people? Because as I say, New Zealand is Maori soil.

Now I want to end this book with a farewell of my own to the old people of Taumata-o-mihi and Tuparoa, who raised me up and looked after me in my childhood days.

Hei whakamutunga mo tenei pukapuka, he mihi naku ki aku matua, tipuna hoki, nana nei au i poipoi, a, ka tangata — engari kua kuia hoki inaianei. Ko nga ingoa enei o aku matua, tipuna hoki; Hakopa Haerewa raua ko tana rangatira Te Awhimate; Hunia Te Iri raua ko tana rangatira Tapita; Paora Wharepapa raua ko tana rangatira Hana Tiki. Ahakoa kua mate koutou katoa, engari ko te aroha kai te mau tonu.

Ki taku tungane hoki ki a Te Warihi Tako korua ko to rangatira ko Wini;

Kawhia Milner korua ko to tuahine ko Mami, koia nei te wahine tino pakeke o te Tai Rawhiti; Maraea Ngarimu; Bobby Maru me te whanau; Maraea Te Kawa; Pipi Tawhai; Whaia McClutchie; Heni Nohoaka; Pane Kawhia; Mauhoe Farr; Wawata Rangi me te whanau; Matemoana Grace; Hine Munroe; Iritana Stirling; Te Iwa Eruera — tena koutou katoa. Ki a Ani Kahutawhiti Walker hoki, na taku koka hoki i whakatipu tenei wahine, tena koe e Ani.

He mihi hoki naku ke te wahine nei ki a Ani Salmond, mo te pai ohou e hine ki te tuhituhi i tenei pukapuka; ma te matua i te rangi koe e manaki, e tiaki.

Hei whakamutunga mo tenei pukapuka he waiata, e ki nei o tatou matua he waiata hei whakareka i nga korero.

> Moumou tatari au
> E hine i to moenga
> Moumou awhi ki to pera urunga e
>
> E Miri e ia
> Taihoa e haere
> Kia mutu taku riringi roimata e
>
> Ka hua au e hine
> Nahau te korowhiti
> Kaore na te manu rere i runga e
> > na Ngati Porou tenei waiata
>
> E rere e te ao ra runga o nga hiwi e . . .
> E whanatu ana koe ki aku kai ngakau e . . .
> Inaia te wa i tau ai ki raro ra
> E tu ke ana koe ka motuhake mai au e
> Te tahuritanga mai kai rawa i ahau e . . .
> > na Mihi Kotukutuku tenei waiata
>
> E rere ra e nga wai o Matarau
> Kia inumia iho hei manawa e . . .
> > na Eruera Kawhia tenei waiata

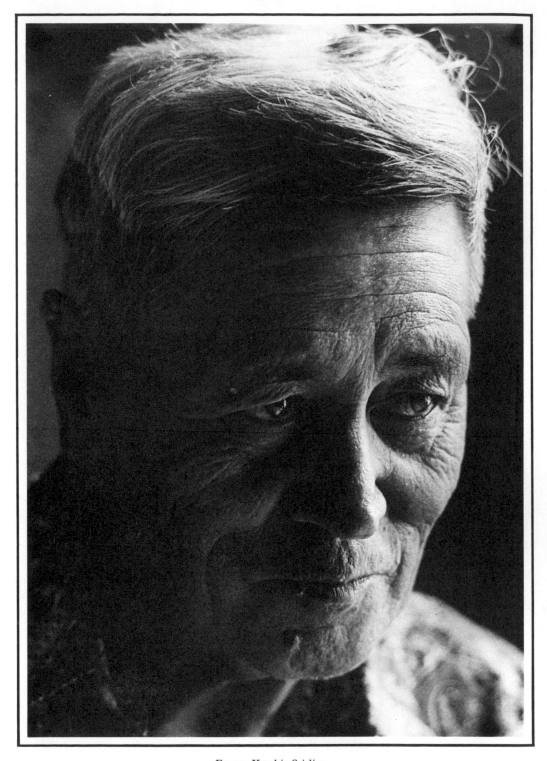

Eruera Kawhia Stirling.

The Young Life Of Eruera Kawhia Stirling

Well, I have to go back now, and remember what happened when I was born. It was on the thirtieth of March 1899, at a special place called Pohaturoa where my mother had been born and all of my great-grandfather's family before her. Pohaturoa was a point near Raukokore; when the ancestors came in their canoes from Hawaiki, somewhere round about Raiatea or Tonga, they saw this reef of rocks pointing out into the sea just like a point way back in Hawaiki, so they called it by the same name.

I was Mihi Kotukutuku's second son, and when the time came for my birth my mother moved outside to the place where my brother was born — there was a big pile of stones my grandparents had put there to mark the spot. She stayed there for a while but no, the baby wouldn't come. Some of my mother's aunties got a bit worried, so they sent word to an old lady who was well known to everybody for seeing signs in the heavens and listening to the owls and all these things. Her name was Hiria te Rangihaeata; she was a relation of my mother's and she lived about three miles into the bush.

Well, the old lady looked up to the stars and noted the ebb and flow of the tide, and she sent a message back to say that they'd have to move my mother, I wasn't meant to be born at that place. So the people took my mother to a wharepuni back in the hills on the Kapongaro block. When she started to labour, Hiria came and said no, the child should not be born there, and she told them to take my mother across on to the Kaikoura block, to a big karaka tree planted there by my great-grandpeople years back. When they got to that place Hiria te Rangihaeata looked up to the sky and she said,

"I can see the star Poutu-o-te-rangi just rising on top of Tikirau mountain, and the waters of Te Kopu-a-Hine-Mahuru are starting to move. Once the tide comes in the child will be born . . ."

The stars were bright beneath the karaka tree and as the tide came in I was born to the world. After everything was finished they took my mother back to the old people's home, back to Maaka te Ehutu and his wife Ruiha.

As soon as I was young enough and able to look after myself, when I was about two and finished with my mother, the old lady Hiria came to her and said,

"We're taking him as our mokopuna, Mihi, we want to take him away from you. We can see all the signs on him, he will be the one to hold the mana and the traditions of his great-grandfather."

I had two moles, one on my lower lip and one on the chin. The first was the sign of te kauae runga, the upper jaw which holds on to the prestige and mana of everything, the oratory, the tapu and the sacred things; and the other was the sign of te kauae raro, the lower jaw, for the modern college, the knowledge coming from below. Those were the signs that I was going to take both the top and the bottom, that I should be put through the ritual of my grandfather.

So the old lady took me, and we went to her whare nikau in the bush. I lived there with Hiria and her husband Pera Kaongahau until I was about seven years old. Pera was a first cousin to my grandfather, but he was the one who'd been through the channels of the tapu line, holding onto all the history of Whanau-a-Apanui and Ngati Porou and all the other tribes. During the Maori Wars he had joined up with the Ngati Porou under Major Ropata Wahawaha and travelled around, and that's how he met Hiria te Rangihaeata of Ngati Raukawa, and they decided to get married. Pera was the one and only from the Kirieke Whare Wananga, the school of learning that held all the tribal genealogies for the Whanau-a-Apanui, and Hiria had been in the school of Maori studies too.

Our toetoe hut was pretty nice. It was warm and well-kept, with plaited flax mats and a special place to light the fire. I enjoyed staying with them because I got plenty to eat, they gave me the best of food. Mainly we had pigeon, tui, wild pig or fish, but one of the special delicacies my grandparents liked was the grey rat — that was their special. When it's cut up properly and cooked it's something like the bird, eh, and I just followed their way and ate up the meat and everything. One day I saw them catch some of those rats in a snare; they put them in a big calabash, and when they wanted some to eat they'd just take them out and skin them. That was one thing with the old people, they always liked you to eat, and if they saw that you weren't eating they'd get worried and try to find something that you wanted.

There were a lot of birds in the bush around our hut, and one of the most important birds to the old people was the owl. If the owl came at certain times of the night it was bringing good news or bad news and when the owl started to talk my grandfather stood up in the whare puni and he'd growl at it, calling it all sorts of things. The owl would speak more softly then, and the old man would talk back.

There are different tones of the owl and Pera knew them all, if someone had died he always knew about it even before the messenger came to our nikau hut. Pera had pet parrots too, and he taught them how to speak Maori. They could talk and sing and whistle, they could do anything.

As I grew a bit older the old man started to teach me history; now and again and little by little he'd try to teach me, and then he'd go on to talk to me about genealogy. He'd tell me about the mana on the land, how each ancestor came to own the land and how it was passed on in history right down to now. He told me about all the big blocks around Raukokore — Tawaroa block, Matengareka block, Pouerua block, Whangaparaoa block, Marae-kahu, Kapongaro, Kaikoura, and the boundaries around each one. They were divided through different ancestors but it all came back to the one person, and he gave me all these lectures about it.

I suppose I was about four years when I began to understand, and when I got further, somewhere about six years old, I'd sit together with the old people and they'd ask me, who are the ancestors of Pohaturoa block, and Kapongaro, and Tawaroa and so on. I would answer, and in the end it was automatically in me. If I got something wrong I'd feel the hair of my head starting to pull, and then it would come back to my right mind.

The old man took me back through the genealogies little by little, he didn't hurry, but we went right back to the canoes — Horouta, Tainui, Te Arawa, Matatua, Takitimu and the rest.

It had to be tapu everytime. First of all the foodstuffs were moved out of the house, then we went to a special part of the house that was kept sacred, there was never any food allowed in there. The old man would start to chant, spiritually he seemed to know when it was time for us to go through the right channels of karakia, and we always opened up by praying to the gods. That was the mana and the tapu, it was there.

One day the old people called me, and the two of them sat together then Pera said,

"You go and sit over there."

He went back on these things all over again, and the old kuia asked me questions too — I answered the whole lot. When I had answered everything Hiria said to the old man,

"Well, I think it's about time you should take him to the wai tapu."

My grandfather held me by one hand and the old lady held me by the other and they started chanting. After the karakia Pera said to me,

"Tomorrow morning when the star Pou-tu-o-te-rangi comes above the mountain we will take you on to the waters of the Puru-o-Whakamataku."

There was a sacred pool where the water springs out of the ground, and it still is there today. I felt myself ready and I wanted to get it over; I slept well that night, I was happy.

In the early hours of the morning we all got up and had our karakias, then we walked a long way out of the hills, past the marae and up into a gully. When we got there grandfather started his special chants, and when his ceremony was finished, he and I both had to go into the water. He got hold of me and he said,

"As we dive you must grab a stone from the bottom."

Then he put his hand on my head and we both dived down, but that first time oh! It was too cold, I wanted to come up. He kept his hand on my head and he was still praying, then he said,

"You *must* bring up that stone."

The second time it was still too cold, and the old man knew I hadn't caught a stone. So the third time we dived, he kept his hand on my head so I couldn't come up, and the stone came automatically into my hand. As soon as we came up he said,

"Have you got the stone?"

"Yes."

I passed it to him. Then he started with all the karakias to the moon and the stars, and the heavens above, and all the waters of the earth, calling on the gods to support me, to let me take the mana of history and carry on for the rest of my days. When he was finished we came out of the pool and he dressed me, then we went home. The old man said to me,

"E tama, now the mana and the mauri rest upon you; I have given you the power of your ancestors, and it will lead you for the rest of your days. No one will ever come across your way. You have been through the Faith and you go in light; one day you'll be helping your people."

After that ceremony I still lived with my grandparents for a while and I was happy, I was getting the best in the food line and I was having my good sleep, I enjoyed those years with them. But when I was about seven, word came from my mother that I had to go home to attend the Native School. My father came to ask the old man to send me home, and that was one very sad day. I saw the old people just sitting there and I knew that it was a big shock to them, my parting away. My grandmother pulled my hand and said,

"Oh well — haere e tama.... Go child, but we have given everything to you, and it will stay with you for the rest of your life."

Then the old man wept to me, and I was very sad too. When I arrived at the home of my father and mother, well, I wasn't happy with the pakeha way. My father was speaking English to my brothers and I didn't know what he was saying. Every time he spoke to me, my brothers had to interpret what he wanted. One thing though, my mother was very good to me. She really looked after me and she always talked to me about the old people.

The first day I went to school I didn't like the children, I didn't want anybody. I was more interested in the birds flying around; when I saw the sea-birds I called out to them in Maori, and the next thing the teacher gave me a hiding. He kept talking to me and I didn't know what he was saying, and pretty near every day I'd get a hiding.

One day he gave me a very strong thrashing and the marks showed on my hands. When I went home I showed it to my mother and she cried, she was so furious with the schoolmaster. My father was building at Cape Runaway, and when he arrived home that night Mum told him about it and showed him the marks, and he was *wild*. He went and saw Mr Mulhern and told him off about it. I remember he was mentioning something about the Irish, and he kept pointing to his hands; anyhow he gave the schoolmaster a good talking-to.[24A]

"This son of mine is the only one in this whole school who has been through the channel with the old people! You've got to give him time to pick up, I don't want you to punish him again; their way is different and you have to help him and be good to him, so that he'll forget about the life of his grandparents ..."

The next day when I went to school Mr Mulhern got his daughter Kathleen to come and give me special lessons. I didn't like her at first, but she kept on with it and gave me a pencil, and started to point out the writing to me, and in the end I listened to her. She was nice. I picked up and I picked up, and after a while I was shifted back into the schoolroom to sit next to my brothers and a few others.

When I started my schoolwork in a proper way I went on quicker than my own brother, although he was two years older than me. I kept on with school, and I advanced and I got away. In those days when you got into the sixth standard you had to sit proficiency, and after that some of the boys were selected to sit for the scholarship to Te Aute. When it came to the scholarship I beat my brother and I got the scholarship to Te Aute for four years. I believe it was the schooling from my old people that gave me the strength to go through.

I was glad to go to Te Aute, and I did well there. In my second year I sat the Junior Civil and in the third year I sat for Senior Civil Service, and I got them both; I was all prepared to sit for Matriculation in the fourth year when a letter came from my mother to say that I had to go home. The Land Court was going to sit

---

[24A] Mr John Mulhern was head teacher at the Raukokore Maori School from 1897–1905 with his wife as sewing mistress and his daughter as assistant. To do him justice he is remembered in the school's Jubilee publication as a "very popular teacher" (page 19); it mentions that the children used to cluster round him every morning when he came to school.

in our area and she needed my help. She wrote to Apirana about it and he explained to the Headmaster that my mother needed me to help look after her interests in the Maori Land Title Investigation for Raukokore.

The headmaster came to me and said,

"Well Stirling, I think you'd better go.'

"No! No, sir, I want to stay here.'

"Well, which is the more important — your mother's land or your school?"

When I got back home my mother said,

"You're not going back to Te Aute, you're going to get married. Your elders and your uncle Hakopa have agreed to this match, and this woman is going to be your wife."

I tried to say something but she said,

"If you don't listen to me, you go — get away! There'll be no land for you."

That was the tone of things, eh. I was still going around with a few girls but that was all finished. I couldn't argue, and the day after I got back home old Hakopa arrived with Amiria and my cousins.

When I saw her she was a fine-looking woman, and I agreed anyway — had to. She was the one, she didn't want me, I think she had an eye on my elder brother. But she had to do what the people said and so did I, otherwise I'd have got kicked out. That was 20 December 1917.

We were married on the 8th of May 1918 at the Moutara marae. Canon Pahewa and Bishop Herbert Williams gave the service in the Raukokore Church of England, and that night there was a dance in the old Moutara hall.

All the people from far and near came to attend our taumau wedding. The chiefs from Whakatohea were Warakihi Waiapu, one of our best men; Tane Tukaki, and Waikura Tautuhi-o-rongo; Te Aranga-a-Moki, Tohi Kopu from Whanau-a-Apanui; and Hoani Retimana, the son of Eria Retimana, was the best man representing the Ngai-te-Rangi tribe of Tauranga. Then followed the Ngati Porou chiefs, Hakopa Haerewa, Tamati Kaiwai, Ani Parata, Keriana Tupaea, Whaka Parakau, Hukarere Taitua, Waikohu Waenga, Ue-ana-te-whare Waenga, Te Huna Houkamau, Te Hati Poutu, Henare Ahuriri; and the chiefs of the local tribes Manihera Waititi, Paerau te Kani, Hohepa Karapaena, Kanarahi Pururangi, Rawinia Ropiha, Mika Eruera and Mihi Kotukutuku.

The others included James Swinton, Duncan Stirling, William Ellison; the local pakehas James Walker, Frank Walker, Mr and Mrs Rutledge, J. S. W. Neilson, W. S. Saunders the schoolmaster, and Jack and Ernest Kemp; Moana Waititi, Sid Waititi, and Hirini Puha, Kahu Puha, Wi Pahuru Heremia, Marama Paraone, Hauraki Tawhai, Paratene Hia Takimoana, Paretio Tupaea and Wi Tupaea, Parekura Brown, Tumau Koria, Tame Koria and Hinekino Koria.

Of all these names I have mentioned, there are only one or two still living today.

After the wedding Te Huna Houkamau stood up in the dancing-hall and invited the wedding party to visit all the marae on the East Coast, and the old people agreed that we should go after a few days' rest. On the 10th of May the *Mako* arrived with two tons of potatoes, fruit, tinned meat and all the sweet drinks for the wedding.

We waited awhile, and on the 15th of May I called Wirihana Tatai to come back and take us along the Coast in his big buggy. We stayed at Hicks Bay on the 19th with Te Huna Houkamau and his people, and on the 20th we were given a reception in the old meeting-house Tumoana-Kotore by the old chief Wingara Houkamau, Te Huna's uncle.

Then an invitation came from Henipepi Houkamau, Henare Ahuriri, Ani Kaniroki and Wi Taotu, Dr Wi Repa and Reweti Kohere for us to call and stay at Hine Rupe meeting-house at Te Araroa marae.

At Te Araroa, Watene Waititi invited us to call in at Kiwikiwi for a while, then we moved on to Rongomaianiwaniwa meeting-house at Tikitiki marae where we were welcomed by Rauhuia Tawhiwhirangi, Te Koroneho, Maraea Te Iritawa and others.

That night Pene Heihi, known as Te Kai Rakau, invited us to his marae at Reporua, and at Reporua James Heihi and Mata Nuku told us that Kereama Aupouri wanted us to go to Tuparoa. At Tuparoa we were given the highest of home greetings. The speakers were Te Hati Pakaroa, Awatere Ahipene Mika, and Ruka Haenga, and they gave us the last invitation from Materoa Ngarimu, to go to Te Poho-o-Materoa at Whareponga.

The next morning we all went, some by way of the beach and the rest on horse-back across the hills to Whareponga and when we arrived there all the people from Waipiro Bay and Hiruharama were already assembled. Tuta Ngarimu, Tuhere Maraki, Piripi te Awarau stood to greet us, and Materoa Ngarimu was the last speaker. She gave the lines of tribal genealogy that linked us, then she promised that as soon as we were settled back at home the relations would give us as a gift of 500 head of sheep and 14 milking cows. That was the last marae we visited. There ends the travelling of the marae pohiri after our wedding, arranged in the old Maori custom.

In January 1919 the Maori Land Court sat to investigate the land titles at Raukokore, and the judge was Judge Brown. I had no fear of the old people, Manihera Waititi and the Te Kanis and all those people; I knew they were great orators on genealogy, but I was sitting on top of the world with the knowledge my grandfather had passed on to me.

When the Court opened at 10 o'clock, there were three elderly kaumatuas, all grey-haired old chaps who were going to oppose me for the land titles. Te Kani, Waititi and the Waengas all put claims on the ancestral rights to our land. My grandfather had told me in the days of our teaching,

"Your great-great-grandfather was the man who controlled all of this area, and your ancestors occupied this land right from the time the canoes came until now."

Then he taught me all the whakapapa.

When Judge Brown opened the court he saw me sitting there, and he knew that I was only young to face those old chaps, so he explained what the Court was going to do, and how we should make our claims, then he held off the proceedings until 2 o'clock. After that he said to me,

"Are you going to act for your mother?"

"Yes."

"All right. Now, I'm going to ask the clerk to give you the minute books of the Title Investigations into this land. You have a good look, and make sure you write down everything important."

When everybody had left the meeting-house the judge told me I could stay in there and take my notes. When I looked at the minute books, ha! The first thing I saw was the first sitting of the Maori Land Court in Opotiki 1886 — Maaka Te Ehutu had established his claim for the whole of our district by way of tribal occupation or papatipu, and the original ancestor was Kai-a-runga-te-rangi. I took all those records and wrote them down before the Court opened. After a while the judge and the clerk came back, and the judge said to me,

"Have you taken the evidence of your grandfather?"

"Yes, I've got it here."

"All right. Let the other people make their claims, and then I'll call you to come into the box. You ask them where they were born, and whether they have ever lived at Raukokore. Can you give the genealogy of the Te Kanis and the Waengas and the Waititis?"

"Yes.'

So at 2 o'clock the judge called out to Waititi and he put in his claim — finish. Then Te Kani, then Waenga — finish. After that the judge called out to me.

"Well Mr Stirling, have you got any questions?"

I asked Manihera Waititi,

"Where were you born?"

"At Whangaparaoa."

"Have you ever lived on this land?"

"No."

That was the end of those questions. Then I asked Te Kani the same, and then Te Waenga. The judge said,

"Well Mr Stirling, are you objecting to these people claiming ancestral rights?"

"Yes! They have no rights here whatsoever, their ancestors have never had permanent occupation on this property — only my great-great-grandfather."

"Oh. And on behalf of your mother, can you give the genealogies of this tribal area?'

I gave him the genealogies of all the descendants of Maru-haere-muri — there were seven in the family, and I brought it right down to Te Kani, Te Waenga, Manihera Waititi and my mother.

Then the judge said,

"According to the minutes of the Maori Land Court at Opotiki in 1886, no-one contested the claim of Mr Stirling's grandfather to this land at that time. You people have no right to come from Cape Runaway and claim this land. I will vest the title of all this area in Mihi Kotukutuku, and if she wishes to divide the land, it's up to her."

When the Court was over, I said to my mother,

"Oh, we'll claim the whole lot, never mind about giving it to the other people."

"No — we can't do that. You must give aroha to the people, they're part of you too. If your grandfather was alive today he'd give that land."

"Oh Mum, we had to fight today for our land, otherwise they would have taken it from us!'

But my mother still said,

"No! If you go back in your whakapapa, Manihera, Te Kani, they're *yours*, your own."

I was disgusted with Mum. In the end she was the one that put so much for the

Te Kanis, so much for the Waengas and so much for the other families. She told me,

"The main thing is to love your people. You have to look after them, because they're your *own*."

Well, that was my first experience, and after that I got further and further into the Land Court. I won all my cases because of the knowledge handed down to me by my grandpeople, and it was a big help to my mother and the family.

Eruera Stirling.

The Story Of The Tiki Mahu-tai-te-rangi

In the early days on the East Coast there were two brothers called Porourangi and Tahu-potiki, and they could never get on together. Porourangi was the high chief because he was the eldest, but Tahu-potiki was spoiled. When he was born his mother just adored this baby, so she called him "taku tahu", "my darling", and "tahu potiki", "the beloved child", and everything was for him first before the other children. As they grew older the people looked to Porourangi for everything because he was the eldest, so Tahu-potiki got jealous and tried to have an affair with Porourangi's wife. Then Porourangi said,

"You keep away from my wife, Tahu, or I'll be the man to put this taiaha through you! This is my warning — if ever I find out there's been something going on between you and my wife, I'll kill you."

Some of the people overheard the argument and they decided that the two young men should be separated. They couldn't talk to the mother because she was all for Tahu the younger son, so they went to the father and said,

"You'll have to tell Tahu to go away. Give him a canoe so he can find his own country and rule in his own way, and then he won't interfere with Porourangi. If he stays here he'll get killed for what he's been doing."

The father had a shock to hear them say this, but he called Tahu-potiki and told him that the people had something to say. One of the elders stood up.

"Tahu — we've been looking at the way you behave to your older brother and it's not right, because Porourangi is the chief around here. This is what we want you to do. . . . We want you to go and find your own country then you can rule it in your own way; but not here — the East Coast is Porourangi's. So Tahu, there's a canoe — take it and any of the people who want to go with you, and find a new home."

Tahu was excited to get a canoe just like that, so he jumped aboard and called out to the people,

"Let us get out of this country, let's find our own country — Porourangi can rule here! We'll find our own place, come on — haere tatou!"

A lot of people went with him. They had battles all the way to Wellington, and when they got to Wellington Tahu said,

Amiria wearing the tiki Mahu-tai-te-Rangi.

"We're still on Porourangi's land. Why can't we be like our ancestors who came from Hawaiki and crossed the ocean? Perhaps on the other side we'll find a new country and we can live there as chiefs. . . . How's that?'

"Yes!"

They took off on the boat and they rowed and rowed. In the end, hello! there's land. They went ashore and the first thing they saw was greenstone. When they pulled the canoe onto the land they found a river and it was full of greenstone, so they screamed and picked up these stones and threw them into the air.

"Oh! Look at this! They haven't got anything like this on Aotearoa. We're rich now . . . richer than Porourangi!"

Then they named the land "Te Wai Pounamu" or "Greenstone waters". When they looked around they saw karaka trees growing by the river with their dark green leaves, so they named that type of greenstone "karaka". The next thing someone came rushing over to Tahu-potiki,

"Leave that there — it's nothing! Come in this cave and have a look!"

"What is it?"

"There's solid greenstone in there!"

"Well, bring some out."

"We can't, it's a great big rock . . ."

They chipped off a piece and showed it to Tahu, and it was lighter in colour than the greenstone in the water. I suppose the sun had been beating down on the river greenstone for years and years and turned it that dark green colour, but the greenstone in the cave was hidden away and it had stayed very pale. They were trying to think of a name for it when somebody spotted some herrings in the river.

"Hey! He inanga — herrings! It's pale like those herrings," so they called the greenstone from the cave "inanga".

The people decided to make something from that first chip, and because it was the chief it had to be something very fine.

"How shall we carve it?'

"Oh . . . you design it like a man, he'll be the one to lead us. Give him hands and a face and everything."

"Yeah, but don't put his tongue out because we don't want a fighter. If he's going to be our leader we need someone who can talk to us and tell us what to do. Just leave his mouth open as though he's saying 'Go this way . . . no, not that!' "

"And don't put a hole through his head, we don't want him dead. Just put the string through his arm and keep his hands up, because if his hands are down that means his work is finished — ka pu te ruha, ka hao te rangatahi — the old net is set aside so you young people go fishing. But this man, no! He's going to live with us forever and be our guide to tell us what to do and what not to do."

So they carved the tiki Mahu-tai-te-rangi with one hand on his hip, and his face looking up at you all the time.

Tahu-potiki settled down in the South Island and he did very well there, and his South Island descendants are called Ngai Tahu to this day. When his elder brother Porourangi died years later, Tahu went home for the tangi, and he took the tiki Mahu-tai-te-rangi with him. He stayed there for a while, but after the tangi the people had a shock to find that Tahu had gone back to the South Island and he had taken Porourangi's widow with him. In her place Tahu had left the tiki as a gift for his people; because of this they didn't make trouble, they didn't try to chase him.

In the following years Mahu-tai-te-rangi was passed around from one chief to another along the East Coast. Every time there was an important tangi the tiki was brought out and placed on the coffin, and after that it was buried again because it was too tapu to have around.

It was generations later when Keita Horowai, Mihi Kotukutuku's older sister, died. The people brought the tiki from Ngati Porou to lay on her coffin because she was Ngati Porou on her mother's side, and it was decided that this time Mahu-tai-te-rangi would be put inside the coffin and buried forever. Maaka Te Ehutu, her father, was the man that took it out. His last living daughter Mihi Kotukutuku was very sick at the time; they had taken her to all the different tohungas but every time she came home she fell sick again, so Maaka thought that this tiki was the last chance to save her. He took it from the coffin and hid it, and after the tangi he told his wife what he'd done. She was wild because the tiki was too tapu to have in the house, and in the end he passed it on to someone else.

Over the next years Mahu-tai-te-rangi travelled around the Bay of Plenty, and landed up in Opotiki. Someone in that family died, so the people decided to pass the tiki back to Mihi Kotukutuku because they knew it wasn't theirs, they had no connection to it. She came to the tangi and after the burial the people asked her to stay behind, to let her people go but to stay at the marae herself because they had something important to say to her. That night they started to talk about the tiki Mahu-tai-te-rangi and Mihi said,

"Oh yes, I know that tiki — it was buried on my sister Keita Horowai."

"No it wasn't, Mihi," and they told her all about it. "It's here and we want you to take it with you.'

"No! I can't do that! I'm frightened of that tiki, it's too tapu. My husband is a pakeha and he doesn't know about those things, he might take food near it or anything. You people keep it."

"We don't want it, Mihi — it's yours, not ours."

She still refused so the next day they took it to a tohunga, then they brought the tiki back to the marae.

"Mihi . . . here is your ancestor Mahu-tai-te-rangi, take him. He's all right now, he's a pakeha like your husband. We took him to the tohunga and he washed off all the tapu, you can keep him in the house and everything."

The old lady was glad then, and she took Mahu-tai-te-rangi home with her to Raukokore. When she died in later years the tiki was passed over to Eruera because he was the eldest of the family still living, and Mahu-tai-te-rangi remains with us today.

Amiria Stirling.

Amiria – A Discussion

"Ani, no wonder we hit it. We were both born on the sixteenth!—Amiria Stirling, 1964.

I met Amiria and Eruera Stirling for the first time at a party; it was during my first year at the University of Auckland and the daughter of some friends of a friend was going overseas. I suppose Amiria would have been sixty-eight then and I was just eighteen. We sat down in a corner and talked, then the old lady started one of her stories and I was caught and held. That night we began a friendship which has grown into something more, and which has led us to the writing of this book.

Not long after our first meeting I went to visit the Stirlings at their small house in Herne Bay, an old place with green-trimmed windows and a red roof, and it's verandah sitting in flowers right next to the footpath. After a cup of tea we went into the living-room, then Amiria said,

"When were you born, Ani?"

"Sixteenth of November, 1945. Why?"

"Oh, the sixteenth! I was born on the sixteenth too . . ."

She crossed the room to a table in the corner and began turning over the pages of a hefty family Bible until she came to Proverbs.

"There you are — Proverbs 16, verse 16. That's us . . . 'To get wisdom is better than gold; to get understanding is to be chosen rather than silver'."

Then she showed me Eruera's verse — "The lion, king of the beasts, who fears no man" (Proverbs 30, verse 30).

Eruera is the head of an old-school chiefly family and his proverb is undeniably apt — his willingness to share his fund of traditional knowledge takes no account of possible critics, to the great benefit of those who wish to learn. Amiria on the other hand is, in her own words, "not so high up in birth', but her joyfully unaffected stories of Maori life have their own wisdom to offer. They cut to the heart of Maori experience, and I think you could say that they reflect that understanding which is better than silver.

"Societies, like lives, contain their own interpretations. One has only to learn to gain access to them . . ." — Clifford Geertz, "Deep Play: Notes on the Balinese Cockfight."

The nice thing about this account from the ethnographer's viewpoint is that it arose out of deep personal friendship and not the other way around. Usually the anthropologist goes into the "field" with a project in mind, recruits his informants and then if he's lucky, makes friends with them, but in this case the Stirlings and I had already moved to a sort of "grandparent-grandchild" closeness before we ever did fieldwork together. When I came back to New Zealand in 1970 after

Anne Salmond.

finishing my doctoral papers in anthropology at the University of Pennsylvania, Eruera and Amiria took me to visit marae throughout the country so that I could study Maori gatherings or "hui". For two years we travelled together, and it was towards the end of that research that the idea of this book emerged.

With this life, then, there never was a problem of access, because by the time Amiria was beginning to realise that her personal history might be more than just a series of casual yarns to be told in the meeting-house at night or in passing to family or friends, I had already heard most of them; and when the suggestion was made that they might be collected and published, it came from her. We had been attending a tangi at the Tira Hou marae in Panmure, and that night while we were having a rest in the meeting-house, the old lady turned to me and said,

"Hey, Ani — what do you think of a book about my life?"

Immediately it seemed a good idea, and in 1973 we set to work. Over the next two years forty tapes (1 track, 5-inch) were filled with anecdotes, songs and reminiscences, not collected in any particular order but as they came to mind. In general we tried to keep the material in English although most of our conversations are something of a medley between English and Maori; this was because the final account was to be published in English and a minimum of translation seemed desirable. For all that there were large stretches of Maori in the tapes, especially if Amiria was recalling conversations with her elders or characteristically Maori events (e.g. speeches on the marae, meeting-house construction, matters involving tapu), and these have been translated as naturally as possible.

As we taped I tried to keep pace with the work of transcribing the material, but after 24 tapes I gave up and Mrs Rangi Motu took over, supported by a generous grant from the University Grants Committee.

Late in 1975 the task of turning the tapes into a book began. Amiria's exuberant narrative needed little alteration, and editing was more a matter of cutting, trimming and re-arranging rather than extensive re-writing. All the same there had to be some transition from the spoken word to a written version, and at that point I decided to change some recurrent "Maori English" tense and plural constructions to their more familiar New Zealand written forms. This was not because they were regarded as mistakes or deviations, but simply because they tended to catch the eye in places where it was important that the reader should not be distracted. Idioms and turns of phrase on the other hand have been left intact, and I hope that the end result still sounds very much like Amiria Stirling. Readers who wish to judge this for themselves can consult the tapes (lodged in the Archives of Maori and Pacific Music at the University of Auckland) or the transcripts (lodged in the University of Auckland and the Alexander Turnbull Libraries).

Because I am convinced with Geertz that lives, like societies, contain their own interpretations, I have resisted any anthropological tinkering with the main text. Footnotes are explanatory rather than analytic, and the only anthropological discussion comes in this section. It seems to me that Amiria Stirling interprets her experience with exemplary skill, and that any re-processing on my part would be beside the point.

"We can only teach . . . [Maori] culture according to our tribe" — John Rangihau, a Tuhoe elder, 1975.

It should be clear from what I have already said that I regard the account which follows as something more than a fascinating exercise in idiosyncracy. It is true that it is the life story of a single woman and a rather unusual woman at that, and in no sense can it be regarded as a definitive statement about "Maori society".

But then over the past few years I have seriously begun to wonder whether there is such a unit as "Maori society" in any case, or whether there ever has been. A closer look at what actually happens reveals a wealth of tribal and individual difference, and these differences are not accidental but critical to the way that Maori people interact in Maori contexts. "Maoritanga" seems to be built on these critical differences (of tribal history, contact experiences, marae etiquette etc.) as much as it is on shared values, concepts and strategies, and this is something which has been consistently underestimated by its scholarly interpreters. In such a situation a text of this kind can be a useful corrective, because it is founded on both personal and tribal individuality, and yet it evokes in compelling detail some of the central Maori themes (tapu "the sacred"; mana "prestige, virtue"; leadership and the handling of childbirth, adoption, marriage and death).

"The culture of a people is an ensemble of texts, themselves ensembles, which the anthropologist strains to read over the shoulders of those to whom they properly belong" — Clifford Geertz, "Deep Play: Notes on a Balinese Cockfight."

I think Amiria Stirling's life story can be seen as one of those texts which illuminates its cultural setting. Her early childhood on the East Coast with its movement between her grandmother's raupo hut and the silver, china and polished floors of the Williams homestead gives a heightened example of the discontinuities of experience shared by other Maoris since contact, and the mixture of Maori and European attitudes which results is characteristic. It is a very Maori account, and one which other Maoris ought to find authentic.

Here it differs from most works by anthropologists, historians and other scholars, disciplined as they are by models from outside the Maori tradition. Their explanations are customarily directed towards a European audience and are both valuable and valid in that context, but to a Maori audience they can sound quite alien. New Zealand is just not like the usual situation in which European scholars of exotic cultures have been trained to work; there is almost none of the accustomed geographic and cultural separation between the studying culture and the studied.

So again the account which follows comes as a corrective, because it discusses Maori experience in a Maori way. Amiria's stories are neither romantic or didactic, and the reader can learn a great deal from them without ever realising that he is being taught. The text is one which is freely and gladly shared, and for once the interested student is not left peering over the shoulders of those to whom the culture belongs — with true Maori aroha they turn and for a time, invite him to share their lives.

"Ko Hikurangi te maunga, ko Waiapu te awa, ko Ngati Porou te iwi."
Hikurangi is the mountain, Waiapu is the river, and Ngati Porou the tribe.

"Ko Whanokao te maunga, ko Motu te awa, ko Te Whanau-a-Apanui te iwi."
Whanokao is the mountain, Motu is the river, and Te Whanau-a-Apanui the tribe.
Tribal proverbs (ancient).

The East Coast or Tai Rawhiti (here roughly defined as the rural district between Opotiki and Gisborne) is an area with a fascinating past. It is mainly a Maori area in population and perhaps because of that its history is not widely known, and yet it makes a story well worth the telling. The proverbs of its two major tribes Ngati Porou and Te Whanau-a-Apanui begin appropriately enough with the names of mountains, for it is a land of formidable hills and rocky coastline, facing the sunrise and looking out to sea.

Amiria Stirling was raised by elders of the Ngati Hinekehu sub-tribe of Ngati Porou, who trace their descent back to Toi-te-huatahi, the original captain of the Horouta canoe; Paoa, its later commander; and Paikea, who came from Hawaiki on the back of a whale.[25]

Paikea was the first-born son of the great ariki Uenuku; he was almost drowned with most of the other young aristocrats of Hawaiki when the canoe in which they were sailing was scuttled by his younger brother Ruatapu in a fit of jealousy. As Ruatapu was about to attack him in the water, Paikea was rescued by an ancestor who came in the form of a whale and carried him off to Ahuahu (Great Mercury Island). Eventually he made his way to a place between East Cape and the Waiapu River where he married the daughter of Whironui from the Nukutere canoe, and founded a line which leads to Porourangi, the naming ancestor of Ngati Porou. The Ngati Porou people still often perform a chant which recalls his exploits:

Uia mai koia	*Ask me*
Whakahuatia ake	*To name*
Ko wai te whare nei e?	*This house?*
Ko Te Kani!	*It is Te Kani!*
Ko wai te tekoteko kei runga?	*Who is the carved figure up there?*
Ko Paikea! Ko Paikea!	*It is Paikea! Paikea!*
Whakakau Paikea	*Paikea swam*
Whakakau he tipua	*The sea-god swam*
Whakakau he taniwha e	*The taniwha swam*
Ka u Paikea	*And Paikea landed*
Ki Ahuahu pakia	*At Ahuahu*
Kei te whitia koe	*You are changed*
Ko Kahutia-te-rangi!	*To Kahutia-te-rangi*
Me awhi o ringa	*Give your hand*

[25] Readers who wish to pursue this history in all its complexity should consult the *Rauru-nui-a-toi Lectures*, Sir Apirana Ngata, Victoria University 1972; *Te Tini o Toi*, Rongo Halbert, Whakatane and District Historical Society Memoir 1; "Hawaiki to Whangara", Tiki Riiti, in *Echoes of the Pa*, Tai Rawhiti Assn pp. 108–118; and *Nga Wahine Kai-Hautu o Ngati Porou*, Apirana Mahuika, M.A. thesis, Univ. of Sydney.

Ki te tamahine	To the daughter
A Te Whironui!	Of Te Whironui!
Nana i noho	Who sat
I te kei o te waka	At the stern of the canoe
Aue! aue!	Alas! alas!
He Koruru koe, koro e!	You are a carved face on a house, old man.

Ngati Porou also trace their descent from Ruawharo and Tamatea of the Takitimu canoe.

The history of the Whanau-a-Apanui (the tribe into which Amiria married) on the other hand, has largely remained in the realm of oral tradition.[26] Its descent lines go back to Muriwai from the Matatua canoe; Tama-te-kapua the captain of the Arawa canoe; and from Paikea to his descendant in the senior line, Apanui Waipapa. Ngata also mentions a pre-migration people called Ngariki with their leader Motatau-mai-Tawhiti, who were important Whanau-a-Apanui ancestors.[27]

Eruera Stirling's mother Mihi Kotukutuku was chieftainess of the Whanau-a-Apanui people, and her sub-tribe Te Whanau-a-Maruhaeremuri had long-time links of alliance with the Ngati Hinekehu people of Ngati Porou. It was partly to reaffirm these traditional ties that Amiria's marriage to Eruera was arranged.

European contact with the East Coast began in 1769 when the cabin boy on the *Endeavour* sighted land off Gisborne. The local Maoris according to Polack decided that the ship was an enormous bird carrying "party-coloured beings",[28] but when they went to challenge the visitors in traditional style the challenger was shot. After that relations were anything but cordial, and it wasn't until the *Endeavour* sailed north to Tolaga Bay that Cook and his men were welcomed ashore. Banks[29] described the people of the area as living in profound peace in scattered houses, with a large and affluent population working extensive cultivations, and this description is backed by an account in Nicholas[30]; in which he was told that "the people of the East Cape, though very numerous, were yet of an unwarlike turn of mind. . . . But this disposition, with the resources produced by their superior skill and industry, served only to expose them the more readily to the devastating incursions of their rapacious neighbours."

These local attacks, however, were quite overshadowed in the post-contact period 1818–24 by a series of raids from the North. Parties of Nga Puhi warriors armed with muskets descended upon the East Coast from the sea, killing, plundering, and taking great numbers of prisoners. It was because of bitter memories from this time that Amiria's Nga Puhi grandfather Wiremu Parata was almost killed by the Ngati Porou when he was shipwrecked in their territory.

Traders and whalers kept away from the area in those years, but shortly after the last of the Nga Puhi raids Australian schooners established a regular trade of produce for guns along the Coast. During the 1830s there was a boom in the flax

---

[26] See only Stirling, E. K., *Te Whare Wananga o Kirieke*, in press, Victoria University; and *Raukokore School Jubilee Booklet, Gisborne Herald*.
[27] Ngata, A. T., *The Rauru-nui-a-Toi lectures*, p. 4.
[28] Polack vol. 2, p. 15.
[29] Banks.
[30] Nicholas, vol. 2, pp. 219–20.

trade, and trading stations were established ashore by Montefiore and Co. of Sydney. One of their traders, "Barnet Burns", who was captured and tattooed in an inter-tribal raid, later published his memoirs under the title *A Brief Narrative of a New Zealand Chief*.[31] Other traders who left descendants in the district were Thomas Halbert, George Taylor, James Walker, William Martin, Capt. David Bristow, Charles Goldsmith and a Spanish trader "Manuera".

The demand for dressed flax dwindled in the mid-1830s, and maize, pork and potatoes replaced it as the main items for trade. The East Coast tribes put their traditional agricultural skills to work and before long they were running their own flour mills, trading schooners and establishing stores. In the same period whaling became a popular pursuit and some of the Maori chiefs acquired their own whaling boats as well. Whalers who left descendants in the area include Sam Delamare, Robert Espie, and Billy Brown, and whaling continued to be practised there until the time when Amiria and Eruera were both children (1890–1910).

Christianity came to the Coast in the 1830s as an indirect result of the Nga Puhi raids. A number of East Coast captives who had been taken North came into contact with the mission stations there, and in 1834 a group of these people were returned home by Rev. William Williams on the *Fortitude*. One man in particular, Taumata-a-kura, became an enthusiastic evangelist, and Christianity spread like wildfire along the Coast. The early Church in the district was run almost entirely by Maori catechists, and it wasn't until the 1840s that William Williams established his mission station near Gisborne and other European missionaries were sent to Rangitukia, Te Araroa and Tolaga Bay. The diocese of Waiapu has been distinctively Maori since it was established in 1858, and the first Maori clergy to be ordained in this country came from the East Coast.

In the early years of settlement almost no land sales were made on a regular legal basis in the district but neither did many of the settlers pay leasehold rent for the land they used. This and the prices paid for produce led to deep resentment, and when the movement to establish a Maori King began in the 1850s, its emissaries were well received on the Coast. The great East Coast chief Te Kani a Takirau was said to have been one of the first leaders approached to take up the Kingship, but he refused saying "My mountain does not move."

Hostility to the Europeans was not unanimous, and among the prominent loyalist chiefs were Iharaia Te Houkamau of Te Araroa; Mokena Kohere of Rangitukia,[32] Henare Potae at Tokomaru Bay; Hotene Porourangi at Waerenga-a-Hika, and Major Ropata Wahawaha,[33] the 'grandfather' of Apirana Ngata, at Waiapu. When fighting broke out in 1865 the opposing parties occupied separate pas, and at first the anti-European faction held the advantage. Before long however the loyalists received military support from the Government, and the "rebels" were decisively routed from Waerenga-a-Hika Pa after only eight months of hostilities.

Among the prisoners deported to the Chatham Islands after this battle was a

---

31 Burns, 1844.
32 See *The Story of a Maori Chief*, Reweti Kohere.
33 Refer *Major Ropata Wahawaha*, Lt. Colonel Porter, *Gisborne Herald*.
   Ropata Wahawaha, who was childless, was actually Apirana's great-uncle. (Sir Robert Hall, private communication).

man called Te Kooti Rikirangi, who was sent off at the instigation of some local chiefs although he had in fact fought on the Government side. During his two-year imprisonment on the Chathams Te Kooti developed a messianic cult among the exiles, and when he led an escape on the schooner *Rifleman* it was as a prophet leading his people to the Promised Land.

Te Kooti planned to travel to the Waikato to usurp the Maori Kingship, and although he warned the Poverty Bay settlers not to hinder his passage he was attacked by troops who were still in the area. In revenge he swooped down on the settlement at Matawhero and killed some 30 Europeans and many more Maori. Over the next four years he was chased around the inland territory of the Urewera by a Government contingent that included Ngati Porou troops (among them Eruera's "grandfather" Pera Kaongahau), led by Major Ropata Wahawaha. Te Kooti successfully eluded capture and escaped to the King Country where he was pardoned in 1883. The Ringatu religion that he founded was particularly influential in the Bay of Plenty, and Eruera's mother Mihi Kotukutuku and her people were followers of Te Kooti until Mihi married Duncan Stirling and changed to the Church of England.

The Ngati Porou people on the other hand, remained under the constant influence of the Williams family[34] and the Church of England, and Hauhauism was only briefly in vogue in their territory. When the Waiapu Diocese was founded William Williams became its first Bishop; his nephew Samuel Williams was in charge of Te Aute College near Napier, which for many years was dominated by pupils from Ngati Porou; and in 1894 his grand-nephew Thomas Sydney Williams came to manage the 20,000 acre Tuparoa leasehold run in the heart of Ngati Porou country.[35]

T. S. Williams built his homestead Kaharau near the small marae of Taumata-o-mihi where Amiria was living with her "grandmother", and the old lady Mereana Mokikiwa became his first cook-housekeeper. Amiria talks of a sale of land between Mereana and T. S. Williams, but it wasn't quite that simple. According to the Land Inquiry Officer of the Tai Rawhiti District of the Maori Land Court, Mereana Mokikiwa was an owner in the Ngamoe Block which became part of the Kaharau Blocks under the Tuparoa Consolidation Scheme 1932, and there was no recorded sale from Mereana to T. S. Williams. In fact the original agreement over the Kaharau site was a leasehold transaction with the local hapu, with Mereana no doubt as a major member; the land was not bought until later.[36]

In any case, when the house was finished Thomas's wife Agnes (who was a grand-daughter of both Henry Williams and James Busby) came to join him, and their family of five children grew up at Kaharau; Eva, Rachel, Oswald, Harold and Colin. Amiria had her first schooling with the children's governess, and she later spent two years (probably 1915–17) at Kaharau as a housemaid. T. S. Williams took over the Tuparoa lease on his own account until it lapsed in 1914; in 1897 he acquired Pakihiroa station where he trained a number of local men in agricultural techniques. When Eruera Stirling went to Pakihiroa with Amiria in 1919 he was one of the last of these trainees.

[34] See *Through Ninety Years*, Fred Williams.
[35] Refer *Farms and Stations of New Zealand*, vol. 2, pp. 404–5.
[36] Mr Harold Williams (now deceased) — private communication to Sir Robert Hall.

In the 1870s and 1880s a number of large sheep-runs were developed along the Coast by European farmers, some on confiscated land but mostly on leasehold, and the local sittings of the Native Land Court became a major focus of interest. Teams of surveyors began working in the area, and the courthouse at Waiomatatini was thronged with Maori litigants. Relatively little East Coast land was sold outright, but areas were leased (typically for terms of 21 years) to European settlers.

Under the provisions of the 1885 Native Lands Act only the ten major shareholders of each block received title, and even when the titles were widened the senior people were awarded majority shares; as a result the Maori aristocrats of the area became very wealthy for a time. Either they farmed their own land (by 1873 there were 14,000 Native-owned sheep on the southern side of the Waiapu River alone) or they leased it; either way their cash income was considerable.

For some years before fractionation of title really became a problem, the leaders of each tribal and sub-tribal group lived in style, building elegant wooden homes with tennis courts and stables, dressing in full Victorian respectability and operating their own gigs and buggies. At the same time they cared for their people, making livestock and land available to aspiring farmers, financing the construction of churches and meeting-houses, and contributing largely to the upkeep of the local maraes. Eruera's mother Mihi Kotukutuku was a chieftainess in this tradition, as both Eruera and Amiria's accounts of her have shown.

In the mid-1870s, there was great European excitement over the possibility of a major oil strike in Ngati Porou territory, and a number of wells were sunk. The local Maoris were not in the least surprised when these went dry; they attributed the oil springs in the district to the carelessness of an ancestor Rongokako who had dropped a whale on the ground as he stepped from Mahia Peninsula to Whangara.

Produce from the stations — at first mainly wool and maize — was shipped out by schooner, and coastal settlements such as Tuparoa, Waipiro Bay and Tolaga Bay boomed. Amiria's mother Ani Kahutawhiti lived at Tuparoa during its heyday when there were two hotels, a wool-store, Post Office, a boarding-house, two large stores, stables, a smithy, billiard saloon and a dumping-shed in the settlement on the beach, and her Irish husband Harry O'Hara was the local tailor.

From Gisborne to the Waiapu River a coach service ran along the beaches, and from there most travel was by horseback along inland tracks, with ferries crossing the main rivers. At each such crossing there was a hotel or store, and by 1880 there were 52 establishments selling liquor between Gisborne and Hicks Bay alone, which helps to explain the recurring upsurge of Prohibition sentiment in the area.

Apart from the schooners, launches and surfboats and later steamers called regularly at the coastal settlements, but this sea traffic began to decline as the inland route was upgraded from 1910, and it was largely replaced by motor vehicles in the 1930s. Over this same period the coastal townships declined, and a small inland settlement called "The Crossroads" or "Manutahi" (Amiria's second name) grew into the country town of Ruatoria.

The early years of the twentieth century were a difficult time for the people of the East Coast; fractionation of land titles became a problem as large families succeeded their parents' lands, and a series of severe epidemics (typhoid in 1891, 1911 and 1913–14; and pneumonic influenza in 1918) wreaked havoc in the area.

Land tenure and health were problems demanding urgent attention, and when the Te Aute Students Association was formed in 1899 to advocate improved sanitation, education and industry among Maoris its young reformers received a more sympathetic hearing than might otherwise have been possible. Apirana Ngata, a former Te Aute student from Wai-o-matatini, became the Association's travelling secretary, and when he added a concern for communal agriculture and the fostering of Maori arts to its policies he was elected to the Eastern Maori seat in 1905.

Ngata had a B.A., M.A. and LLB from Canterbury University but for all his scholastic brilliance he remained deeply Maori in his attitudes and political strategies, and this made him an ideal leader for the Ngati Porou, hard-headed pragmatists and proud traditionalists at once. In Parliament he went from strength to strength, eventually becoming Native Minister in 1928 and shepherding some major legislation on Maori lands and Maori arts and crafts through the House. Ngata is perhaps one of the most fascinating of all Maori leaders in modern times, a wily strategist, compelling orator and an idealist with a deep and unquestionable allegiance to his own people. He was the hero of Amiria's young girlhood, and he remains the hero of many East Coast Maori people today.

In the mid-1920s Ngata almost single-handedly established a dairying industry on the Coast, raising finance to purchase quality stock for farms that were often operated on communally-owned lands. Ngata was instrumental in having 660 grade Jersey heifers and calves and 36 pedigree bulls brought from Taranaki to the Coast in late 1924; and in 1925[37] the "Ngati Porou" Co-operative Dairy Company was founded with 58 suppliers producing 61 tons of butter in its first season; by 1937 there were 377 suppliers producing 744 tons. Ngata also led a revival in the arts of meeting-house construction and helped establish a new art-form, the action song, in his area; and when World War Two broke out he channelled local patriotic fervour to the support of the Maori Battalion.

In 1943 Ngata lost the Eastern Maori seat to a Ratana candidate, and in the years afterwards the migration to the cities began to take its toll. "Ta Apirana" died in 1950, the same year that Eruera and Amiria bought their home in Auckland, and in the 25 years since then the history of the East Coast has been one of increasing difficulties with land tenure; farms falling under the control of the Maori Affairs Department, and running up prohibitive development debts; an out-migration of local residents and an annual in-migration of summer tourists; and the deaths one by one of the local elders. Many of the maraes are falling into disrepair because there are no longer enough people to "keep them warm", and although tribal sentiment remains strong among East Coast people in the cities, it becomes increasingly difficult for them to return home to tangis and other gatherings.

The story of Amiria's life, then, may be the chronicling of the twilight of a tribal area. From the time of Cook onwards, observers of the East Coast have been impressed by the enterprise and vigour of the Ngati Porou and Whanau-a-Apanui peoples, and if this enterprise takes them into the mainstream of urban Maori life I suppose one can't object. But as an anthropologist and something of a romantic I'm glad that Amiria Stirling has captured part of the essence of early twentieth century Maori life on the East Coast and given it for us to share.

Anne Salmond.

---

37 Graeme Butterworth (private communication).

Seven Ngati Porou Maraes

TAUMATA-O-MIHI MARAE
  Rauru-nui-a-Toi meeting-house
  Ngati Hinekehu tribe
  Elders: Hakopa Haerewa
          and his daughters Areta, Titihuia and Kareti
          Mereana Mokikiwa, widow of Henare Kaiwai
          and her son Tamati Kaiwai, his wife Te Waihuka
          Paora Wharepapa and his wife Hana Tiki
          and their children Wi Te Arakirangi (♂), Keriana (♀), Tamati (♂), Tarati (♀)
          Hunia Te Iri and his wife Tapita
          and their daughter Hariata Te Iri, who married Moko Nepe of Waikato

HIRUHARAMA MARAE
  Kapohanga meeting-house
  Te Whanau-a-Te-Aowera tribe
  Elders: Materoa Reedy
          her brother Hamuera Ngarimu

KARIAKA MARAE
  Ngati Porou meeting-house
  Ngati Porou tribe
  Elders: Eruera Kawhia
          and his son Raniera Kawhia
          and his grandson Dan Kawhia and his wife Pane Ngata
          Hekiera Rewarewa and his wife Te Huinga Uaea
          Henare Pokai
          his brother Tokena Pokai
          Orewa Goldsmith
          Te Poa Smith
          Tom Reedy and his wife Heni Whangapirita
          Frank Harrison
          and his children Riria (♀), Te Harangi (♂), Henare (♂), Robert (♂)

TUPAROA
  Ruataupare meeting-house
  Te Whanau-a-Ruataupare tribe
  Elders: Te Hati Pakaroa and his wife Apikara
          Te Aperahama Tatai Koko (the minister)
          Hati Whangapirita
          Ahipene Mika
          Hone Haenga
          Petuere Awatere and his wife Heni Hautao
          Ihaka Turori
          Ngatoto and his wife Harata Tuhaka
          Ruka Haenga
          Niha Pei
          Hotene Porourangi

Pera Tawhai
Opotiki Walker
  and his children Heni (♀) who married Hati Whangapirita
    Hera, who married Raniera Kawhia, then Aperahama Tatai Koko
    Mereana, who married Wihiroki Grace
Hera Kaiwahie (♀)
Piniha Maru

HICKS BAY
Tumoana Kotore meeting-house
Te Whanau-a-Tumoanakotore tribe
Elders: Wingara Houkamau
      Wi Poutu
      Rawiri Bristowe
      Hori Stainton
      Piri Arapeta

TE ARAROA
Hine Rupe meeting-house
Te Whanau-a-Hinerupe
Elders: Henare Ahuriri
      Hatiwira Houkamau
      Heni Houkamau Brown
      Manahi Parapara

TIKITIKI
Rongomai-aniwaniwa meeting-house
Te Whanau-a-Rongomaianiwaniwa
Elders: Henare Rukuata
      Te Koroneho
      Piripi Rairi
      Paratene Ngata
      Apirana Ngata
      Akuhata Kaua
      Te Kaahu Tuhaka
      Henare Matanuku
      Maraea Te Iritawa
      Te Kairakau Heihi

Glossary Of Maori Terms

ae	yes
anei!	here!
aroha	love, friendship, compassion
a tena!	well then!
aue	alas
e hine	girl (address), daughter
e hoa!	lit. friend! — an exclamation of surprise, disgust
e koro	old man, elder (address)
e tama	child (address)
e tau ki raro	sit down
haere atu ra	farewell!
haka	war chant with actions
hangi	earth oven
haramai	welcome, come here
hika ma!	lit. people! — exclamation of surprise
hinu	oil
hui	gathering; Maori ceremonial gathering
ika a Pou	Pou's fish (the first fish of the season)
kahikatoa	red tea-tree
kai	food
kai kanga	maize eaters (Te Whanau-a-Apanui's nickname)
ka mau te wehi!	lit. hold the fear — exclamation — that beats everything!
kanga pirau	rotted corn
kanga waru	scraped corn
ka pai te wahine nei!	what a good woman!
karakia	incantation, prayer
ka rawe	lovely
ka tika	that's right
kauae { runga / raro	upper / lower } jaw, chin
kauta	cooking-shed
kei te pai	all right, that's right
kei whea koe?	where are you?
kia kaha!	be strong!
kia ora!	greetings! (lit. be well)
kina	sea urchin
koa	glad
kouka	cabbage tree
kuia	old lady
kumara kao	dried sweet potato

makutu	bewitch (v); black magic (n)
mana	prestige, 'virtue', authority
manuka	tea-tree
maoritanga	maori-ness, maori culture
marae	ceremonial centre with meeting-house
mauri	life principle, essence
mere	a stone or bone hand-weapon
mihi	greeting
mokopuna	grandchild
nanakia	trick (n)
pa	village, fortification
pae kare	by golly
pai ana tena	that's all right
pai noa	good enough
pakeha	European
paua	haliotis sp — a mollusc with an irridescent shell
pohiri	action chant of welcome
ponga	tree-fern
porangi	mad
potiki	youngest child
puha toroi	fermented sow's thistle
rangatira	chief
raupo	bulrush
Rerenga Wairua	the Leaping Place for Spirits — Cape Reinga, Northland
tahu	darling
taiaha	carved longstaff
Tai Rawhiti	lit. Coast of the Rising Sun; East Coast
takou	red ochre
taku korero ki a koe	my words to you
taku tamaiti kua mate!	my child has died!
Tama-nui-te-ra	Great Son of the heavens — the sun
tangi	funeral, weep
tangata kino	bad person
tapu	sacred
taumau	arranged marrage
taurekareka	slave
tawhao	driftwood
tekoteko	carved figure (usually at gable of a meeting-house)
tena koe	greetings to you (sing.)
tena koutou	greetings to you (pl.)
tino kino	very bad
tipuna	grandparent, ancestor
tito	lie, fabrication
toetoe	sedge species
tohunga	a priestly expert
tukutuku	woven wall panels in meeting-house
turehu	a light-skinned fairy people
uru mahora	flowing hair

wahine	woman
wai kohua	boiled water
wai tapu	sacred water
wareware	forget
wehi	awe, fear
wiwi	rushes
whakaika	to mound up (e.g. kumaras)
whakapapa	genealogy
whare	house
whare nikau	house made from nikau palm
wharepuni	sleeping-house
whata	elevated storehouse

Bibliography

Anderson, L., *Throughout the East Coast: The Story of Williams and Kettle Ltd*, Pictorial Publications Ltd, Hastings, 1974.

Burns, Barnet, *A Brief Narrative of a New Zealand Chief, being the Remarkable History of Barnet Burns, an English Sailor*, R. and D. Read, Belfast, 1844.

Butterworth, G., *Sir Apirana Ngata*, A. H. & A. W. Reed, Auckland, 1968.

Condliffe, J. B., *Te Rangihiroa — the Life of Sir Peter Buck*, Whitcombe and Tombs Ltd, Wellington, 1971.

Cranwell Pub. Co., *Farms and Stations of New Zealand*, Cranwell Publishing Co., 1958.

Faram, T. C., *Memories of the East Coast*, Gisborne Herald Ltd.

Geertz, C., "Deep Play: Notes on The Balinese Cockfight", in *Myth, Symbol and Culture*, ed. Clifford Geertz, W. W. Norton, 1974.

Gisborne Herald, *Raukokore Maori School Jubilee Booklet*, 1962.
        "The Sad End of A Settlement . . . ", 13 October 1972.
        Centenary Special, Jan. 5 1974.

Gisborne Times, "Life in Early Poverty Bay", based on *The Gisborne Times Golden Jubilee Supplement* May 1927.

Halbert, Rongo, *Te Tini o Toi*, Whakatane and District Historical Society Inc., Memoir No 1, from vol. IX, no. 3, 1961.

Hiruharama Maori School Jubilee Programme, 1961.

Journal of the Polynesian Society, "Sir Apirana Ngata Memorial Tribute", *vol. 59*, no. 4; *vol. 60*, no. 1 (Reprint no. 5).

King, Michael (ed.), *Te Ao Hurihuri: The World Moves On*, Hicks Smith & Sons, Wellington, 1975.

Kohere, Reweti, *The Autobiography of a Maori*, A. H. & A. W. Reed, Wellington, 1951.
    The Story of a Maori Chief (Mokena Kohere), A. H. & A. W. Reed, Wellington, 1949.

Lambert, Thomas, *The Story of Old Wairoa and the East Coast District*, Coulls, Somerville and Wilkie Ltd, 1925.

Mackay, J. A., *Historic Poverty Bay and the East Coast*, J. G. Mackay, Gisborne, 1949, reprinted 1966.

Mahuika, Apirana, *Nga Wahine Kai-Hautu o Ngati Porou*, M. A. thesis (unpub'd), University of Sydney, 1973.

Morrell, W. P. (ed), *Sir Joseph Banks in New Zealand*, A. H. & A. W. Reed, Wellington, 1958.

Ngata, Sir A. T., "A Scene from the Past", in *Ngarimu VC Investiture Souvenir Programme*, 6 Oct. 1943.
    A Map of Maori Tribal Boundaries 1800 and 1840, held in The Alexander Turnbull Library, Wellington
    The Past and Future of the Maori, Christchurch Press, 1893.
    The Rauru-nui-a-Toi lectures and Ngati Kahungunu Origins, Victoria University 1972.
    The Treaty of Waitangi: an Explanation, Maori Purposes Fund Board, 1922.

Oliver, W. H. and Thomson, J., *Challenge and Response*, Gisborne Herald, 1971.

Nicholas, J. L., *Narrative of a Voyage to New Zealand, 1814-15*, Black, London, 1817.

Pocock, J. G. (ed.), *The Maori and New Zealand Politics*, Blackwood and Janet Paul, 1965.

Polack, J., *New Zealand: Being a Narrative of Travels and Adventures*, Richard Bentley, 1838.

Porter, Frances (ed.), *The Turanga Journals 1840-50*, Price Milburn, 1974.

Porter, Lt. Colonel T. W., *The History of the Early Days of Poverty Bay: Major Ropata Wahawaha*, Poverty Bay Herald Co., (2nd ed.), 1923.

Ramsden, Eric, *Sir Apirana Ngata and Maori Culture*, A. H. & A. W. Reed, 1948

Rosevear, W., *Waiapu: The Story of a Diocese*, Pauls Book Arcade, 1960.

Stirling, E. K., *Te Whare Wananga o Kirieke*, in press, Dept of Anthropology, Victoria University.

The History of Te Whanau-a-Maru and Ngati Hinekehu of Tapuwaeroa Valley, unpub'd.

Tai Rawhiti Maori Association, *Echoes of the Pa: Proceedings for the Year 1932*, Gisborne Publishing Co. Ltd, 1932.

Williams, Frederic W., *Through Ninety Years, 1826-1916*, Whitcombe and Tombs Ltd., 1940.

Williams, Nigel (ed.), based on Williams, G. M., *The Williams Family in New Zealand 1823-1973*, Paihia 1973.

Williams, Bishop W. L., *East Coast (NZ) Historical Records*, reprinted from the *Poverty Bay Herald*.

Index

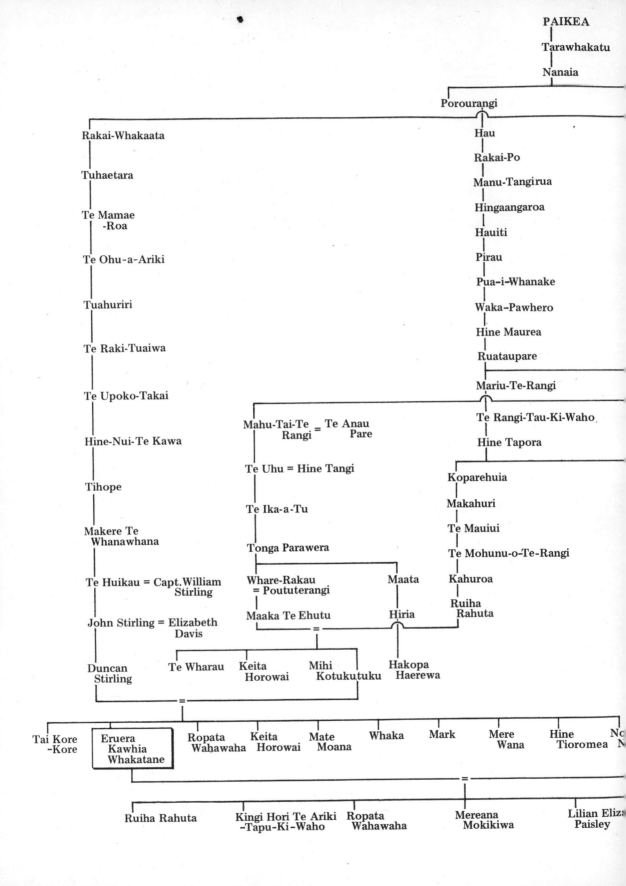